DAVID DARLINGTON

ANGELS' VISITS

An Inquiry into the Mystery
of Zinfandel

HENRY HOLT AND COMPANY

NEW YORK

Library of Congress Cataloging-in-Publication Data
Darlington, David.
Angels' visits : an inquiry into the mystery of Zinfandel / David
Darlington. —1st ed.
p.   cm.
1. Wine and wine making—California.   I. Title.   II. Title:
Zinfandel.
TP557.D37   1991
641.2'223—dc20   90-5288
CIP
ISBN 0-8050-1608-2
ISBN 0-8050-2093-4 (An Owl Book: pbk.)

Henry Holt books are available at special discounts
for bulk purchases for sales promotions, premiums,
fund-raising, or educational use. Special editions
or book excerpts can also be created to specification.
For details contact:
Special Sales Director, Henry Holt and Company, Inc.,
115 West 18th Street, New York, New York 10011.

First published in hardcover by
Henry Holt and Company, Inc., in 1991.

FIRST OWL BOOK EDITION—1992

DESIGNED BY KATE NICHOLS
MAP BY JEFFREY WARD

Printed in the United States of America
Recognizing the importance of preserving the written word,
Henry Holt and Company, Inc., by policy, prints all of its
first editions on acid-free paper. ∞
1   3   5   7   9   10   8   6   4   2
1   3   5   7   9   10   8   6   4   2
pbk.

ANGELS' VISITS

ALSO BY DAVID DARLINGTON

In Condor Country

For John Raeside
and Steve Aibel

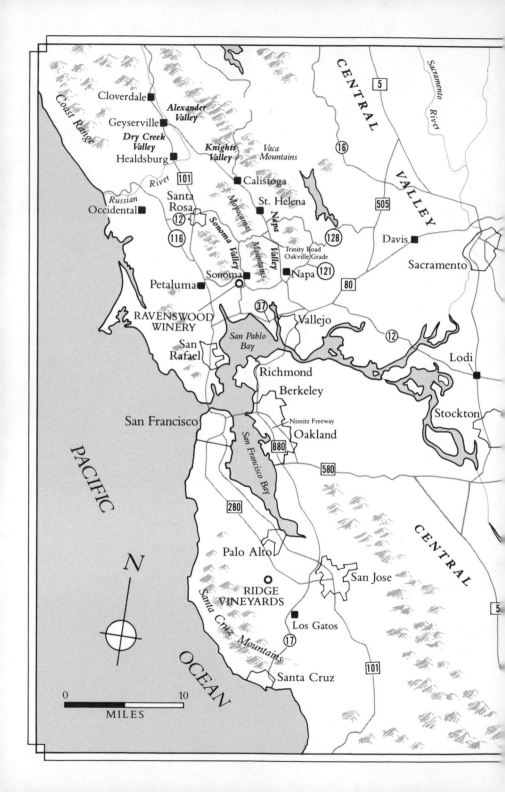

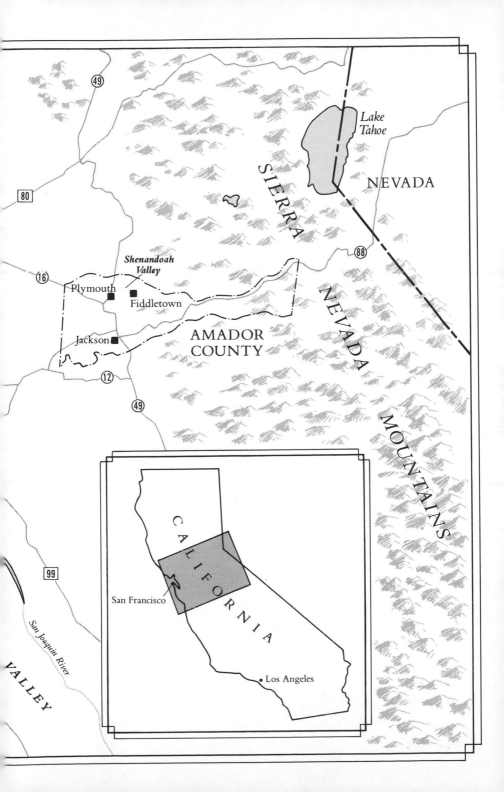

*I have yet to see the red wine of any variety [that]
I would prefer to the best samples of Zinfandel
produced in this state. Unfortunately these* best
*samples are like angels' visits, "few and far
between."*

GEORGE HUSMANN,
*Grape Culture and Wine-Making
in California,* 1888

In the spring of 1985 the following news item appeared in the *Vinifera Wine Growers Journal*, a Virginia-based quarterly:

BATF FORBIDS USE OF "ZINFANDEL" BY ITALIANS

Following a complaint by Rich Kunde, president, Sonoma County Grape Growers Association, Santa Rosa, California, to the Bureau of Alcohol, Tobacco, and Firearms, that Italian wines made from the Primitivo grape are being labeled and sold in the U.S. as Zinfandel, BATF ordered importers to eliminate "Zinfandel" from such wine labels.

According to "WINEWS," Jan.–Feb. 1985 . . . Mr. Kunde had seen an Italian wine labeled Zinfandel which also stated, "It can now be affirmed with resonable [*sic*] certainty . . . that the Primitivo grape cultivated in Puglia, Italy, and Zinfandel are the same vine. Zinfandel was first introduced into the United States by Agoston Haraszthy, the father of California viticulture. . . ." Mr. Kunde claimed that the name Zinfandel is used only in

1

the United States, and that Italian growers should not apply the name to Primitivo.

The article included comments on this action from several experts. Charles Sullivan, a California wine historian, debunked the long-held notion that the legendary Hungarian Count Haraszthy had introduced the Zinfandel grape to California. Sullivan held that Zinfandel had originally come to the West Coast by way of New England, where it had been grown as a table grape since the 1830s. Betsey Bradford, acting chief of the product compliance branch of the Bureau of Alcohol, Tobacco, and Firearms (a grouping of responsibilities that reveals much about social attitudes toward wine in the United States), said that federal law requires imported wines to conform to their legal designations in the countries where they originate; since Zinfandel is not included on the European Economic Community's list of Italian grape varieties, wine cannot be imported here from Italy under that name. To the argument that it was hypocritical for the United States to censure an Italian "Zinfandel" after long sanctioning a California "chianti," C. S. Ough, chairman of the viticulture and enology department at the University of California at Davis, flatly replied: "Two wrongs do not make a right. California has worked very hard to develop and promote varietal names rather than using the European names, mainly because of continued whining about it from Europeans. Why should the Europeans now want to get on the California bandwagon?"

To many ways of thinking, there was no small irony in this fuss. For more than a century vintners in the United States have been making and naming wines after the respected products of Europe—not only chianti but champagne, burgundy, Rhine wine, claret, chablis, et al. Moreover, most of these domestic offerings have made no attempt whatsoever to match the quality of their Old World counterparts, but rather have been simple, unremarkable jug wines—the sort of product that until very recently defined the U.S. wine market in general and the California wine industry in particular. Only in the last few decades have Americans, in an effort to stimulate interest in fine wine varietals while severing themselves from the hegemony of Europe, widely begun naming their wines not after Old World viticultural regions but after the grapes that the wines were made from. Not incidentally, in the same era the status of American wine has risen to rival that of Europe, and even prior to 1976— when a California Chardonnay and Cabernet Sauvignon outscored a French white Burgundy and red Bordeaux in a blind tasting at the Académie du Vin in Paris—Europeans had been heartily hailing the California bandwagon: fermenting their wines in stainless steel rather than wood, pressing them off the grape skins early, filtering them heavily, and, yes, even naming them after grapes instead of regions.

The remarkable fact in the Primitivo case, then, was not that Europeans were emulating American wine but that they were seeking to hitch themselves to a wagon pulled by Zinfandel, a grape that has never been considered the equal of the *vignobles* of Europe—which had, in fact, been the primary ingredient in the generic red jug products of California's past, and a wine that, to the extent that it had any reputation at all, was traditionally known as a "cheap claret" suitable for picnics and everyday drinking but certainly not for elegant dinner parties or occasions of any importance. Even more telling, if less surprising, was the spectacle of the California contingent, led by Mr. Kunde of Sonoma County, rising to defend the name of a varietal that had always been known as a poor man's grape because of its high productiveness and low price. In a stroke, it showed the extraordinary loyalty that Zinfandel enjoys in a certain segment of the wine community—a following that, considering the mystique surrounding the nature of the wine and origins of the grape, could almost be called a cult.

"If an absence of apparent ancestors is proof of divine origin, certainly the Zinfandel grape is entitled to a whole collection of legends," Frank Schoonmaker wrote in *American Wines* in 1941. Unlike the so-called noble grapes—Cabernet Sauvignon, Pinot Noir, Chardonnay, and Riesling—Zinfandel has no forebears associated with regions of Europe. In the University of California/Sotheby's *Book of California Wine*, Paul Draper—winemaker at Ridge Vineyards, the California winery more closely associated than any other with fine Zinfandel—calls it "the Horatio Alger of varietals, the 'True American.' Born of peasant stock somewhere in Europe, Zinfandel did not make its name and fortune in its native land. It did not come to the attention of its monarchs nor was it tutored and polished by the English wine trade until worthy of knighthood. Not until it was planted on the hillsides of California's cool Coastal Range did it find its ideal soils and climate." Zinfandel clearly belongs to the *Vitis vinifera* family (of which all fine wine varietals are variations) and is therefore of European ancestry, but until recently it was known to grow only in California, where for more than a hundred years it has been the most important grape raised for the purpose of producing wine. In the late nineteenth century its wine was touted as a possible domestic alternative to French claret, and during the great grape-planting boom of the 1880s it was the most widely cultivated varietal in California. It survived Prohibition largely because of this foothold and because of its popularity among home winemakers, many of whom were immigrants favoring the sort of robust, straightforward beverage that Zinfandel could make. Subtlety is not an attribute generally ascribed to this grape, which produces a racy, spicy wine historically lacking in the refinement and savoir faire of its "superiors." While it is acknowledged to be "among the pleasantest table wines of the world" (Schoonmaker), it nevertheless "falls short of a titanic reputation for lack of the extra depths or infinite layers of flavor that define great wine" (Hugh Johnson). It is usually described as redolent of raspberries and recommended for consumption while young—viewpoints that have (after the initial hopes for a domestic claret were scaled back) at times caused it to be nominated as an American version of Beaujolais.

In fact, with the possible exception of Pinot Noir, Zinfandel is the world's most versatile grape, capable of conferring a panoply of wine styles from a light, refreshing rosé to a dense, rich port. The adaptability—not to mention the sheer available acreage—of the varietal has encouraged winemakers to experiment with it, and over the decades Zinfandel styles have swung wildly from moderate claretlike table wines to lurid alcoholic essences to pink soda-pop-like aperitifs. Unfortunately, this chameleonlike character has served to camouflage it in the marketplace, as, from year to year and label to label, the casual consumer could never be sure what he or she might get when choosing a bottle of Zinfandel from a shelf. The typical buyer browsing for an innocuous dining companion who instead wound up with a wild buckeroo was not likely to invite Zinfandel to a meal again in the near future—despite the fact that most of the other choices on the shelf would, in all likelihood, have been models of discretion with little of interest to say either for or against the food.

This lack of a coherent Zinfandel tradition is, however, another thing that makes it a purely American wine. Like the country in which the vine found a home, the wine had no precedent and hence had to invent itself. Makers of California Cabernet know that their yardstick stands in Bordeaux; producers of Pinot Noir and Chardonnay compete with the climate and soils of Burgundy; American Rieslings are judged by how well they evoke the valley of the Rhine. These standards have developed in Europe over several centuries, while the vines that produce such wines in the United States have scarcely been in the ground for decades. The world's oldest *Zinfandel* vines, however, are growing in California. Its tradition—such as it exists after only a hundred years—has evolved along with American winemaking and is still evolving. For better or worse, Zinfandel has been California's native contribution to the international world of wine.

This partly explains why, despite Zinfandel's second-class reputation and roller-coaster career, the grape growers of Sonoma County are so tenacious in claiming it. But the motivation goes deeper than that. Considering that wine itself has accompanied Western man in all his incarnations (winemaking first occurred in the Caucasus seven thousand years before Christ and spread through the succeeding ages to Egypt, Phoenicia, Greece, Italy, North Africa, Spain, France, Germany, and the New World), its role in history now looms larger than that of a simple beverage. In fact, wine has come to represent the essence of civilization (a point clarified by Webster's, which defines *essence* as "a substance distilled or otherwise extracted from a plant, drug, etc., and believed to possess its virtues in concentrated form; also an alcoholic solution of such a substance," and *civilization* as "advancement of social culture"). As the history of California testifies, whenever Europeans have colonized a place, they've gotten right to work making wine in it; apparently we *have* to have it, and see ourselves reflected in it. Hence the sometimes ludicrous tendency—including, to judge by some of the preceding evidence, my own—to describe wines as if they were people.

In this context, the recent rise in status of California wine furnishes subtle signals about the maturity of American culture. In the eyes of the Old World, the fact that fine wine now originates in the United States apparently implies that America has passed out of its adolescence. There seems to exist some tacit notion that if our wines are judged good, we as a people will be also; we will have a chance of being regarded as civilized and humane, not merely as the boorish perpetrators of Coca-Cola. Which serves further to explain why Californians would shout down a coarse European product that presumes to identify itself with our own native wine. As we monitor the progress of Zinfandel, we cast a sweeping sidelong glance at civilization in the New World.

It probably says something not only about me but about contemporary enology that I ascribe the beginnings of my interest in wine to a magazine article about Robert Mondavi. Entitled "A Magnificent Obsession," the piece was written in 1981 for *New West* magazine by Moira Johnston, who chronicled the many-sided existence of the man whose name is most closely identified with the recent status of California wine. Johnston accompanied Mondavi as he hosted tastings, met with his production staff, feted foreign visitors, negotiated with grape growers, and released the first vintage of Opus One, the wine that he produced jointly (and grandiloquently) with Baron Philippe de Rothschild of France. She also detailed the feud that begot the Robert Mondavi Winery, which came into being after its namesake sued his own family for expelling him from its long-standing Napa Valley bulk-wine business.

It wasn't the soap opera scenario that impressed me in this story so much as the varied nature of the wine business itself: its international aspect, its generational history, its financial demands, the litany and poetry of its varietal names, its formal tastings and informal craftsmanship. Above all, it was the passion of the winemakers themselves—the "magnificent obsession" and ceaseless self-questioning that constantly changed the nature of their product, moving it toward some mutable and ineffable ideal. As Johnston herself framed the overarching question, "What is to be served—the palate, the marketplace, or the grape, even if it can be odious?" Given the mercurial influence on that product of climate and geography, the most compelling element in the formula was the fact that these multifarious influences finally came together in one clearly identifiable place: the bottle of wine itself, a point where culture and agriculture met.

To say that Johnston's article piqued my interest is not to imply that I had stumbled upon wine completely unawares. I had, for example, already been living for some years in the San Francisco Bay Area. It's hard *not* to develop an interest in wine in a place where legislators face the problem of whether to allow teachers to lead schoolchildren in daily prayers to Chardonnay and Cabernet. I had perforce participated in the ritual of tasting trips to the "wine country," where the objective was not to taste but to swallow as much wine as possible; my initiation had occurred at Sonoma, where (in a fully sanctified approach) I visited Buena Vista and Sebastiani and then, having consumed my quota of two-ounce allotments, tried to climb Sonoma Mountain on a bicycle—a not uncommon reversal of the saner order of endeavor. It was at Sebastiani that, for the first time, I discovered a wine I could say I actually liked: "Grey Riesling," my selection of which was also quite typical, as most new converts to the faith begin with devotion to off-dry whites.

If I change the working metaphor here from religion to baseball (practically the same thing), perhaps I can say that if the Boone's Farm–Ripple–Thunderbird triangle constitutes a Little League of wine appreciation, I was now beginning to stumble about in the Class D sections of the minors. I quit buying jug wine altogether and started paying more than four dollars for a 750-ml bottle (though my prolonged periods of staring in wine shops involved little evaluation of anything other than labels). I also shifted the focus of my visits to smaller wineries of higher quality—the likes of Clos du Val, Chateau St. Jean, Chateau Montelena (whose Chardonnay had placed first in the '76 tasting-heard-round-the-world), and Joseph Phelps (my favorite, for both its setting and its wines). During these tours I came deeper under the spell of California wine-making—a condition induced by the sweet smell of wine-soaked wood, the cast of sunlight on the vines, the coolness of the cellars on hot summer days. As Robert Louis Stevenson observed in 1883, "the stirring sunlight, and the growing vines, and the vats and bottles in the cavern, made a pleasant music for the mind." In a quiet way, California wineries seemed— like wine itself—to exist as expressions of the landscape.

With such ideas swimming in my brain, I decided to seek employment in the 1984 grape harvest. I asked a chef I knew in Sonoma to keep her ear cocked to the prospect of enological employment, and she soon called to tell me that a Sonoma winery named Ravenswood needed help right away. As it happened, I had recently read about Ravenswood in an article on Zinfandel; the writer had put forth the novel theory that the grape had originated in outer space. My wine-shop trances had also familiarized me with the provocative, enigmatic Ravenswood label—a circular pattern of three ravens joined at the talons. I called the winemaker, whose name was Joel Peterson, and agreed to drive up the next day.

Upon arriving, I perceived a gap between my ideas and reality. The romantic image of the European *cave* is a cobweb-covered cellar crammed with old oak barrels. The typical California winery, by contrast, exhibits contemporary redwood siding and stainless-steel tanks. Ravenswood answered to neither image. The winery was hidden behind a woodworking shop in a prefab warehouse south of Sonoma; its office (which was vacant) was covered with cat hair and newspaper. The closest thing to a tasting bar appeared to be the john, where glasses stood on the toilet tank after being rinsed out in the sink. Rock music boomed through the interior of the warehouse, which was filled to the ceiling with barrels stacked on a vast steel framework. Clouds of fruit flies rose from the fermentors, and interesting cultures grew on the floor. Out back I found a stout young curly-haired man named John, who gave me a pair of rubber knee boots, directed me to wash out twenty-five barrels, and left to deliver a load of wine to Santa Rosa. I spent the rest of the morning lifting sixty-gallon French oak barrels, fitting a spray nozzle to their bungholes, and spinning each one for a few minutes as a thick gunk of pink sediment—"lees"—flowed onto the cement driveway like some wayward strawberry milkshake.

Washing turned out to be the main thing I did that fall. Indeed, for what seemed like a dirty little winery, a tremendous amount of washing went on. John Kemble had a fetish for hygiene wherever contact with the wine was concerned; if I wasn't washing barrels, I was washing redwood fermentors or rubber storage tanks or the hydraulic press or the crusher-stemmer or the pump or the hoses or the floor. Not to imply that washing was *all* I did; oh, no. Most of Ravenswood's winemaking practices harked back to the turn of the century, and that meant, among other things, a lot of hand labor. For example, in order to submerge the cap of grape skins that forms on top of fermenting juice—a layer that, if left alone, soon grows so hard you can walk on it—most modern wineries use machines to pump must (i.e., crushed grape juice) from the bottom of the tank to the top. One of my jobs at Ravenswood was to punch down this cap by hand. This involved sitting, standing, or kneeling on a two-by-ten board (sometimes in the dark, since the warehouse had no lights), jamming a wooden plunger into the skins and stems, occasionally even jumping on them in my rubber boots, all the while pouring sweat thanks to the ninety-degree heat generated by the fermenting wine. (Years later, after the '84 Ravenswood Cabernet was released, someone described it as a mixture of "horse sweat and tidepools," an unfair misrepresentation. The sweat was mine.)

As the reader may discern, what most impressed me about

winemaking at that point was how much drudgery it entailed. Even at a scrupulous operation like Ravenswood's, the glamour of the grape seemed to diminish when mashed, punched, pitchforked, walked on, and shunted through hoses and hydraulic devices in mass quantities. Whereas scrubbing and waxing a fermentation tank or racking (that is, emptying, cleaning of sediment, and then refilling) a few barrels of wine seemed like a relatively honorable pursuit, scrubbing out five fermentation tanks and racking a hundred barrels simply seemed a chore. Many of my duties didn't directly involve *wine* at all; somebody had to stack cases, label bottles, and shovel pomace into the vineyard, and that somebody was me.

Ravenswood's landlord was Angelo Sangiacamo, a grape grower who sold his fruit to vintners throughout Northern California. Sangiacomo grew his Chardonnay directly behind our warehouse, where his crew lived in a cottage frequently overflowing with Mexican music. After Ravenswood wines were pressed (i.e., separated from the crushed grape skins and seeds), I drove a flatbed truck into the vineyard and dumped the dry mounds of grape skins there as compost. We borrowed equipment from Sangiacamo constantly; one time I almost drove his forklift over a twenty-five-foot bank into Sonoma Creek. I entered into reveries whenever I contemplated the gold and crimson vines. I became especially enraptured while making deliveries to Napa Valley, where, in the fairy-tale atmosphere, I found myself fantasizing and free-associating uncontrollably. Napa Valley resembles Oz under any conditions, but in autumn—when the air turns soft, the vines change color, and the earth exudes the warmth stored up over the summer—it becomes utterly hypnotic. On one especially Elysian day in mid-October, John and I drove to Joseph Phelps to buy a load of used barrels, and I was enthralled to be dealing as a worker with the winery that, in my Class D days, had been my favorite major-league player.

At that time Ravenswood was eight years old and producing only 5,000 cases of wine per year (as compared, say, with

Phelps's 60,000 or Robert Mondavi's 3 million). John Kemble was the sole full-time employee; Joel Peterson, the winemaker and principal owner, was also employed as a medical technologist at Sonoma Valley Hospital. When he wasn't working at the hospital, Joel would arrive at the winery in the morning with a caffe latte and his son, Morgan, who at three years of age could already distinguish between Zinfandel and Cabernet. Morgan could also climb the stacks of barrels into the upper reaches of the winery, and I labored in constant dread of rounding a corner and finding his precociousness scattered across the floor. Peterson was then thirty-seven years old, with an appearance confirming his Swedish surname: thin blond hair; pale blue eyes; sparse beard softening a lean, rawboned visage. Before becoming a vintner, he had been a cancer researcher; his father, however, had been a wine collector, and Joel, like Morgan, had been tasting fine wine since he was a child. Given this genealogy and length of experience, his palate and "taste memory" were renowned. They conferred upon him a resplendent command of that specialized vocabulary that so mystifies laypeople—the one that can describe mere bottled beverages as forward, austere, reticent, aggressive, closed, etc., etc. They also helped him produce extraordinary wines.

In addition to the primitiveness of Ravenswood's technique, Joel barred no holds in his effort to squeeze flavor from grapes. Where most modern vintners sterilize their must and inoculate it with a commercial yeast, he allowed his to ferment on its naturally occurring ones from the vineyard, saying that a mixed population of yeasts gave the wine a more interesting nose. He added grape stems to the fermenting must, allowed its temperature to rise into the nineties (temperatures over a hundred degrees Fahrenheit can kill the yeast and stop the fermentation, a severe headache for a winemaker), and sometimes left it on the skins for as long as a month. Most California wine is pressed off the skins before it's dry—i.e., before all the grape sugar has been converted to alcohol, a transformation that takes about a week—but Joel's wine continued to macerate even after the cap had sunk, an event signaling the disappearance of carbon dioxide and the wine's consequent vulnerability to acetic bacteria. This is the point at which untended wine can turn into vinegar, but given the persuading presence of alcohol, it's also when maximum flavor can be extracted from the grapes. Joel thus walked a microbial tightrope, watching and waiting as long as possible in order to make the most intense wine he could. After aging it between fourteen and twenty-four months in French oak—he abhorred American—he bottled the wine after fining (clarifying) it with egg whites, and without filtering.

The resulting wines are almost unparalleled in the wide world of enology. They are intense, dark, powerful, and ponderously deep, to the extent that the words *gothic* and *brooding* have been employed to describe them. They tend to be tannic from the addition of the stems and alcoholic from the ripeness of the grapes; while almost all wines are said to possess qualities of fruits, berries, and generic "spice," Ravenswood wines seem to suggest somewhat rarer commodities—cloves, mint, eucalyptus, chutney. They're complex and well balanced as well as "big"—crafted to command attention and gain interest with age.

That might not sound like American Beaujolais, but in fact, Ravenswood had gained notoriety primarily for its Zinfandels. During that fall of 1984 Peterson took gold medals in both Zinfandel categories at the Sonoma County Harvest Fair, and his '81 and '82 wines received the highest possible rating in the *Connoisseur's Guide to California Wine*. He scoffed at the notion that Zinfandel is an inferior grape. "I think Zinfandel has the potential to be every bit as good as Cabernet—maybe better," Joel once told me, in the manner of someone proclaiming that Willie McGee was a better center fielder than Willie Mays. "Cabernet Sauvignon in most areas of California doesn't really make a pleasant, Bordeaux-style wine. A lot of them get boring after one or two sips; their herbal qualities are too strong. I think Zinfandel is better suited to our Mediterranean climate. Its flavor verges on the exotic; it has all the aging potential of Cabernet, but it comes around early in the nose and can be very charming when young. Cabernet doesn't get really exciting until it's old. In some ways, you might say Zinfandel is the perfect child."

As the weather got colder, the work got easier. By November all the wines had been pressed and entered into various types of storage, beginning their long sojourn of settling and maturation. As the clamor of the crush abated, stillness settled over the winery like snow; the first rainstorm of the season came and went, steelhead returned to Sonoma Creek, and since the warehouse lacked heat as well as light, wool supplanted cotton as the work fabric of choice. I topped up the '83 vintage, clambering among the stacks with a pressure hose to fill each barrel with wine (counteracting the effect of evaporation through the staves), and spent tedious days on end gluing labels to bottles. As the holidays approached, however, there were fewer and fewer things for me to do; I came to Sonoma less and less often, and eventually returned to the city full-time.

As winter arrived, I began convening with a couple of friends to make dinner and drink wine. One of them had lived in New Orleans, where I had recently gone for the first time, to write an article about the Cajun chef Paul Prudhomme. Prudhomme's assistant had sent me home with several pounds of andouille and tasso—an aged, smoked, wickedly spiced ham that served to obliterate my journalistic objectivity. The other member of our cooking group was by nature prone to New Orleans-style indulgence, so it stood to reason that our initial efforts would be Louisianan. From the beginning, the method of the Young Gentlemen's Culinary Society was overkill: We began each meeting with Cajun martinis (marinated with garlic and chili peppers) before tucking into incendiary concoctions of barbecued shrimp, jambalaya, crawfish étouffé, pecan meunière trout, andouille in eggplant with oyster-tasso hollandaise. In the kitchen we were more enthusiastic than efficient, often sitting down to eat around 11:00 P.M. As the evenings progressed, social relations would become rather boisterous, with certain participants invariably ending up on the floor.

The tenor of these events being blatantly bacchanal, only one wine was appropriate to them: Zinfandel. Finer, less robust varietals were no match for the food. Their nuances would have been wasted on our pepper-blasted palates, whereas Zinfandel could stand up and trade punches with the powerhouse cuisine. (This pugilistic dining strategy was called into question as time went on, but that's a later chapter.) Moreover, there was something beyond Zinfandel's piquant flavor that jibed with our ethos. Though it was (probably) no more Spanish than we were, its name rang of spurs and castanets and the string of silver conchas down a gaucho's leg; like our gustatory ardor, it was hedonistic and unpretentious, not coy. It epitomized the philosophy that "Wine is made to be drunk," an adage with which we were eager to comply—and one accommodated by Zinfandel's price, which ran about half that of Cabernet Sauvignon's. (Our first bulk purchase—the inaugural Young Gentlemen's house wine—was the 1980 Rutherford Hill Zinfandel, a 15.4-percent-alcohol bruiser that cost seventy-two dollars for a case.)

In more ways than one, then, Zinfandel was accessible—an easy wine to grow fond of and adopt—and over the next couple of years I cultivated a special interest in it. You might say that, personally and professionally, I joined the Zinfandel flock—which, considering the commercial exile that the varietal was then undergoing amid Cabernet/Chardonnay fanaticism, felt more than ever like a cult.

Meanwhile, Ravenswood was developing a cult of its own. Despite increasing their production (and their prices) every year, Joel, John, and their financial partner, Reed Foster, found themselves unable to meet the growing demand for their idiosyncratic wines. This comforting dilemma was exacerbated by Robert M. Parker, Jr., whose bimonthly newsletter, *The Wine Advocate*, serves as holy scripture for wine buyers around the country. Having gotten hold of some Ravenswood Zinfandels, Parker wrote that they had "dazzling aromas of exotic berry fruit and a heady level of alcoholic punch, but they are wonderfully pure and, most important, thrilling to drink." He called Ravenswood's Napa Valley/Dickerson vineyard "the Heitz Martha's Vineyard of Zinfandels" (referring to the origin of California's most famous and prized Cabernet Sauvignon) and claimed that he had almost mistaken it for a '59 Mouton Rothschild. Eventually Parker chose Joel Peterson as one of his fifteen "winemakers of the year," a worldwide competition. Previously he had accorded Joel an almost as impressive accolade when he proclaimed that Ravenswood was replacing Ridge Vineyards as the world's finest producer of premium Zinfandel.

To many of Parker's readers, that statement was probably tantamount to heresy. The foil in the formula—Ridge Vineyards—was the legendary and long-standing temple of the Zinfandel cult. Founded by a group of Stanford Research Institute scientists in the late 1950s, Ridge had pioneered such now-common California practices as technically informative labels and separate vineyard designations on the bottle. Its estate wine was the expensive, highly esteemed Monte Bello Cabernet Sauvignon, but for decades Ridge had also been renowned for its Zinfandels, which were made from different vineyards all over the state. I had read repeatedly about the Ridge winemaker, Paul Draper, who was considered Zinfandel's leading exponent and one of California's great vintners. Draper had lived in France and Italy and begun making wine in Chile; he was called "a charismatic figure" by one writer (who also threw in "a scientist, a philosopher, a gentleman farmer, maybe even a Beat poet" and summed up by saying that "many people consider him an artist"). In the book *Great Winemakers of California*, Draper was said to possess "the most intellectual approach to winemaking in the state," but also to be as "affable, garrulous, and down-to-earth as a ranch hand."

Explaining his original attraction to winemaking in that book, Draper himself had said, "It was an intriguing idea to take something from the earth, to carry it a step further through artisan ability, and make of it as sophisticated and complex a thing as fine wine, and to have that also be something that would give pleasure." This statement succinctly expressed my own fascination with the craft. As far as Ridge wines were concerned, however, I had one problem: I didn't much care for them. Despite their reputation as huge, inky blockbusters (the Young Gentlemen's accepted quality standard), the Ridge Zinfandels I'd consumed had been mild-mannered, not terribly interesting clarets; they completely lacked the oomph of Ravenswood. To be fair, my prowess as a wine taster, then as now, was quite modest, but my findings were occasionally borne out by more experienced judges. In September 1986 the *Connoisseur's Guide to California Wine* wrote: "As the winery that has been most responsible for elevating Zinfandel into a prestigious varietal, Ridge has sometimes disappointed us in recent years with wines that fell short of the earlier successes. The performance was usually sound without quite hitting the top of the charts and more than a few wines were bothered by a musty, damp wood, mushroomy quality." One night I had accompanied Joel Peterson to a Basque restaurant, where a group of San Francisco enophiles had been meeting weekly for decades, each participant bringing a bottle in a bag; my contribution was a Ridge Howell Mountain Zinfandel, which, when unveiled, created a sensation—but probably not for reasons that the winemaker would have preferred. It was variously deprecated as "stinky" and "defective"; one of the tasters—a commercial wine retailer—suggested that I take it back and demand a refund.

Joel told me that Ridge's reputation for big wines had been built by David Bennion, one of the original partners who had preceded Paul Draper as winemaker. After Draper took over in the early seventies, the winery had maintained its traditional approach—a natural one much like Ravenswood's, employing natural yeasts and minimal filtration—but production had been increased considerably, and the wine style had become more moderate. Recently the entire Ridge operation had been sold to a Japanese pharmaceutical firm, creating minor shock waves in the wine world; after all, Ridge was among the most respected of California wineries, one that had helped revolutionize the industry, and with more and more domestic wineries coming under foreign corporate control (fully one fourth as of this writing), there was wide consternation about what this sale portended. I, for my part, wondered whether it was simply another step on a road that had already seemed to be leading toward commercialization.

Ridge Vineyards became another mysterious element in the Zinfandel story. So, in an effort to unravel it, I gave Paul Draper a call.

I visited Ridge for the first time in August 1987. To get there from my house in Berkeley, I drove through San Francisco and down the Junipero Serra Freeway ("the most beautiful freeway in the world"), a route I had followed frequently when I first moved to California and was going back and forth between San Francisco and Santa Cruz. As I drove, the urban environment receded by degrees; a landscape littered with pastel buildings gradually became oak-dotted pastureland, rising toward a crest of coastal hills topped with a white tissue of fog. After about an hour I left the highway and drove west into those hills, passing a reservoir and a quarry and turning onto Monte Bello Road, which climbs two thousand feet in five miles. My ears adjusted on the climb as I passed picturesque pastures, orchards, old barns, and a ranch called Jimsomare. I counted forty-five bends in the road before I reached Ridge's driveway, where the oaks suddenly cleared out to reveal a panorama of the entire South Bay—Silicon Valley and San Jose sprawled immediately below, the bare brown Diablo Range rising in the east, and the blue-green bay itself stretching away to the north, where San Francisco lay hidden in fog. I drove up a short hill, through a gate, and found the winery—or at any rate the winery's office, a weathered barn with board-and-batten siding.

The sunlit premises were perfectly quiet. I parked my car, turned off the engine, and detected the smell of superheated water; I opened my hood and released the pressure cap on the radiator, which immediately overflowed with sputtering yellow-green water—the legacy of the two-thousand-foot climb. I left the car to cool and wandered down the driveway and through the big barn door. Nobody was about. As I stood looking through a picture window at the mountains to the south, a turtlenecked woman suddenly burst through a side door, singing. When she saw me, she stopped and said, "I didn't know anybody was here." I identified myself and she disappeared.

A moment later a man wearing khaki pants, a blue-and-white-striped shirt, and a salt-and-pepper Van Dyke beard came out to greet me. "David, hi," he said, extending his hand. "Paul Draper." A pair of eyebrows to rival Groucho's were offset by his wire-rimmed glasses; his goatee covered his entire chin up to the bottom of his lower lip, and combined with a cherubic smile, it gave him a slightly elfin (as opposed to strictly intellectual) quality. "We can sit down and talk in just a few minutes," he said, leading me outside onto a deck while explaining over his shoulder that he was dictating a letter protesting the BATF's decision to disallow Ridge's use of certain vineyard names. He gave an exasperated chortle and said he'd return momentarily. Already Draper had displayed two traits with which I would soon become familiar: his low chuckle, which can indicate anything from trepidation to delight (often both at the same time), and an immediate, apparent willingness to launch into a discussion of anything he happened to be thinking about.

He displayed a third when he came back to the deck, carrying a clipboard and saying, "Okay!" to indicate that one task was finished and another could now begin. Draper poured himself some coffee and sat down at the table with his clipboard. I described my interest in wine in general and Zinfandel in particular, and without further prompting, Draper began to relate a saga that he was probably capable of reciting in his sleep.

"From 1965 to 1973 you could name on one hand the interesting Zinfandels in California," he said. "For the first decade of our existence, during the sixties, Ridge was an estate Cabernet vineyard—Monte Bello Cabernet Sauvignon comprised about eighty percent of our production—but we did make a tiny amount of Zinfandel from the Jimsomare and Picchetti vineyards on this hill, so we knew how good—how complex and unusual—those wines from old vines could be. Zinfandel grapes, like Cabernet, have to come from the best areas in California to be top quality; unlike Cabernet, Zinfandel vines need to be considerably older to produce the best fruit with the most intensity. The Zinfandel I've gotten from eight- or ten- or twelve-year-old vines isn't much more than half the quality of wine from sixty- to ninety-year-old vines. But we happen to be incredibly fortunate to have old Zinfandel vines planted in ideally suited soils and microclimates. It's only because we have these old, old vines that we're able to make such unusual wines.

"In the early seventies we had to expand our production in order to become financially viable. It was almost impossible to find old Cabernet vineyards that would produce the quality of fruit we were looking for, but all over the state there were these old Zinfandel vineyards whose grapes were going into the jug blends of the big wineries. They were absolutely first-rate grapes, but the growers weren't being paid any more for them than for grapes that had only been in the ground for six or eight years, producing three times as much fruit at one-third the quality. Many of these people were descendants of the Italians who had originally planted the vines; we bought some of their grapes and identified the vineyards on the label, and when they saw the results, they could take some pride in the fact that superior wine was being made from their vineyards. That enabled us to work with the growers to produce the kind of wine we wanted.

"When my friend Fritz Maytag wanted to plant Zinfandel in his York Creek vineyard up on Spring Mountain, we recommended the clone from the Picchetti vineyard down the ridge here. Today two-thirds of our York Creek Zinfandel comes from that. The other third is a clone from Leo Trentadue's ranch

21

near Geyserville, in Alexander Valley. That would probably be our best Zinfandel vineyard, judging by its consistent performance, year in and year out. There's a series of small blocks scattered around the Trentadue ranch with vines ranging from sixty to a hundred years old. The best ones are in the gravel above the Russian River—the old prehistoric riverbed. There's a particular intensity to the original block, the Heart's Desire vineyard planted by a friend of Luther Burbank's over a hundred years ago.* We've been making wine from that vineyard for twenty-two years; it's one of the longest personal and grower relationships that anyone in California has had. It's about eighty percent Zinfandel, with a small portion of mixed blacks—Petite Sirah and Carignane. At first we didn't realize that those varieties were part of it; in '74 we left them out, and the wines weren't as complex. Now we consciously include the Petite Sirah. You get a different wine depending on whether you ferment the Zinfandel and the Petite Sirah together or apart; if you ferment them together, they're integrated sooner, but if you ferment them separately and then blend them by taste, adding five or ten percent Petite Sirah after about nine months, it can add a cleansing element of spice, and you get a more exciting wine. We believe Zinfandel needs a small amount of Petite Sirah in order to age well; it's more tannic than Zinfandel, it has a different color, and it adds some liveliness. Generally Zinfandel can go about ten years and still be lovely and complex, but that's all. From ten years on, it just depends on the vintage; it may hold after ten years, but not necessarily improve."

The aging question summoned a memory for Draper: "I was at a formal dinner once with some English wine people, and the host brought in two decanters with the main course. He said, 'We can call a halt to this when it ceases to be amusing'—

---

*Most of these vines have since been ripped out and replanted by the property's current lessor, Chateau Souverain (a subsidiary of Wine World, owned by the Nestlé Corporation). Ridge continues, however, to make its Geyserville Zinfandel from the surrounding vineyard.

you don't want to spring surprises on the English—but suggested that we taste them blind. They were magnificent old red wines—rich, full, lovely, complex." With each adjective, Draper sliced the air, making elegant karate chops with his upturned hand. "I said one was an old Médoc. The other I didn't know, but I thought it might be from California; the Englishman thought it was the other way around. It turned out that I was right: One was a 1924 Château Margaux; the other, a '35 Simi Zinfandel. I had detected just a hint of redwood in the Zinfandel, which I thought might have come from an aging tank in California. Simi is an old Italian winery, and in those days they blended Petite Sirah and Carignane with Zinfandel in redwood tanks. The fruit of the Zinfandel would have better survived the tank aging process that way. I'd bet the wine was twenty percent Petite Sirah; it still tasted fresh and young. Anyway, the moral of the story is not that I was so perceptive but that a European could mistake this California Zinfandel for an old French claret!

"Now I'll tell you another rather egotistical story. In 1985 I was invited to be guest of honor at a tasting with the 'California First Crew' club in New York. A lot of retailers and a few writers like Barbara Ensrud and Frank Prial were there. They had asked me what I wanted to taste, so I said, 'Put together the best grouping of '73, '74, and '75 Cabernets from your cellars. Then don't tell anyone, but include our '73, '74, and '75 Geyserville Zinfandels.' Nobody had the '73 Heitz or Stag's Leap Cabernets; they did have Mayacamas, Chappellet, and BV Private Reserve. They also insisted on including our Monte Bello Cabernet, so there were fifteen wines in all. The five from '73 were tasted together, rated, and pushed aside; then the '74s and '75s. The Monte Bello won in every category, but the big surprise was that the Geyserville was second in '73 and '74 and third in '75. In other words, ten to twelve years out, only one of the non-Ridge Cabernets was better than any of the Zinfandels."

Draper got up to get more coffee; I asked him what he specifically liked about Zinfandel.

"From day one, Zinfandel has so much forward fruit that it's sensual to drink right away," he said, continuing to stand while holding his cup. "Its appeal is immediate, whereas Cabernet needs time to develop. You *can* have a very sensual experience with old Cabernet, but you can have a comparable experience with young Zinfandel—which is why, in a restaurant, I'd be more likely to order a Zinfandel than a Cabernet. The roundness and depth of flavor in Zinfandel—it's sheer joy, whereas the pleasure of Cabernet is more intellectual. You might say Zinfandel is romantic and Cabernet is baroque. Zinfandel is perhaps a full orchestera, where Cabernet is a chamber quartet."

The philosopher-poet was going strong, but time was fleeting, so I told Draper my opinion of Ridge wines—at least I told him that they didn't seem as brash and brawny as their reputation had led me to expect—and asked if he'd changed the winery's style since he'd joined on. He looked at me squarely, nodding his head.

"Fifteen years ago," he said, "we made a small percentage of monster wines that walked over everyone else in tastings. People focused on them because they were unusual. In '75, which was a cold year, the wines weren't as intense, and we got phone calls condemning our 'change in style.' In '76 and '77 things were back to normal. In '78 we got overripe grapes, and some of our wines were sixteen percent alcohol. I learned my lesson on that vintage; now we pick within a window of ripeness one-third the size of what we did in '78. In the last five years I've decided that for the quality of a wine over its lifetime, balance (not ripeness) is all. In other words, it's a mistake to make wines that don't give any sensual pleasure when they're young. I think if you can make a wine balanced before it's bottled, it has a chance to be one of the finest wines you've ever produced, whereas if it's undrinkable at first, it won't be one of the greatest. People might think it's great eventually, but it still won't be as fine a wine as the one that was balanced from the beginning. And I happen to think that there's much more flavor in the Ridge '85 Lytton Springs Zinfandel than there was in any Zinfandel of the sixties or seventies. One way to get your name known then was to make a big wine that blew others away in tastings; when you have fourteen or fifteen wines to taste, it's not a pleasurable activity. It's work, and you immediately acclimatize to the wines available. After you taste a huge late-harvest wine, you can't go back to table-style wine and find anything there at all—it will just seem flat and dead. But you can't take that late-harvest wine home and have it with your dinner. That's the trouble with tastings. If a late-harvest wine had shown up on my table when I was thirty-three, I might have polished it off and said, 'That's great.' Back then I could sit down to dinner several times a week with a big fifteen-percent-alcohol wine. Now I wouldn't want it for dinner, except maybe outdoors with a Slovanian picnic. I drink very little port these days; I drink very little Sauternes. I drink mostly table wines, and I rarely drink them without food. If I'm at a cocktail party and somebody hands me a glass of wine, I'll drink it, but after that I have to get some food. For me, wine is food, and I believe it's going to be part of our culture *only* if it goes with food—if it's drunk with a meal, every day.''

A group of people had assembled in the kitchen: a Scottish woman name Wilma Sturrock; Ridge's president, Bill Curtiss; the winemaker, David Noyes* (Draper is head winemaker and chief executive officer); and a muscular, mustachioed young man named Fred Peterson, Ridge's vineyard manager, visiting from his home near Dry Creek Valley in Sonoma County. Draper invited me along on a survey the group was about to conduct of the immediate backcountry, with attention to its prospects for grape growing. "We're negotiating with the county parks district about trading development rights on our land for agricultural rights on acreage adjacent to the winery," Draper said. "The parks would extend their open space; we'd replant the vineyards on the hills. It strikes us both as compatible and historic use of the land."

The group crowded into Peterson's Land Cruiser and inched

*Since this writing, Noyes and Curtiss have departed and Wilma Sturrock is now president of Ridge.

down a steep dirt road behind the winery, probing into the untrammeled chaparral. Among the oaks and manzanita grew wild grapevines, greasewood, and profuse amounts of poison oak. The sunbaked air was hot and dry; perfumed aromas rose from the bush. As we progressed, the road became increasingly rutted and overgrown, and we lurched from side to side, clutching the handgrips.

"I haven't driven these roads in ten years," Draper said, clasping his clipboard and leaning forward to look through the windshield from a back seat.

"I was on a worse road than this last week," said Peterson.

"I'm glad to hear there *is* one that's worse," said Draper.

As it happened, we were traveling directly above the San Andreas earthquake fault, along the boundary of the Pacific and North American tectonic plates. "Hey!" said Draper. "We're getting into limestone here! This whole mountain is unique. It wasn't part of the North American plate. This limestone was laid down by microscopic sea life dying off a hundred and sixty million years ago, at the same time as the huge die-off that created Burgundy and the cliffs of Dover. This mountain was built up near the equator and moved north with the Pacific plate; when it went under the North American plate and continued on to Hudson Bay, this three-thousand-foot mound of limestone was sheared off and left behind."

We could see the blue Pacific through a V in the mountains. The hills were hushed and breathless in the sun. We came to a spring-fed water tank with goldfish in it; Draper said that on his morning jog he turns around at the tank. We were now directly below his house, which was situated on an open knoll beside a row of poplars, olive trees, and European chestnuts with a view of the ocean. Pointing to an adjacent slope that exhibited faint horizontal traces, Draper said, "Those are the old terraces from the original Monte Bello vineyard. If we replanted them, this would be one of the most beautiful vineyards in the world." As it was, it wasn't doing too badly.

The "safari" lasted about an hour; by the time we returned

to the winery, the sun was getting low. I told Draper that I'd like to come back, and he suggested that I attend some tastings.

As I descended Monte Bello Ridge, I contrasted Draper and Ridge with my other primary reference. On the surface, comparing Ridge with Ravenswood seemed like splitting hairs; they seemed to correspond in more ways than they differed. Both espoused dedication to traditional techniques; both made red wine almost exclusively (though both also produced Chardonnay in limited amounts); both were best known for Zinfandel, though both made other, more expensive wines from more prestigious varietals. Still, considering all these congruencies, their wines turned out quite different. This raised the broader artistic question of how and why two similarly inclined practitioners, given the same raw material, can create completely distinctive products.

It occurred to me that if I were to examine both Ridge and Ravenswood in depth, I might find out something about how this process took place. Moreover, I'd undoubtedly learn a few things about the nature of fine wine itself. If, as Robert M. Parker maintained, Ravenswood was replacing Ridge as the world's finest producer of Zinfandel, what exactly did that mean—not only in terms of wine but in terms of the world? Considering Zinfandel's role in California, California's role in the world of wine, and wine's role in the history of civilization— who knew? Perhaps, by pursuing this question, I'd stumble across something more significant in the bargain.

Isn't that what usually happens in a good mystery?

In late August I accompanied Joel Peterson on his pre-crush rounds of premium Zinfandel vineyards. The '87 harvest was shaping up as one of the earliest—and smallest—in the state's history; a warm winter had encouraged buds to break out early, but then a heat wave during the flowering period had shattered much of the fruit, leaving a very light crop on the vines. Joel was wearing a Fort Worth Stockyards T-shirt and a Panama hat; in his Peugeot with "RAVENSW" license plates, we picked up six-year-old Morgan and drove west through the hills, passing small farmhouses whose yards contained horses, mules, date palms, and pickup trucks. When we came to the intersection of Stagecoach Gulch and Adobe roads, Joel referred to it as Ravenswood's Bermuda Triangle. "I don't know what the deal is there," he said. "One time I ran out of gas when the gauge said the tank was half full. More than once I've had to tighten ropes on trucks, and another time a storage tank blew off; I spent an hour looking for the lid and never found it. Last year I came up to that stop sign carrying four tons of Dry Creek Zinfandel; you can square off directly or do it on an angle, and I couldn't see both ways, so I did it on the angle. I hit a pothole and the truck turned over, dumping four tons of grapes into the road."

"What did you do?"

"I called Angelo Sangiacamo, and he sent a crew over to help me scrape up the grapes."

"How did the wine turn out?"

"I'd say it has kind of a tarry quality."

The August air was still and silent. Black-green oaks and shaggy eucalyptus were strewn across the parched brown hills; yellow-topped fennel grew along the road. We passed through the college town of Cotati, which displayed an assortment of green-and-red Dos Equis umbrellas, kids on motorcycles, and young women in tight jeans. I offered a lament to the effect that as one gets older, one's interest in youthful biology doesn't cooperate by subsiding.

"Unfortunately, life doesn't work that way," said Joel, who has a degree in biology. "And doubly unfortunately, the older women get, the tougher and harder to deal with they are."

There exists a long and not necessarily honorable tradition that compares wine with women. I evinced my subscription to it by saying, "Unlike wine."

"I used to drink nothing but old wines," said Joel. "Lately, though, I've come to appreciate young wines. Maybe because I work with them and taste so many of them. You start looking for that life, that resilience."

We passed a sign saying FIRE DANGER TODAY: VERY HIGH.

"Maybe it's just that I'm over forty," Joel said, pulling onto U.S. 101 North.

Evergreens began to appear along the freeway above Santa Rosa. In true California fashion we were traveling from microclimate to microclimate in a matter of minutes. We had started out in the Carneros district, marked by cool breezes and fogs from San Pablo Bay and noted for Chardonnay and Pinot Noir; now we were entering the North Coast region, where the average summer temperature is much warmer and the marine influence comes from the Pacific Ocean. We pulled off near Healdsburg and drove northwest into Dry Creek Valley—a hallowed, historic Zinfandel region, a slender cleft in the coast range whose hillsides were covered with oak, manzanita, fir, and redwood, but whose fertile floor and lower slopes were infused with bright green grapevines.

"There are at least three different environments in this valley alone," Joel said as he drove north in the valley. "There's the valley floor, the east-side benchland, and the small outcroppings of hills on the west. In my first harvest, in '76, I got the grapes from the west side. Now I get them from the east, which ripens a week earlier. It can get very warm here during the day, which is good for sugar, but the marine influence makes it cool and foggy at night, which maintains acidity."

We pulled off the main road, ascended a short hill, and got out of the car. The heat surrounded us like cotton. Here at the end of summer the grapes were being seared, their sugar levels climbing quietly toward the ineffable point where they could produce fine wine. The bunches of grapes were black and shiny beneath their chalky dust of yeast: plump, luscious little globes, gifts from the plant. The vines carrying them, head-pruned in traditional Zinfandel style, looked like miniature trees: independent, self-supporting, their branches radiating from a central trunk free of wires or trellises. Despite their apparent autonomy, their tendrils reached out across rows to hold hands, creating obstacles to foot travel. Joel strolled through the vineyard anyway, picking berries and putting them into his mouth.

"It's going to be a great year, fruitwise," he announced. "These are starting to get real good Zinfandel flavor." He squeezed juice from a grape onto a refractometer, held the device up to the sun, and peered into the eyepiece, where light refracting through the film of grape juice cast a shadow across a scale. "That one was twenty-point-five," he said, meaning that the juice measured 20.5 degrees Brix, or about 20.5 percent sugar. "They're already showing some color in the juice. Usually they don't do that till around twenty-three. There's a tremendous amount of pigment in the skins this year. The wines are going to have rich color."

He continued taking samples at random. "This one's twenty-one. That was twenty-two. That was twenty-three. Here, taste one off this bunch." I put a grape into my mouth, and it exploded between my teeth; the thin membrane burst, and warm juice gushed onto my tongue. "That was twenty-seven," Joel said. "That's what I'd call ripe. It depends partly on where the berry is situated on the bunch; they're higher in sugar up here on the shoulder, but toward the apex the readings are lower. Afternoon readings tend to be higher than morning readings; during the day the vine is busy respiring water. At night it's busy soaking it out of the ground.

"Grapes have a funny way of getting almost ripe and then stopping," Joel said. "But these are real close. Maybe Friday; maybe this weekend."

Joel wanted to harvest the fruit between 22.5 and 23.5 degrees Brix. "We take our grapes a little riper than most people," he said. "I like them rich and flavorful. If you pick too early, you'll be too high in acid, and the wine will taste tart and not have much character. The most important factor, really, is my sense of the flavor development of the grape—what it feels like in my mouth, what kind of wine it'll make. There's also the factor of what the weather's going to do. If the grapes were twenty-two-point-five and the weather was cool, we might wait a few more days for more ripening and less acid. On the other hand, if it's going to be very hot, it'll just dehydrate the berries, and the fruit will deteriorate—particularly Zinfandel, which tends to develop raisining and overripe characteristics. Then there's the question of how full the winery is at the moment—whether we have space in the fermentors and can juggle the different vineyards."

In the distance beyond the glinting acres of grapevines were a couple of massive steel tanks. Joel said they were a crushing station for a rather large, rather well-known Central Valley wine producer. "They're putting a boutique winery in here. It used to be very hilly over there, but they rebuilt the land surface. They knocked the topsoil down the hill, filled the gully with undersoil, and then brought the topsoil back up." As a matter of fact, the grower from whom Joel was buying these grapes was contractually obligated to sell most of them to this producer. We got back in the car to pay the family a visit.

A few minutes later we pulled up in front of a low ranch house with a stack of inner tubes outside. That annual signal for the approach of harvest—"naked lady" flowers, clusters of pink bells dangling from maroon stalks, blooming from bulbs— stood beside the driveway. A group of Mexican girls ran by. In the shade of a walnut tree an elderly lady was conversing in Italian with a mustachioed man wearing jeans, a baseball shirt, and cowboy boots. Joel got out of the car to greet them. He then introduced me to the mustachioed man, who was responsible for the vineyard.

After we had talked for a while, I asked him what the Central Valley winery did with most of his grapes. "Probably throw it in with their other shit to make jug wine," he said. "It would be good for my reputation if I sold all my grapes to Ravenswood, but I ain't gonna bite the hand that feeds me; this year they voluntarily upped the price for my Zinfandel from six hundred fifty to eight hundred dollars a ton. And who else is gonna buy my Palomino? Who's gonna take my Sauvignon Vert? They wouldn't take the junk grapes if they couldn't get my Zinfandel."

"When I first came here, he pulled out some of his own home Zinfandel," Joel said as we drove away. "He told me he made it from the second-crop grapes after selling the best stuff. He said he just threw it all in the fermentor, put a lid on it, and then went on vacation for two weeks; when he came back, it was ready to be pressed. The wine was good, amazingly enough. We sat under that tree all day drinking it. At first he said he couldn't sell me any grapes. Then after about an hour he said maybe he could. After about four hours he said he'd sell me a little. By the time I got up from the table, I could hardly walk. Those grapes have been pivotal to the winery's success."

We turned onto Canyon Road and passed the J. Pedroncelli Winery, longtime producers of sound, basic Zinfandel. Then— again in a matter of minutes—we entered another appellation: Alexander Valley, a broad agricultural basin cradling the Russian River below the eastern eminence of Geyser Peak. We rejoined

Highway 101 and drove north, but Joel missed his exit and we turned around at the town of Asti, driving a few miles back south and turning onto Chianti Road.

The names bespoke the ethnic origins of California Zinfandel. As Idwal Jones wrote of northern Sonoma County in a 1949 book entitled *Vines in the Sun*: "Most of the farmers are Italian . . . their grapes are largely Zinfandel, and their ledgers are balanced. . . . It is not improbable that the growers of tomorrow, if direct from the Apennines, and settled in the right pocket of earth, may produce a red Monte Mario, or a Grottaferrata; but it is more likely they will do nothing of the kind, and hardheadily grow Zinfandel, which on this earth yields a balanced, dusky, and aromatic red wine, so individual that it cannot be mistaken for anything but zinfandel."

The beginnings of viticulture north of San Francisco Bay in the mid-1800s were overwhelmingly German, featuring such Teutonic nomenclature as Krug, Beringer, Gundlach, Korbel, and Schram. The Italian immigration didn't begin in earnest until the end of the nineteenth century. Those Italians who had the means to reach the West Coast of America tended to be better off financially than their eastern cousins; they brought with them the southern European tradition of wine as a daily drink, and they began acquiring vineyards and planting grapes within hours of arriving. In Sonoma County, where the land reminded them of home, alluvial bottomlands were planted to orchards or alfalfa, but gravelly hillsides with good exposure resembled places where wine grapes throve in Tuscany and Piedmont. Italian grape varieties—Barbera, Nebbiolo, Trebbiano, Sangiovese—were generally too shy-bearing to be profitable in California (as, at the time, was Cabernet Sauvignon, whose astringent product also took time to soften). But Zinfandel would produce a substantial crop, generate a second one if a frost or heat wave killed the first shoots, and survive the summer heat with enough acid to make a balanced, readily drinkable table wine—hearty, spicy, fruity wine that tasted terrific with tomatoes and pasta. Blended, as it often was, in the vineyard with the more tannic and spicy Petite Sirah, it would even im-

33

prove for some years if not finished off by fall. Zinfandel vines crept inexorably over the hills of Sonoma County—vines upwards of ninety years old as we drove past them now.

Chianti Road contained entrances to various Alexander Valley wineries: Seghesio, Vina Vista, Geyser Peak. The enological vantage point on the speeding traffic of 101 wasn't terribly bucolic. We drove thorugh a gate and pulled up to an imposing structure on an open slope, done in characteristic style for California boutique wineries: Gentrified Barn with big breezeways and vertical redwood siding. This was the headquarters of Lyeth ("Leeth") Vineyards, a five-year-old winery more emblematic of recent than ancient California winemaking. It was the venture of Munro L. ("Chip") Lyeth, Jr., the forty-four-year-old scion of a Colorado banking family who had bought the vineyard and built the winery following a career as a photographer and airplane racer in Santa Barbara and Aspen. Joel had contracted for twenty tons of Zinfandel from the seventy-year-old vines behind the winery.

"This winery is pretty big," Morgan said as we got out of the car. "How many acres does he own?"

Joel said he didn't know.

"A lot, though," said Morgan. "A hundred? More than Angelo?"

"I think Angelo owns more."

No one was stirring on the grounds. The atmosphere was vacuumlike; the place seemed deserted. We went inside the building, which was equally elegant and eerie, with fine joinery, wood paneling, and French doors leading into an empty tasting room. When Joel announced his business to the receptionist, she said: "People say Zinfandel's making a comeback. I think it never left."

"It never left for people who were making good wine," said Joel.

After a moment Chip Lyeth appeared: a big sandy-haired man wearing jeans, boots, and a plaid shirt. "Hey, Morgan," Lyeth said.

"Hi," said Morgan. "How many acres do you own?"

"About three hundred," said Lyeth.

Morgan rolled his eyes.

"Only about a hundred in grapes, though."

The vineyard behind the winery was on a slight slope amid a range of rolling yellow hills that contained yet more vineyards marching toward the sky. The soil underfoot was sandy gravel. "This soil is similar to what you find in the Médoc," Joel said as we walked. "It's extremely well drained—the water goes straight through the ground. In such a porous vineyard the soil dries out in equilibrium with the vines ripening. The vines get stressed, but not so stressed that they wither. Heat reflects off the gravel and gives you a more even ripening pattern; even on cool days, you get a little bit more warmth."

I noticed that the poplar trees bordering the vineyard were turning yellow, though it was only August. "It's fall up here," said Lyeth. "You might not think so, but ask a grapevine."

"Why are all these leaves on the ground?" asked Morgan.

"Mites ate 'em up," said Lyeth.

"Uh-oh!"

"They should all be dead by now."

"Did you spray for them?" Joel asked.

"You bet," said Lyeth. "The leaves were turning brown before my eyes."

We came to the Zinfandel vines, and Joel whipped out his refractometer. "That one was eighteen," he said.

"Perfect for eating," said Lyeth. "No acid."

"Oh, no, no acid at all," said Joel, munching the grape and wincing at the sharpness of the acid. He picked and squeezed several more berries. Lyeth asked what the average was.

"About twenty-two," said Joel. "I'll have to go back and talk to John, but it looks like Thursday to me."

"Thursday's okay," said Lyeth. "I got smart this year; I've got eight pickers on full-time standby. Next year I'm going to plant a vegetable garden for them."

A single swallow hovered above us, stationary on a stiff

breeze. As we walked back through the vineyard, Lyeth said, "It looks like the winery's going to sell in a couple of weeks."

"Is that right?" said Joel. "How long has it been on the market?"

"Three years."

"Whew!"

Driving back toward the highway, Joel said: "Chip started out with just a vineyard there. He built the winery at his father's behest, even though he already had his hands full. The idea was to produce expensive Bordeaux-style blends; they've made some nice wines, but the winery started consuming all his time, and they were losing money. They had no cohesive marketing program, so they couldn't sell the wine as fast as they needed to, and they ended up sitting on a lot of inventory. A very expensive, big winery like that is a ten-year project, minimum; they gave it four. You can't do it unless you have your heart in it."

In Cloverdale, thirty-two miles north of Santa Rosa, we made a sentimental stop at the Owl Cafe, where Joel's parents had taken him when he was a boy. Now, with his own son in tow and out from under the watchful eye of his wife, Joel ordered a milkshake and a piece of pie. Then we drove a few hundred yards up the road and pulled off to the west, where within view of the cars and trucks passing on 101, a small house stood in the middle of a Zinfandel vineyard, poison oak growing among the vines.

"See the undeveloped grapes?" Joel said, pointing at a bunch of tiny green balls hanging from a vine. "That's from the heat wave in the spring. I see we're already beginning to get some raisining here; last week we didn't have that." He showed me a cluster of grapes exhibiting three different stages of development: pink berries, mature fruit, and shriveled raisins, all on the same bunch. "Uneven ripening is typical of Zinfandel. A lot of people tear their hair out over it, but I'm of the opinion that it contributes to the character of the wine. You get the acid of the unripe grape, the berrylike quality of the mature grape, and the rich intensity of the raisin. Taste how tannic these berries are? Almost as tannic as Cabernet. One of the hallmarks of this vineyard is its astringency. The wine from it has a significant spine, whereas Lyeth has a substantial berrylike center and Dry Creek has an intense black-cherry nose." (All three, blended together, would enter the shelves of retail wine shops as Ravenswood 1987 Sonoma County Zinfandel.)

On the opposite side of a dirt road was a yard full of vines that had been devastated by deer. Looking at the naked branches and unmowed rows, Joel said, "That's what happens when you don't take care of a vineyard. Those are probably Sauvignon Vert and Palomino. I'm not much interested in old white vines in California; there's really no white equivalent to Zinfandel." We picked a couple of oranges from a tree as we walked toward the ruins of an old stone winery that stood beyond the vineyard. A group of black-faced sheep ran away from us. The oranges were very sweet. The winery was a relic from the nineteenth century.

"You can see in the strata of stone where the builders quit for the day," said Joel, examining the walls of the roofless building. Inside were piles of brittle, uprooted black grapevines and rusting agricultural equipment—hay balers, harvesters, barrel hoops. "This was the tank room," said Joel. "See the rectangular cement pits on the hill? That would have been the fermentation room; they probably had the press basket over there and ran the wine down those little sluices through pipes to the tank house. A classic gravity-flow operation." Joel picked some blackberries from bushes growing over the walls. "Mmm!" he moaned. "Delicious!" As he surveyed the ghostly ruins, he mused: "They probably expected this operation to last for hundreds of years."

We got back in the car and returned south on 101, stopping in the tiny town of Geyserville for motor oil and juice. Then we got on 128 East and passed a crew of dust-covered Mexican grape pickers. Here in Alexander Valley the harvest was already under way. We crossed the Russian River. A fire truck went by. Morgan said, "Daddy, did you know firemen don't get paid?"

"Who told you that?" asked Joel.

"Our next-door neighbor. He's a fireman."

"He gets paid," said Joel.

"*Dad*," said Morgan. "He knows. *You* don't know."

We ascended into Knights Valley between Napa and Alexander valleys. "See that house?" said Joel. "I'll be getting several rows of Cabernet from over there. It's cooler here than Napa Valley, and they get a little more rain. The grapes bud out and ripen later; they're fruitier, with higher acid, thick red skins, and rich, intense flavor. I get my darkest, most intense Merlot from here. We're trying to put together a partnership to buy that Merlot vineyard."

The grapevines disappeared momentarily as we entered a classic California landscape of dry yellow hills and scrubby oaks hung with gray moss. We crossed the Napa County line, and as we wound our way down to the mud-bath and mineral-water realm of Calistoga, the brown volcanic cliffs of Mount St. Helena came into view. Sometime after we turned onto Highway 29, we passed a group of tourists having their picture taken next to a sign:

WELCOME TO
THE WORLD FAMOUS WINE GROWING REGION
NAPA VALLEY

A highway worker in an orange suit held up a stop sign. Somewhat emblematically, having spent the day roaming freely around Sonoma County, we had entered Napa Valley and immediately gotten caught in a traffic jam.

"Great," muttered Joel, looking at his watch. He wanted to reach an olive oil factory in St. Helena before four-thirty. "Why anybody scheduled roadwork for Napa Valley during harvest season is beyond me."

As we slowly neared St. Helena, a roll call of wineries flowed past: Frog's Leap, Stonegate, Freemark Abbey, Charles Krug. The grand chateau of Christian Brothers displayed a banner advertising a Harvest Brunch. "It must be great to have a staff handling PR and all the social aspects," said Joel. "Over here I'd just be another shop along the road. The number of wineries along here always amazes me; you wonder how they all survive. I remember what it was like trying to sell my wine when I wasn't so well known as I am now; a lot of these newer wineries are in that position. I guess what most of them have that I don't have is a tasting room—one condition of my use permit with Sonoma County is that they didn't want a 'bar' on my corner."

We passed the Beringer winery, ensconced in the great arbor of trees at the north end of St. Helena. The sidewalks of the town swarmed with fashionable people. The pastoral life of the wine country impressed me as I looked down an alley from Main Street and saw a blonde woman in bright red lipstick and a bare-chested, well-built young man posing for a photographer. We turned off the highway and parked in front of the olive oil factory, a white barnlike building that turned out to be filled with gourmet mustards, mushrooms, cheeses, salamis, pastas, fruits, and olives. I brought a couple of dried dates to the counter, and the proprietor waved his hand: "You take." Outside under an olive tree (from which a corkscrew dangled on a string), Morgan was conversing with an elderly Italian, though the man, playing solitaire at a picnic table, appeared not to hear a word that the verbose youngster uttered. Here in Napa Valley the appellations were becoming quite complex: We'd just gone from a very cool region to a very warm one—Hollywood to rural Tuscany—in barely a block.

I wasn't alone in being jarred by these juxtapositions. The Napa County Board of Supervisors has expressed concern about commercialization and gentrification that threaten to overwhelm the valley's agricultural traditions. Where twenty years ago there were two dozen wineries in Napa Valley, there are now more than two hundred. Along with worldwide fame and prices upward of forty thousand dollars per acre for vineyard land, this explosion has brought tourists, traffic, and tackiness in amounts approaching critical mass. In 1988 the board of supervisors declared a moratorium on applications for new wineries and winery expansions in Napa Valley, and a coalition of vintners, growers, and civic groups banded together to block the introduction of a sightseeing train that proposed to shuttle tourists from winery to winery. (They failed.) Napa growers think Napa vintners should buy 75 percent of their grapes in Napa Valley; the growers also want to divide the wineries into categories by age, with on-site marketing activities—for example, the tasting rooms that Joel had singled out as so important to a young winery's survival—severely restricted at none other than the youngest wineries.

"A lot of people with a lot of money got into the wine business in Napa Valley for what I consider the wrong reasons," Joel said as we waited for a break in the traffic on the highway. "In Sonoma Valley they tend to be in it because they love the land, they love the soil, they love the grapes. They're not doing it for status or glamour, and they help each other out. Over here there's too much infighting."

We turned west onto Zinfandel Lane and drove toward the Mayacamas Mountains, at the far western edge of the valley. The late sun threw its rays across the ridges, which receded in shades. Along a dirt road behind a line of walnut and eucalyptus trees, we entered one of Ravenswood's sources of premium vineyard-designated wines: forty acres of sixty-year-old Zinfandel owned by William Dickerson, a Marin County psychiatrist. The vineyard was immaculate, its orderly rows of head-pruned vines luxuriating in manicured red earth.

"Rumor has it that growing red wines in red soil is beneficial," Joel said as he got out of the car. "It does seem to work out pretty well; it indicates high iron content. The soil here is very deep. It isn't gravel; it's clay loam, typical of Napa Valley. The French talk a lot about soil differences, but I'm not convinced it's all that important; climate has more influence on flavor. There isn't as much marine influence here as there is in Sonoma Valley. The nights aren't as cool, the sun day is longer, and the fruit tastes plummier. The wine from this vineyard has a very distinctive raspberry-cinnamon-cedar-eucalyptus quality, an incredible opulence in the nose. If people pick up a bottle of Dickerson Zinfandel, they know that's what they're going to get. I think it's important that a vineyard-designated wine perform in the same manner, year after year."

Joel walked into the vineyard and picked a few grapes, which measured nineteen and twenty degrees Brix. Then he walked back and started the car. "I've got all I need to know," he said. "The grapes aren't going to come in this week."

We continued south past Grgich Hills, Beaulieu, Franciscan, and the Robert Mondavi Winery, its architecture mirroring the missionary role that its namesake has assumed for California wine. Then we turned west onto Oakville Grade, which climbs seven hundred feet in one mile before dropping into the middle of the Mayacamas Mountains: supernal shaded oak woodland and dense California chaparral, home to coyotes, foxes, and mountain lions. We went over a narrow bridge and up again, negotiating a series of excruciating hairpin turns. Turkey vultures circled overhead. The air got cooler. My ears popped. At the crest of the range, redwoods appeared, contributing their inimitable cathedral light. Soon after that Sonoma Valley began to reveal itself in glimpses stretching away to the northwest; it confronted us in CinemaScope as we descended Trinity Road, a veritable parachute drop to Highway 12 and the floor of the Valley of the Moon. Civilization on the Sonoma side was perceptibly funkier than that of Napa. Rude, disheveled little shacks were hidden among the oaks; we passed piles of hubcaps and a sign saying CAMPER SHELL 4 SALE. Joel seemed to breathe a sigh of relief.

We had one more vineyard to visit, that from which Ravenswood produces its most expensive Zinfandel—at thirteen dollars per bottle,* one of the costliest versions of the varietal

*In 1987.

ever placed on the market. The vineyard was situated behind Sonoma State Hospital for the mentally disabled, and as we approached this secret entrance, we passed people studying bushes intently and making explosive sounds, rendering the location that much more exotic. We turned down a narrow, overgrown dirt lane and suddenly burst into a sunlit field of vines: the Old Hill Ranch.

"This is one of my favorite vineyards for the feel of it," said Joel, driving slowly in the shade of the oaks that bordered the ranch. "It brings a sense of other bodies having been here doing what you're doing."

The vineyard stretched away from us in a series of gently rolling knolls. At our backs was Sonoma Mountain, former home of Jack London; in front of us were the wild Mayacamas, former hideout of the bandit Joaquín Murieta. Ancient vines slouched before us like old haystacks, bedraggled and unkempt; the undisked ground between them was rife with burs and dry brown grass. Compared with the impeccably groomed Dickerson vineyard, this one looked like a collection of fright wigs. Joel described it as "benevolently tended."

"If it looks ratty, it's a lot better than it was," he said. "It used to be full of blackberries, saltbush, and poison oak. An eighty-year-old organic farmer named Otto Teller bought this vineyard five or six years ago. He doesn't use any chemical fertilizers or pesticides; he uses praying mantises and ladybugs instead. He thinks that if you leave the grass, you get the good mites preying on the bad mites. To stimulate growth, he sprays the vines with foliar kelp. The foliar feeding combined with deep roots makes for exceptional wine."

We strolled into the vineyard. "These vines are probably a hundred years old," Joel said. "Old vines by their nature don't produce much; they settle down and mellow out, whereas young ones are rambunctious and erratic. The low-growth pattern here is sort of like a French vineyard. The French consider crop levels to be critically important—they rigidly control their tonnage at about one and a half to two tons an acre. If you produce four tons per acre in Montrachet, they declassify the wine; instead of charging forty dollars a bottle for it, they call it Bourgogne Blanc and charge three. Economically, most growers in California think they need to get at least six tons to an acre. We ask for less tonnage but pay more for the grapes. It does a number of things for Zinfandel: It gives you a darker, richer berry that's more flavorful and intense; the bunches sit apart from each other on the vine, so they don't rot; and during harvest the fruit can hang out longer and you get more mature grapes.

"This vineyard usually produces about a ton an acre," Joel said. "This year it'll be even less because Otto pruned the vines back severely. The normal procedure is to leave about twenty buds on a vine, and these have about seven. If you don't force the vine to put all its energy into producing fruit, it'll work on storing carbohydrates in the foliage and end up being better nourished. Producing grapes is like childbirth—it takes a lot out of the vine."

Joel began testing and tasting berries: 20, 22, 21, 20.5, 21 . . . 17. "See the virus in these leaves?" Joel said, referring to the last vine, whose leaves were turning red and curling at the edges. "That's leaf roll virus. It clogs the veins, and the plant can't photosynthesize; it can keep the fruit from ripening. But slow ripening can also give you more maturity. Some people think viruses contribute to the flavor of the grape. Those big bunches over there are Carignane. Chew on one of the berries— they're sweeter and more tannic than Zinfandel. If we picked this entire vineyard, Carignane would probably make up fifteen percent of it. Old Italian vineyards like this almost always have Carignane, Petite Sirah, and Alicante-Bouschet mixed in with Zinfandel. It drives Otto crazy that I don't take all the grapes; he hates to see the Carignane hanging out on the vines. It's a real grapy grape, and it makes a real winy wine, but it doesn't contribute much when you're striving for varietal character in Zinfandel. I had a bottle of '35 Simi Carignane at a dinner party the other night. It must have killed people when it was young because it still had a lot of tannin and life in it. It was remarkably good."

Light departed from the vineyard as the sun went behind

Sonoma Mountain, the dominant climatic influence in this part of the valley. "Sonoma Mountain protects this area from the ocean, and you don't get the Carneros winds this far north," said Joel. "This is the Sonoma banana belt; it can get pretty warm here. The Zinfandel from this vineyard is tremendously deep and complex, peppery and aromatic. It has an exotic, almost Oriental quality. It's entirely different from Dickerson; the fruit tastes more like blackberries than raspberries. With all its flavor and vigor, Dickerson is like a flashy one-night stand, whereas Old Hill is like a long-term relationship. When the Dickerson is no more than a song in your mind, the Old Hill will still be trudging along, giving you more and more stuff."

Joel pocketed his refractometer. "I think this one looks like the middle of next week," he said. "We'll be all right here for that long. If I had to call it right now, I'd say we had all the earmarks of a great vintage. The crop level's not very high, and the summer weather has been consistent. If anything, it's been a little too fast. If the grapes sugar up too rapidly, they're technically mature, but the flavors don't develop in coordination with the sugar. But the quality looks very good, for the fourth year in a row. It's been a remarkable string of vintages; '84, '85, and '86 were all superb. Every year now I say the same thing: It's the best vintage I've seen since last year."

I revisited Ridge the last week of August. I met Draper at his office; as we got into his car (a white Acura Legend coupe with "70 MBCS" on the license plate) and drove farther up Monte Bello Ridge to the upper winery, he explained that he was about to give a tour for a group of sommeliers visiting from Japan. "They're from the leading hotels and restaurants in the country," he said. "We've been sending them Zinfandel, but their focus is likely to be on our Monte Bello Cabernet. A lot of Japanese wine tasting is snob tasting—they're connoisseurs, they have the whole world to choose from, and they tend to feel that Europe manufactures better quality. They drive Mercedes, BMW, and Volvo; in wine, their standard has been France. California is a new thing for them, but how it compares with France is of great interest to them. Last week we had a group of Japanese collectors here; they bought five or six thousand dollars' worth of wine and took it home on the plane."

The upper winery was also a barn—a larger one this time, at the bottom of a hill. Alongside it a purple waterfall poured forth from a pipe, and the smell of wine pervaded the vicinity, intermingling with oak and bay laurel. On top of the hill a gondola of grapes was being emptied into a big crusher-stemmer, with the must proceeding downward by gravity into stainless-steel tanks. (Here was at least one place where Ridge differed from Ravenswood.) On our way inside the building to get some wineglasses, we passed Draper's office; on top of a rolltop desk there were bottles from Château Latour dating back to 1918. There was also a photograph of one Gérard Jaboulet, which was inscribed: "After a rough day up here at 'La Chapelle,' I kick back and break out the Ridge Monte Bello Cabernet. . . . It's superb!"

Clutching the glasses and a bottle of Ridge Chardonnay, Draper and I went back outside and walked farther downhill. Behind the winery we found eleven Japanese sommeliers in a semicircle, all dressed in white and all wearing running shoes except for one iconoclast in cowboy boots. Draper shook hands with their American guide—a writer named Wes Benson, who has lived in Japan since 1946—and distributed the glasses.

"I thought because it is a warm day and you have been traveling, we would start with a taste of Chardonnay before we taste the red wines," Draper said, carefully enunciating each syllable for his foreign guests. As he poured the wine, the sommeliers swirled their glasses, holding them not by the bowl or the stem but by the base at the bottom of the stem, and smelled the wine.

"This is from vines that are quite old," said Draper. "It is made in the old and simple way—it is fermented in the barrel. The one place we use French oak is in Chardonnay; at Ridge we have championed the use of American oak. Some of the best oak is grown in America. The grain is very tight. It's very good for the wine because the liquid cannot penetrate the wood."

After everyone tasted the Chardonnay for a few minutes, Draper led the group inside the building, passing under a purple and yellow stained-glass window in the wall above the door. Draper said the window had been made by Blanche Rosen, one of Ridge's original owners. "We have to pass the equinox before we get sunlight coming through," he added. Tree roots protruded from the gray limestone walls. In the half-light were rows of new flesh-colored barrels, full of '87 Chardonnay. The grapes had been crushed the previous week, and the room was filled with the meaty smell of the new wine. Fermentation was proceeding with force: Yellow liquid fizzed and sputtered up through the air locks in the bungholes. It looked exactly like my car's radiator after ascending Monte Bello Road.

A Hispanic man with a headlamp moved among the rows of barrels. "The insulation between ourselves and the floor above is earth, so here we have the natural coolness and humidity of an old wine cellar," Draper said. "It's quite damp, but there's still evaporation, so Raul must come through every two weeks to top up the barrels. This building is a hundred years old. It stopped producing wine thirty years ago, and twenty-five years ago we started again. For small California wineries, we're among the oldest. We use old-fashioned techniques; we've found that the way winemakers in Bordeaux and Burgundy did things a hundred years ago was correct. In California, individuals are learning this now, usually after leaving the university, where they're taught that the shortest distance between sugar and alcohol is best. We use the natural yeast on the grape to ferment the wine; if a commercial yeast is used, it dominates the entire fermentation, but with natural yeasts, one will begin the fermentation and die off, then another will take over. When the second one begins, there can be a hesitation, and you develop side effects that contribute to the complexity of the wine. We also allow the wine to go through malolactic fermentation, and we clarify the wine by settling—we avoid filtration and centrifuging. We believe filtration should be used only when absolutely needed, at the end of the aging process when the wine is about to be bottled. Every time we've blind-tasted filtered wines versus nonfiltered wines at three to five years of age, we've always preferred the nonfiltered wines. Yet many times you must filter for stability. The most open filtration is the best, if it can give you the level of stability you require. A sterile filtration won't give you as complex a wine."

We followed Draper up and down two steep flights of heavy

wooden stairs. The winery had three levels supported by red-wood posts and beams. The cellars were staggeringly pictur-esque, with spotlights creating studio effects among rows of barrels stacked six-high. Draper stopped beside a row that had "86GZ" chalked on the barrelheads; he reached among the bar-rels, removed a silicon bung, drew out some red wine with a slender glass thief, and distributed it among the sommeliers' glasses.

"This is Zinfandel," he said. "It is a European grape, but they have not yet identified where it came from. It was grown on the East Coast of the United States and also in England, of all places, two hundred years ago. There is a similar grape in southeastern Italy, but it wasn't grown as early there as it was on the East Coast of the U.S. So the origin of the grape is still unknown.

"This wine comes from a vineyard near Geyserville in Son-oma County. It is very young, so you don't have to drink it, you can spit it into the gutter. But there is nothing wrong with it, so you may drink it if you wish."

After tasting the wine, most of the sommeliers spit it into a narrow trench in the floor equipped with a grate for drainage. Draper led them around a corner, deep into a canyon between two walls of barrels.

"Our most important wine is our estate wine, Monte Bello Cabernet Sauvignon," he said. "The vineyard is right here on the property, almost eight hundred meters above sea level. We make ten different wines from our Monte Bello Cabernet grapes, from ten different sections of the vineyard, and we choose only the finest of those for our Monte Bello Cabernet Sauvignon. In 1984 thirty percent of the wine was good but not exceptional, and it was left out. In 1985, an extremely good year for Cali-fornia, forty-five percent was kept aside. With Monte Bello, we are trying to make one of the great wines of the world.

"This is probably the very coolest region recognized as pro-ducing fine Cabernet Sauvignon," Draper said, reaching be-tween the barrels again. "My friend Christian Mouiex, from

Château Pétrus in Bordeaux, believes that the Santa Cruz Mountains produce the finest Cabernet in California. I like old Bordeaux very much—the table in my office is covered with old Bordeaux bottles—but we are attempting to make great Cabernet Sauvignon from Monte Bello, not Bordeaux from Monte Bello. The soil here is different, and the soil here is unique. The climate is also different, and it makes unique wine if we allow the soil and climate to show through.

"This is our 1986 Monte Bello," Draper said, distributing the wine. "You can smell the fruit in it; you can also begin to smell the oak. '86 was a cool year, and in a cool year the style will be very elegant. By *elegant* I mean that it has excellent fruit but is not excessively tannic. It's good in restaurants and good when young. In a warm year the style will be richer, and the wine will need more aging. 1985 was a warm year, and the '85 Monte Bello is big and intense. We think the '85 and '86 vintages may reflect the two styles perfectly."

The wine stimulated some murmuring among the sommeliers; there wasn't so much spitting this time. We went back upstairs and outside onto a concrete pad that supported several ten-foot-tall stainless-steel fermentors.

"These tanks are filled with fermenting wine," Draper said. "We are the only winery in California that uses a submerged-cap fermentation for the majority of its reds. A steel grate inside the fermentation tank holds the grape skins down in constant contact with the wine. This is an old method which is used very little in the U.S. When we changed from wood to steel tanks, it was difficult to adapt the system, but we continue to use it because we think it gives a gentler extraction."

Grasping his glass, Draper bent over and twisted a spigot near the bottom of one of the tanks. Out sprayed a raspberry-colored liquid that foamed up in the glass, forming a pink head.

"This is Merlot from Sonoma County," Draper said, pronouncing the word with the French inflection ("mare-," not "murr-," "low"). "We also use Merlot that we grow here for blending with the Monte Bello Cabernet—usually about seven percent. When wine is this young, you can taste little difference between Merlot, Cabernet, and Zinfandel. You may not wish to drink it, but again, it will not hurt you."

The sommeliers filed up to the spigot. One of them opened the tap too abruptly, and a geyser of wine gushed forth from his glass, decorating his white shirt with a bright swatch of red. His ten mates erupted with mirth. Draper, chuckling, said, "Oh, no!" But the drenched connoisseur reacted quickly, asserting that all he needed now was 93 percent more Monte Bello Cabernet. Not for nothing do the Japanese have American business bamboozled.

As if to address this issue, Draper answered a question about the sale of the winery to Otsuka Pharmaceutical. "Before the sale Ridge had been equally owned by eight people, plus some other shareholders, including three Nobel Prize winners. Most of the owners had been with the winery for twenty-five years. Two were in their seventies and wanted to retire. We had other interested parties—one Canadian and one European—but they wanted to change the approach and increase our size, whereas Mr. Otsuka wanted to change nothing. Under Otsuka, decisions are still ours and all profits are put back into Ridge. We have a board meeting every six months to discuss our plans. No one from Otsuka is on our staff, except for one apprentice studying winemaking. Mr. Otsuka said he would buy the winery only if I stayed on; he offered to let me retain my part-ownership, but I felt that where before I had been an equal partner, now I would be a minor one. Better that he should be the sole owner.

"Personally I don't know what Mr. Otsuka is getting out of this, other than prestige. Mr. Otsuka is a wine collector, and he purchased the winery as a collector's item. He simply wants us to continue to make the best wine in the world.

"Okay!" Draper said abruptly. "I think we're set up for tasting down below."

On a knoll next to the lower buildings, four picnic tables were arranged in a square. There were fourteen place settings, each containing a water glass, an empty cup for spitting, and a semicircle of wineglasses, into which had been poured a Ridge 1981 Monte Bello Cabernet, a Ridge 1983 York Creek Petite Sirah, a Ridge 1984 Jimsomare Cabernet, and a Ridge 1984 Howell Mountain Zinfandel. As the sommeliers sat down and began swirling and sniffing, Draper introduced the wines.

"The Jimsomare Cabernet comes from a vineyard just down the hill," he said. "It's owned by the Schwabecker family—Jim, Sophie, and Marie Louise. Of the vineyards we use, we think it's second in quality only to Monte Bello. There's a slight difference in elevation, but the Jimsomare wine is so tannic and austere that we can't include the press wine in it. The '84 is young, rich, and opulent, whereas the '81 Monte Bello is an elegant, older vintage. '81 was a relatively cool year; we had rain in September, and everyone was worried that winter had arrived early, but then the weather in October was nice. The fermentation was cool, the sugars were modest, and the wine was lower in alcohol—twelve-point-two percent, with moderate tannin. It's much more what we've been looking for in our Monte Bello since then.

"Because the quantity of Monte Bello is so small, we must make other wines to be profitable. For Zinfandel, the best vineyards are in Sonoma and Napa counties; we believe the Howell Mountain and York Creek vineyards are two of the finest of their kind in California. The Howell Mountain vineyard is at five hundred feet of elevation; the vines are very old, and the wine has considerable spice. '84 was a warm year and a rich vintage, which tends to mask the wine's tannins. This wine is soft enough to be enjoyed when young.

"1983 was a high-tannin year in California, so we were very gentle with our '83 Petite Sirah. It was pumped over less than usual, and fined early. As a result, it's one of the softer, more approachable Petite Sirahs that we made in the eighties—not like some others that need five or ten years of aging. Petite Sirah is one of the traditional old California varietals. It's like Zinfandel in the sense that it doesn't have a counterpart in Europe, though there are indications that it's similar to the Duriff, a Rhône grape.

My friend Gérard Jaboulet, in the Rhône, used to slip our '71 Petite Sirah into tastings with his European distributors and ask them how they liked it, then pull it out and say, 'Aha!' We feel that, grown in the right climate and made with care, Petite Sirah is a premium varietal—not just imitation Rhône wine. In the early seventies a New York writer named Gael Greene wrote that our '71 Petite Sirah was the best California wine she'd ever tasted. It was one of the first statements in the American press that California was capable of making truly fine wine."

The Petite Sirah and the Jimsomare Cabernet were ripe, sweet, and earthy. The flavors in the Monte Bello were much smoother, rounder, and more refined. The wine had layers of interest; it made you want to hold it in your mouth and furrow your eyebrows while staring at the tablecloth. The Zinfandel wasn't nearly as complex, but it was more provocative—it hit you in your sixth chakra. It occurred to me that this must be what people mean when they say a wine is "forward"—that it isn't hard to get.

After twenty minutes most of the sommeliers' glasses were still almost completely full. When I mentioned this to Draper, he said quietly: "If the taste of a wine turns out to be good, the nose is the most important thing. When I taste several wines, I go through the nose of every one first; then, after one taste, the ones that I've decided are out I push back and don't taste again. But if the taste and feel in the mouth of one live up to its smell, I say there's the winner. A lot of old Frenchmen I know always have a cigarette hanging out of their mouths; they're great tasters, but if they stop smoking, they have to learn a whole new way of tasting. At dinner your nose will recover faster than your palate, even if there are a lot of smells around the table. After a certain point in a long meal you don't need any more liquid, but you find yourself still sitting there, smelling the wine. Eighty percent of the quality of the pleasure is in the smell."

A truck loaded with grapes honked its horn on the way to the upper winery. One of the sommeliers got stung by a bee, and a Ridge employee—the Scottish woman Wilma Sturrock—

applied a papaya enzyme solution to the wound. In the setting sun the Japanese took many pictures of one another high above Silicon Valley—an exercise rife with symbolism of all sorts—and dinner was served under the oaks. Afterward "Draper-san," as he was now being called, autographed the Merlot-spattered shirt, which somehow never received its rightful portion of Monte Bello Cabernet (maybe the Americans aren't so bamboozled after all). Draper announced that he expected to be visiting Japan periodically, and bid the sommeliers a safe trip back.

"The Japanese are good tasters," Draper said, carrying wineglasses into the kitchen after his visitors had departed. "They're very focused." When I asked what he thought made "a good taster," Draper said: "Broad experience of French, Italian, German, and California wines—a broad background in which to place a wine. If you have eight wines, all of which are acceptable, a group of experienced tasters might have different rankings for numbers one and two according to their personal preferences, but they'll probably all agree on the top four. Of course, everyone is right about taste; but there's amazing agreement among connoisseurs about what is exciting. I think *excitement* is the key to a great wine; if you have a lot of bottles on the table, some will inevitably go down faster, due to the level of excitement that they offer. The others might be decent wines, but there's no excitement—nothing to bring you back after the first sip.

"Recently a taxi driver in New York said to me, 'What I want in a bottle of wine is to be surprised.' I agree. When I go into a restaurant and look at a wine list, I order something that I don't know what to expect. European wines, because they're handmade, with more mistakes, tend to come up with those earthy, contradictory, surprising flavors more often; they might not be perfect and clean, but by God, they're pretty interesting. I think Joel Peterson plays with that same line, and Ravenswood wines are ones that I'd order from a wine list. Whatever else you might say about them, they offer the possibility of a surprise."

Ravenswood harvested the Old Hill vineyard on three different days of 1987. The hilltop grapes, which dried out sooner and ripened quicker, were picked on August 28—very early for Zinfandel. I drove up to witness the second picking on September 1. To reach Sonoma, I crossed San Pablo Bay on the undulant Richmond-San Rafael Bridge and headed north on 101. Then I shot east on State Highway 37, past the mouth of the Petaluma River and across the broad alluvial plain along the north shore of the bay, making the final approach north into Sonoma along eucalyptus-lined Highway 121. This route leads through the "cool and foggy" Carneros district into the "banana belt" of Sonoma Valley. So it was odd to see the sun shining on the southern part of the drive, while at 7:30 A.M. the Old Hill vineyard was still obscured in fog.

When I arrived, Clyde Crawford, one of Ravenswood's "cellar workers" (in fact, there isn't any cellar), was standing by himself in the middle of the vineyard atop a truck that held three empty four-by-eight-foot blue bins. The sound of rattling dishes could be heard from the door of the wood-frame house next to the vineyard, but despite the fact that it was prime time for grape picking, no grape pickers were in sight. A few minutes later Joel pulled in, wearing a hooded red sweatshirt. "Where is everybody?" he asked. He walked into the vineyard and took a few samples with his hydrometer, then got into his car and drove through the vineyard and across Highway 12 to Otto Teller's house.

"I don't know what's going on," Joel said. "We don't refrigerate the grapes, so it's imperative that they be picked in the morning. If they get too warm, fermentation starts too rapidly and the must overheats."

A white egret flew overhead as we pulled up alongside Teller's barn. Inside, long tables with red-and-white-checked cloths supported boxes of organically grown melons, red bell peppers, plum tomatoes, acorn and yellow squash. Garlic braids hung from the walls, dried yellow asters and purple zinnias from the ceiling. We located Otto's foreman, Jorge, who said he'd be over with his crew in a few minutes—he'd only just been informed that Joel wanted to pick today.

"In my first Old Hill harvest three years ago, I let the grapes get too ripe," Joel said as we walked back to the car. "I looked at them and thought they'd hold for a few more days; then it got hot, and they went to twenty-four. It made a plummier, more raisiny wine. I'm not going to let that happen again; he's known for a week that we were going to pick today." At that moment, perhaps in defense of its master's honor, a dog rushed out from behind a parked truck and tried to bite *me* on the leg.

Half an hour later, as the sun began to lift over the Mayacamas and burn through the fog, eight pickers ambled into the vineyard. All were wearing baseball hats with emblems proclaiming various allegiances: Cadillac, Löwenbräu, Ace Hardware, L.A. One wore a cowboy shirt with a cactus embroidered on the front and "Mazatlán Venemos" on the back. Each man carried a white plastic bucket and a short curved knife in a holster on his belt. Joel told Jorge that he wanted only Zinfandel to be picked: "No Carignane. No second crop. But feel free to bring in the raisins—I have no problem with those."

With his knife, one of the pickers began to free bunches of grapes from a vine and toss them into his bucket. "Señor, no," said Joel. "That's not Zinfandel. Zinfandel has spiky little leaves. This is Carignane. It's big and bushy."

The picker pointed to another vine. *"Este no?"* he asked.

"Este no," Joel confirmed. "Alicante. Squeeze the grape; you can tell because it has bright red juice."

The men began to go leisurely about their business. "I love these guys," said Joel. "You can tell that Otto pays them by the hour—it takes them two days to pick this bloody vineyard. You should see the hotshot crews who get paid by the bucket. Guys jumping over the vines to get back and pick more fruit."

Joel departed, leaving Clyde to supervise the operation. A breeze began to blow out of the north. As the sun continued to climb, the pickers strolled to the truck by turns and offered their buckets to Clyde, who hoisted them up and dumped the contents into the four-by-eight bins, each of which was capable of holding two tons of fruit. Slowly—very slowly—a hill of black grapes mounted: springy, supple, shiny and plump, full of freshness and life. Occasionally Clyde tossed out the unripe second-crop bunches, which were more pink than black—high in acid, low in sugar. By 10:00 A.M. the sky had cleared completely. Joel wanted picking to stop at noon, but when that hour arrived, only one of the three bins had been filled. One of the pickers climbed onto the truck to survey the tally. *"Mucho flojo,"* he commented. Apparently at least another day would be required to complete the picking of the twenty-acre vineyard.

It was a different story four days later, when the Dry Creek vineyard was harvested. The day began ominously when Clyde ran out of gas on Dry Creek Road just after sunup, but then— apparently through some sort of divine intervention—Joel's grower, the mustachioed Italian in the cowboy boots, came along in his pickup carrying a can of gas. Eight pickers were again marshaled for the morning task; this time, however, they were paid by volume, and in marked contrast with the restful exercises performed by the pickers at Old Hill, the Dry Creek vineyard became a maelstrom of activity. Each man was assigned a number, which he called out to Clyde (*"Tres!," "Seis!," "Número uno!"*) upon delivering a tub of fruit to the truck. Clyde kept a tally of each picker's production as the men sprinted back into the vineyard. You could see the vines shaking and rattling as the pickers, knives flying, denuded them of fruit, throwing bunches into the tubs with one hand while cutting more bunches with the other, then running back to the truck, literally sending up clouds of dust. By ten-thirty all the four-by-eight bins were full, and the vineyard owner saw fit to open two sixpacks of Budweiser.

There was more beer back at Ravenswood, where Clyde delivered the grapes after stopping to weigh the truck in Vineburg. At the winery another whirlwind was under way: Joel, John, another Ravenswood employee named Thijs (pronounced "Tice," as in "mice") Van Stigt, and a temporary helper named Steve dashed about in gym shorts, tank tops, and black rubber boots, tending pumps, pulling hoses, and clambering over tanks. In the time since my tenure at Ravenswood, technological advancements had been made: Instead of pitchforking the grapes from the truck, John now upended the four-by-eight bins with a forklift, and a rotating auger transported the fruit to the stemmer-crusher. "Life's getting pretty easy around here," Joel observed. "I can see how people get into crushing thousands of tons of grapes."

"Sure," said Steve, who had apparently worked at several wineries before this one. "You can go bankrupt that much quicker."

Inside the warehouse thirteen redwood fermentors were waiting. Most had 1,350 gallons of capacity; some already harbored the fermenting wine from Old Hill, Lyeth, and Cloverdale, which had been picked during the last days of August. On the staves of the tanks, figures were scrawled in chalk, recording the dates, the temperature of the fermenting must, and the Brix levels as grape sugar was converted to alcohol. One of the Old Hill tanks read:

8/28	8/30	9/1	9/2	9/3	9/4	9/5
63	68	82	86	89	85	87
21.6	22.9	17.2	14.7	10	5.4	3.8

On September 1 the Old Hill grapes I had watched being picked were added to the hilltop grapes, which had been picked on August 28. On September 3 a cooling wand was placed in the tank to keep the skyrocketing temperature from killing off the yeast (hence the decrease from eighty-nine to eighty-five degrees Fahrenheit). The initial increase in the Brix reading—from 21.6 on August 28 to 22.9 on August 30—illustrated Louis P. Martini's observation that Zinfandel is the only grape that goes up rather than down in sugar for the first few days after picking, the result of the marinating raisins' releasing their concentrated sugar into the juice. Apparently the hilltop grapes hadn't ripened as quickly as Joel had thought; 21.6 was a full degree lower than he preferred at picking. However, this was inadvertently and ironically balanced out by the Old Hill crew, whose leisurely approach had allowed the last batch of grapes to ripen all the way to 24 by the time they were fully harvested on September 3.

I climbed to the top of the Old Hill tank and looked inside. Someone had dug a hole in the cap of skins and stems and stuck a colander into it; maroon liquid bubbled up violently in the little reservoir. I lowered my face into the tank, sniffed, and was blasted backward by carbon dioxide shooting into my sinuses.

The Dry Creek must was now emerging from a wide red hose into an adjacent fermentor—a rich red-purple mass of skins, seeds, and liquid piling up in the tank. Smelling the fresh, fragrant noncarbonic grape juice was no problem. I followed the hose back outside past the laboring pump to the crusher-stemmer, which was spitting green grape stems cleanly onto the concrete as the hose carried away the must. Joel would reserve some of these stems and throw them into the fermentor, a French technique for adding tannin to the wine (as opposed to adding Petite Sirah, à la Ridge).

"You also get spice and pepper from the stems," said Joel. "The amount of stems I add depends on the year and on the vineyard. In a hot year the grapes will naturally have more tannin, and they'll also have more flavor to support it. Then you'll get other years that are pretty warm but the grapes don't end up getting quite so much sun, and they don't develop as much tannin as flavor. Those need more stems. Proportionately I add more stems to Dry Creek, less to Old Hill. The Old Hill vines have lower production and thicker skins; Dry Creek lacks that backbone.

"Some people think my wines are too tannic, especially when they're young," Joel acknowledged. "But building them with a little excess tannin is my hope for the future. The wine needs it to age properly; the phenolics and color components combine to give you bottle bouquet later on. To put it very simply, the phenolic compounds in wine link together over time to form longer polymers, which is why a wine tastes and smells different as it gets older. When the polymers get too long, they drop out of suspension and we say the wine is over the hill. But the more extract you have—the more tannin, the more spice, the more phenolics—the more things there are that can hook together over a period of time, and the greater chance for a complex, rich, interesting wine down the road."

This sounded suspiciously like a "bigger is better" philosophy. I mentioned Paul Draper's position—i.e., that "balance is all," even when the wine enters the bottle.

"Balance is important," said Joel. "Balance isn't *all*. Taste a young Latour—it's tannic and it's hard. The great Bordeaux aren't necessarily pleasant to drink when they go into the bottle, but they have sufficient fruit and tannin, and later on they turn out to be great. The great old vintages of Bordeaux stay vibrant year after year; you taste the '49 and you ask, 'Is this wine really aging?' I don't think even Bordeaux starts out as tannic as my

Zinfandel, but Zinfandel tends to soften more rapidly, so with a little bottle age it becomes balanced. I don't pattern my Zinfandel after Bordeaux anyway; Zinfandel is more like a Côtes-du-Rhône. Rhône wines are made from fatter, more berrylike grapes; they have higher alcohol, and they're fuller and richer. When people call my wines monsters, I don't think they know what a monster is. Sure—if you spend your life drinking rosé."

It took about ten minutes to crush six tons of Dry Creek grapes. When all but a quarter of a bin had been pumped into the fermentor, I backed a pickup truck up to the crusher and John detached the hose from the tank. Then he rerouted it toward my pickup and pumped the remaining Dry Creek Zinfandel into five plastic garbage cans on the bed of my truck. I tightened the lids with elastic cords and drove away, retracing my route through Carneros, Marin, and Richmond to Berkeley, where my cooking partners helped me wrestle the grapes into my garage.

Yes: The Young Gentlemen's Culinary Society was about to join the long tradition of Sonoma Zinfandel artisans. After all, how could we not?

Getting such grapes was a coup, of course. Many California home winemakers have to content themselves with Central Valley or second-crop fruit; to gain access to premium Zinfandel from old Dry Creek Valley vines was a tremendous privilege, but one that Joel was willing to bestow (for a reasonable price, of course).

We had decided that we wanted ten gallons of a nouveau style that could be bottled by Thanksgiving and drunk right away. In that batch, where fruitiness was essential and complexity was beside the point, Joel advised us to include whole grape clusters in the vat and inoculate the must with commercial yeast. However, for our main batch (the "Big Zin," as we hopefully called it), we flew in the face of the advice dispensed by every UC Davis enology professor, every book on home winemaking, and practically every professional winemaker in California: We decided to ferment the grapes on their natural yeasts.

The method for doing this isn't terribly complicated: You let the crushed grapes sit there, and after a while they start fermenting. The supposed risk is that you don't know what type of yeast you're getting or if it will do its job "properly." If fermentation stops—or fails to start—the wine can be ruined, developing off odors from ethyl acetate or other types of volatile (as opposed to fixed) acidity ("VA"). This is why 99 percent of California winemakers inoculate their must with commercial yeast. But the Young Gentlemen didn't want 99 percent of the wine in California; we wanted one that was *bigger and better*.

For days we watched and waited. The nouveau batch began fermenting right away, but the uninoculated grapes just sat there. Mold began to form among the grape skins that clung to the sides of the fermentors; Joel said to mix it with the juice and it would go away. It did. I optimistically fashioned a punch from a piece of plywood and a two-by-four, planing and sanding the handle down to a smooth grip. Three days after picking, the grapes still sat there. Soothsayers both private and professional warned us about the bad road we were taking. Finally we decided that if fermentation hadn't begun naturally by the fourth day, we would inoculate with commercial yeast.

On the morning of the decisive day, I rose from bed, donned my jacket, went outside, raised the garage door, lifted the lids from the cans, and was greeted by a firm cap of dark red grape skins pushing their way up out of the juice, boosted by a healthy level of carbon dioxide—a product of fermentation.

Eureka!

In his article on Zinfandel in the University of California/Sotheby's *Book of California Wine*, Paul Draper had gone into some detail concerning the grape's origins on the East Coast and in England. In the article Draper said he'd gotten most of his information from Charles Sullivan, the wine historian who in 1985 had commented on the BATF's rejection of Italian Zinfandel. Joel Peterson had told me in passing that Sullivan's son owned the Acme bakery, where people line up in the morning to buy bread around the corner from my house in Berkeley. The Acme is in wine merchant Kermit Lynch's building alongside Café Fanny—Alice Waters's Chez Panisse spin-off, where the citizens of Berkeley park their Volvos, Mercedes, and BMWs and pay eight dollars to stand at a counter drinking coffee from a bowl and eating a sandwich you could swear was an hors d'oeuvre.

I suffered the odium of the Nimitz Freeway to talk to Charles Sullivan, who lives in a ranch home in a Los Gatos housing tract at the edge of the foothills of the Santa Cruz Mountains. I suspected that I'd found the right place when I saw a car whose license plate said "ZINFDL." Sullivan came to the door wearing a corduroy sports jacket and a mustache and ushered me into his office, which was lined with old wine bottles, carafes full of corks, pictures of grape leaves, and Chez Panisse posters. A big table was covered with papers and books (I noted *A History of the Modern World* by Palmer and Colton, and Ergang's *Europe Since Waterloo*), notecard files, a magnifying glass, and a microfilm reading machine—something I couldn't remember ever seeing outside a library. A Caymus Cabernet Sauvignon label had been taped to a sliding glass door, and several issues of the *Connoisseur's Guide to California Wine* were lying around the room; Sullivan explained that he was preparing to make his '85 Cabernet purchases.

When I asked how he'd gotten interested in the history of Zinfandel, Sullivan lit his pipe and explained that he was chairman of the social studies department at Leland High School in San Jose. "I did my master's thesis on twentieth-century German-Baltic history, and the only people who ever read the damn thing were other historians," he said. "I'd gotten interested in wine during the fifties, and I found that the only published history of the California industry was a dissertation from Johns Hopkins. It only covered the period from 1830 to 1895; the author didn't care about wine, and he didn't do any digging. So I started visiting wineries and talking to the old mustachios. From 1967 to 1975 I just collected stuff."

"What sort of stuff?"

"I read *Wine and Vines* and the *Pacific Wine and Spirit Review* as far back as 1920 and all the San Francisco newspapers from 1850 to 1930. I took notes on anything I thought was important. I looked through old agricultural publications at the National Agricultural Library in Beltsville, Maryland, and the library of the Massachusetts Horticultural Society in Boston. In 1973—when I got to the point where I couldn't remember where things were—I spent a year indexing my notes. Finally Dave Bennion suggested that I do something with the material."

"Dave Bennion," I said. "The first Ridge winemaker?"

"Right."

"Go on."

"History always derives from a question, so I asked myself what the mysteries were in wine history. The mystery, of course, was Zinfandel. So I did what I call a data dump—I looked under *Z* in my index, pulled out everything I had on Zinfandel, and put it all in chronological order." Sullivan handed me a copy of the result, a heavily footnoted article entitled "Zinfandel: A True Vinifera," published in a 1982 issue of the *Vinifera Wine Growers Journal*. In the introduction, Sullivan wrote: "The Zinfandel was a moderately popular table grape grown in New England under glass as early as the 1830's. It was brought to California by New England horticulturists in the early 1850's. I have developed a hypothesis, only now very faintly supported by Old World primary sources, that the wine was brought to New England from England as a table grape. Colonel Haraszthy is not guilty of having claimed to have brought the vine to California. It was his son years later that made the claim for his father."

The colonel to whom Sullivan referred was Agoston Haraszthy, the so-called father of California viticulture, a Hungarian nobleman who for nearly a century had been credited with introducing Zinfandel to California. The legends surrounding this belief are various. One—circulated in 1884 by Charles Wetmore, California's chief viticultural officer—held that Haraszthy had "known" the grape in Hungary and included it among the thousands of vine cuttings he acquired on a trip to Europe in 1861. The version promulgated by Haraszthy's son Árpád maintained that the former Hungarian minister of war General Lazar Mészáros had sent the Zinfandel, along with a great many other grapes, to Haraszthy in San Francisco in 1852. Yet another theory, set down by Alexis Lichine in his *Encyclopedia of Wines and Spirits*, was that Zinfandel was among a hundred grape varieties that Haraszthy planted in San Diego in 1851. Whatever the year and the place, the popular story held that by the time Haraszthy received the vine, the name on its identifying tag had been muddled or mixed up with another—in all likelihood the Zierfahndler, a white wine grape from Germany.

The confusion is partly due to the chaotic rush of exotic plantings that occurred in California in the mid-nineteenth century. It's also encouraged by the fact that Haraszthy's biography is among the most apocryphal and colorful of polychromatic pioneer America. His story has been told and retold, by, among others, Charles Sullivan, who, along with his piece on Zinfandel, handed me a four-part article he'd written for *Vintage* magazine entitled, "A Man Named Agoston Haraszthy."

Over the next few hours (then days, weeks, and months), I pored over Sullivan's work, as well as that of other California historians, piecing together an epic romantic triangle: the story of Haraszthy, nineteenth-century California, and Zinfandel.

Agoston Haraszthy was born in the province of Bácska in the ancient kingdom of Hungary, where his family raised silkworms and wine grapes on its estate near the village of Futak (which today lies within the borders of Yugoslavia). As a teenager he became an officer in the royal bodyguard, a traditional repository for aristocratic youth, and eventually aligned himself with the radical Lajos Kossuth, who was arrested for treason in 1837. It is often therefore deduced that Haraszthy was a political refugee when he came to the United States in 1840 (though Sullivan writes that "Haraszthy was not fleeing anything so much as he was seeking opportunity"). In partnership with an Englishman, he bought ten thousand acres along the Wisconsin River, and after returning to Europe to collect his family, he never again set foot in Hungary.

In Wisconsin Haraszthy quickly became one of the preeminent frontier empire builders of his time. He introduced sheep and hogs to the territory, built a sawmill, grew hops and grain (he was unsuccessful with wine grapes there), operated a ferry service, established a Humanist Society, and founded a town called Széptáj (Beautiful View), which was later renamed Haraszthy and ultimately Sauk City. Large, dark, and black-bearded, he cut an imposing figure, galloping through the woods on horseback, wearing a green silk hunting shirt and red sash, guffawing as the thorns and brambles tore at his clothing. As Sullivan wrote, "Had Agoston Haraszthy never left Wisconsin, his name would have lived as one of the most noteworthy frontier entrepreneurs of the Territory and State." But following a pattern repeated throughout his life, Haraszthy's financial affairs fell apart despite his prodigious talents as an organizer and developer. Moreover, he had asthma and one of his sons had gout, so when gold was discovered in California in 1848, the Haraszthys joined a wagon train bound for the Santa Fe Trail.

Upon arriving in California, Haraszthy ignored the goldfields of the north and headed instead for San Diego, a southern frontier village of 650. His farsightedness enabled him to see that agribusiness—not precious metal—was the place to realize long-term profits. (Indeed, all the gold produced in California in the century following the gold rush was worth less than the state's agricultural output in 1960 alone.) In San Diego Haraszthy duplicated his Wisconsonian behavior, planting orchards, opening a livery stable and a butcher shop, and speculating widely in land. Somewhere along the way he picked up the popular rank of colonel, and in 1850 he was elected sheriff of San Diego County; soon after that he was appointed town marshal. Meanwhile, his father, Charles, became a magistrate and land commissioner, establishing a greater oligarchy than any that the family had enjoyed in Bácska.

The most notable illustration of the Haraszthyan headlock on San Diego affairs was the building of the local jail. The city council, presided over by Charles, awarded the construction contract to Agoston despite the fact that his price of five thousand dollars more than doubled the lowest bid. As the story goes, the jail's first prisoner broke through the wall to have a drink at the bar across the street, whereupon the council awarded Agoston another two thousand dollars to upgrade the questionable construction job. The money was raised through the issuance of scrips, which Haraszthy sold before leaving town;

the incident has been called California's first occurrence of municipal graft. In the 1850s, however, California was a place where such comportment could be seen as enterprising. Never one to be deterred by disgrace, Haraszthy next sought higher office and allied himself with an ex-Mississippian and pro-Southern militant, William Gwin of the California Democrats, in calling for a north-south division of California. The ostensible rationale was an unbalanced tax structure that favored the north, but the pro-Southern leaders also hoped for a transcontinental railroad from New Orleans to terminate in San Diego. Campaigning on this platform, Haraszthy won a seat in the state assembly, which brought him north to the state capital for the first time in 1852. Soon thereafter he liquidated his Southern California holdings and moved to San Francisco.

Nobody knows exactly why Haraszthy decided to pull up stakes (again), but obviously conditions in San Francisco were irresistible to such an opportunist. In 1847, the year before gold was discovered at Sutter's Mill, the city's population had been 459; by the time Haraszthy arrived in 1852, it was 35,000. The citizenry was overwhelmingly male, and the economy was one of scarcity. The number of laundries (and the length of their waiting lists) was such that dirty clothes were sent to China to be washed, and modest fortunes could be amassed by people who knew how to bake pies. In 1851 the *Daily Alta California* observed: "The miners are beginning to discover that they are engaged in a science and a profession, and not in a mere adventure." More than anything other than fortitude, these so-called scientists needed supplies.

One who essayed to provide them was Frederick W. Macondray, a native New Englander who first visited San Francisco as a teenaged ship crewman in 1821, carrying wheat from Chile to Monterey. Macondray had originally gone to sea at the age of nine in the War of 1812; eventually he entered the merchant shipping business, crisscrossing the Pacific between China and South America. When the gold rush trumpet sounded in 1848, he made for San Francisco and founded a mercantile firm—

F. W. Macondray & Co.—to look after miners' gold. Soon he was also exporting furs and importing everything from tea to elephant tusks. Macondray quickly became a prominent San Francisco citizen: He was elected to the board of aldermen in 1850; he was president of the Chamber of Commerce and—as a formerly active member of the Massachusetts Horticultural Society—of the California Agricultural Society as well. Reputedly he was a "moderate" member of the city's vigilance committees—groups of merchants who, exercising a private interpretation of local law, lynched four men, deported twenty-eight, and, in an effort to get their taxes reduced, managed to bring down the city government in 1856.

In 1852, the year Haraszthy arrived in San Francisco, gold production in the mines reached a peak of $80 million. With a handful of other Hungarians the colonel opened a metallurgy firm, and through his Democratic political connections—notably President Franklin Pierce—was soon appointed assayer, melter, and refiner for the brand-new U.S. Mint. He held these positions for three years; when he resigned, he was charged with fraud and indicted by a grand jury for embezzlement of $150,000.

The government's case against the colonel was made by J. Ross Browne, a special agent for the U.S. Treasury who had a curious second career as a humorist. Browne was suspicious of Haraszthy's friendships with private refiners, of his substantial amount of personal property, and of an attempt he had made to purchase the mint's sweepings. However, after four years of hearings and appeals, the charges against Haraszthy were dropped. From 1855 to 1857, the years Haraszthy worked at the mint, more than a hundred million dollars' worth of gold had been processed; the furnaces ran twenty-four hours a day, and blowers were used to force a draft. As it eventually turned out, scrapings taken from roofs near the mint revealed a considerable quantity of gold.

Haraszthy was thus exonerated, but he hadn't exactly been idle while awaiting the outcome of the investigation. Upon arriving in San Francisco, he'd purchased two hundred acres near Mission Dolores and started a nursery named Las Flores. Here he had again planted grapevines, but he found the weather far too cold and foggy—in fact, during California's period of Spanish occupation, Dolores was one of the few Franciscan missions where wine grapes had failed to prosper. Winegrowing in California had begun with these Spanish padres, who—besides having been raised in the European gustatory tradition—required wine as a religious sacrament. (The first written reference is by Father Junipero Serra, who in a letter dated December 18, 1781, expressed to an associate at San Diego the hope that "the grape vines are living and thriving, for this lack of altar wine is becoming unbearable.") The padres stationed Indians in the vineyards with drums to scare away the birds, then marshaled the neophyte Christians to pick and crush the grapes. Unfortunately the native varieties—*Vitis californica and Vitis girdiana*—made abysmal wine. The predominant grape that the friars employed was the so-called Mission strain of *Vitis vinifera*, which, like Zinfandel, had originated in Europe under obscure circumstances. It was apparently brought to the New World by Spanish conquistadors and to Alta California by Serra. Low in acid and undistinguished in flavor, the Mission grape produced a pretty dull beverage, but it throve in the hot climate of Southern California—a single vine in Santa Barbara was said to produce eight tons of grapes in a year.

By the early 1830s the missions were growing more than three hundred thousand vines, half of whose total product was distilled into *aguardiente* (brandy) for purposes of preservation. But after 1834, when the missions were secularized by the Mexican government, most of the vineyards fell into disuse and decay. A partial exception was Mission San Francisco de Solano in Sonoma, thanks to the efforts of General Mariano Guadalupe Vallejo—Indian fighter, horticulturist, and *comandante general* of the Mexican Army in California, who had been sent to Sonoma in 1834 to oversee secularization and check the aspirations of the Russians on the coast. An avid experimenter with exotic fruits,

Vallejo planted cuttings from the Mission vines behind his adobe on Sonoma Plaza, and a few seasons later they gave him three hundred gallons of wine and sixty of brandy, made with the help of his homeopathic physician, a Frenchman named Victor Faure. Vallejo also raised cattle and crops on his rancho near Petaluma; foreseeing the future of the region, he wrote to a Mexican acquaintance: "Is not the land capable of every product, and yet do not the Californians purchase brandy from Catalonia, tobacco from Virginia, vinegar from Marseille, cloth from Boston, manufactured goods from everywhere?" Having been born in Monterey in 1808, he always maintained more allegiance to California than he did to any mere nation. However, his wife's sister (and two of his own) married U.S. citizens, and in 1845 Vallejo began openly to promote the American doctrine of Manifest Destiny, making it somewhat embarrassing when he was taken prisoner in the Bear Flag Revolt of 1846.*

When the United States gained control of Alta California, Vallejo adjusted quite smoothly. He expanded his own holdings to 150,000 acres, and beside the spring that watered Sonoma he built an American-style estate called Lachryma Montis (Tears of the Mountain). He and his boorish brother Salvador continued planting grapevines right along; his mother-in-law had a vineyard at Rancho Cabeza de Santa Rosa, and his brother-in-law maintained one alongside Sonoma Creek. By 1854 Vallejo himself was growing some five thousand vines, whose

---

*A ragtag assortment of hunters and trappers appeared on Vallejo's doorstep one morning, and when the general came out in his bathrobe to meet them, they announced that Sonoma was now the capital of the independent "California Republic" that they had just formed. Vallejo invited the men inside, and after some hours discussing the matter over aguardiente, several of the rebels fell asleep. But the teetotalers among them still managed to incarcerate the comandante, who—with the blessing of the eccentric American Captain John C. Frémont—spent an inglorious two months in jail. He was released only after the Bear Flaggers decided that their cause would be better served by the U.S. government, which propitiously chose that very time to declare war on Mexico.

fermented products annually brought him about twenty thousand dollars—a fact of great interest to an enterprising Hungarian the general had recently met at a special session of the state legislature: Agoston Haraszthy.

Haraszthy was five years younger than Vallejo. The two men, equally enamored of California's agrinomic potential, became friends. At the time Southern California was still producing most of the wine in the state, and San Francisco was annually importing some twelve thousand casks (thirty-seven thousand cases) of French claret, fifteen thousand barrels of white table wine, a hundred thousand bottles of Champagne, and a thousand barrels of sherry. Haraszthy, whose many business pursuits had included the brokering of fresh grapes, posited that the exploding population would soon demand a nearer source of supply. Moreover, he could see that beyond the chilly confines of the city proper, the moderating influence of San Francisco Bay contributed to a table-wine-growing climate superior to that of the blistering south. After his grape-growing experiment failed at Las Flores, he had tried again south of the city near Crystal Springs Reservoir, but in 1855, when Haraszthy visited Lachryma Montis and tasted wine from the vineyards planted by Salvador Vallejo east of Sonoma, he apparently realized an end to his search for a place to grow good grapes. He bought the property the following year and by the end of 1857 had more than tripled the vineyard acreage of Sonoma Valley—in that year alone he planted eighty thousand vines and made six thousand gallons of wine. He soon acquired several thousand more acres in the Mayacamas foothills and, envisioning an agricultural empire there, erected a white Pompeiian villa on the property. Again he named his domain for its beautiful view, but having wisely acclimated to the region's traditions, this time he translated it "Buena Vista."

Neither the language nor the architecture was chosen arbitrarily. As historian Kevin Starr wrote in a chapter entitled "An

American Mediterranean" in his book *Americans and the California Dream*:

> Riding horseback on the Los Angeles plain through man-high mustard abloom in vivid yellow under a Levantine sun, travelers recalled the Holy Land, and perhaps even the parable of the mustard seed. As they sailed off the coast, they thought of Morocco, Sicily, or Greece. Silhouetted at sunset, a row of cypresses outside of Fresno in the San Joaquin brought to mind a similar day's end in Lombardy or the Campagna; and, of course, the vineyards of the Bay counties suggested the south of France. . . .
> Obviously symbolic of civilization, the vines planted by Spaniards suggested to those Americans who first saw them that California was not an unrelieved wilderness. Like the missions themselves, the vines of California bespoke history, solicitude, and patience.

To Haraszthy, of course, they also bespoke profits, and now that he'd found a salubrious spot, he set about promoting viticulture in earnest. He attracted several new winegrowers to Sonoma (among them Charles Krug, who later moved on to Napa) and pioneered the techniques of dry-farmed vineyards and redwood fermentation. In 1858 his wine beat out Vallejo's for first prize at the state fair, prompting Haraszthy to proclaim: "It is beyond doubt that California will produce as noble wines as any part of Europe." The State Agricultural Society (presided over by F. W. Macondray), impressed by Haraszthy's accomplishments, asked him to share his expertise, and his consequent *Report on the Grapes and Wines of California*—the first American explication of traditional European winemaking practices—was reprinted and distributed around the state.

In a word, the time for grape growing was ripe. If everybody's fingers in San Francisco had recently seemed to glow of gold, the thumbs now appeared to be brass: They turned green as the area underwent a horticultural boom. The gold rush had passed its apogee, and given California's accommodating climate, agriculture was a logical alternative for argonauts who stuck around. Nurseries sprouted all over the state, and at the southern end of San Francisco Bay the Santa Clara Valley gained a reputation as the "Garden Spot of the World," attracting a sizable coterie of French nurserymen led by Antoine Delmas. (Delmas, who raised fruit trees, ornamental plants, and grapes, hispanicized his name to Antonio soon after arriving in California but retained his Gallic tastes: Besides being the first person to import vine cuttings from France, he introduced *Helix aspersa*, a snail whose slime trail can now be traced to every garden in Northern California.) In Napa the reigning nurseryman was J. W. Osborne, another native New Englander, who joined Haraszthy at the state fair in preaching about California's agricultural promise. Partly as a result of their efforts, in 1859 the state legislature exempted new vineyards from taxation, and multitudes of grapevines entered the earth in a frenzy.

Most of the plantings consisted of Mission grapes, but Haraszthy and others properly believed that more varieties would be necessary if California hoped to rival the enological products of Europe. "If we make such good wines already from one [variety] of our native grapes," the colonel proposed, "how much better wines will we make when we have differently flavored varieties of grapes for it in a certain proportion mixed together? To illustrate it to persons not acquainted with winemaking, I will say that carrots will make a vegetable soup, but it will be a poor one; but take carrots, turnips, celery, parsley, cabbage, potatoes, onions, etc., and you will have a superior vegetable soup. So with grapes." Antonio Delmas, who won the grand prize at the 1859 state fair for red wine (the *Alta California* referred to it as "French claret,"though it had in fact been made from Black St. Peter's grapes "selected more as table fruit than for wine making"), offered 105 different varieties, including the "Cabrunet" and "Médoc." But another name was beginning to appear in the state records: In 1857 a "Zinfindal" grape was presented by Macondray and Osborne at the Mechanics Institute Fair in San Francisco, and the year after that a Sacramento grower named A. P. Smith exhibited a "Zeinfindall" variety at the state fair.

"Zinfandel originally came here as a table grape," Sullivan said to me. "When you look at it, you can see that it has big upright clusters; it's really good to eat. People were also looking for a cheap way to make good red wine, and they were trying everything because nobody knew what would work—they had no system of classifying the climate aside from this vague sense that it was 'Mediterranean.' There was a great urge to find out what other people were doing. You have to remember that these people were in business; they were selling the stuff that they grew. They were doing the same things with pears and peaches, but progress with grapes was slower because wine took a long time to make."

In 1861 Haraszthy petitioned the state legislature to appoint three commissioners to travel abroad in search of better wine grapes for California. The idea was applauded by the Agricultural Society and the press, and Haraszthy himself was naturally named one of the commissioners "as a dignity without emolument." Despite the fact that no provision was made for his expenses, in June of that year the prodigal colonel sailed for Europe. His third son, Árpád, who had abandoned civil-engineering classes in Paris, was studying the making of sparkling wine in Champagne, and over the next five months the energetic pair amassed a prodigious collection of horticultural information. In his report Haraszthy said that he "purchased in different parts of Europe 100,000 vines, embracing about 1,400 varieties and small lots of choice almonds, olives, figs, pomegranates, Italian chestnuts, oranges, and lemons." He placed orders for cuttings in Bordeaux, Genoa, Heidelberg, and Málaga and authorized still more from Greece, Egypt, and Portugal. (Interestingly, he skipped Hungary.) In a subsequent book published by Harper Brothers, entitled *Grape Culture, Wines and Wine-Making, with Notes upon Agriculture and Horticulture*, Haraszthy described the practices of every important European winemaking region; one reviewer noted that "in pace and gusto it recalls as much as anything the novels of Jules Verne." The colonel concluded that "of all the countries through which I passed, not one possessed the same advantages that are to be found in California, and I am satisfied that even if the separate advantages of these countries could be combined in one, it would still be surpassed by this state when its now dormant resources shall be developed."

Alas, Haraszthy's role in this development was to be frustrated when he returned in December. He requested no payment for his services abroad but did ask to be reimbursed for the twelve thousand dollars he had spent procuring the vine cuttings, which he planned to distribute throughout the state. Unfortunately the United States was by that time engaged in a civil war, and California was experiencing its worst winter flood in recorded history. Charles Sullivan writes: "As Sacramento dug itself out of the mud and as news continued to arrive of Confederate successes in the East, the legislature was in no mood to appropriate money to a wealthy Hungarian grandee for a vacation in Europe." Nor was a Unionist state inclined to support someone who continued to align himself with the Southern faction. Haraszthy was never reimbursed; no distribution system was ever established for his hundred thousand vines; the collection was eventually scattered and wasted. What's more, in autumn of 1862, the fruit of the 1859 planting boom entered into production, and in the first example of a phenomenon that continues to the present day, the grape-growing industry overexpanded, creating a glut of California wine.

Haraszthy, who appeared to be nearing another nadir, was bailed out by a group of investors headed by William C. Ralston, head of the Bank of California and the state's leading capitalist. Ralston and his partners incorporated the Buena Vista Viticultural Society, giving Haraszthy a sizable share and a supervisory position. The colonel built new tunnels and tanks, experimented

with vine propagation by bending old canes earthward and bury-
ing them—a technique that eventually transformed the vineyard
into an impenetrable thicket—and turned the winemaking over
to Árpád, who in concert with his brother, Attila, married General Vallejo's twin daughters, Jovita and Natalie, in the spring.
Then came California's worst drought in a quarter century, and
following a few successful experiments, Árpád botched ten
thousand bottles of Buena Vista champagne. He was pressured
into resigning his post, leaving Agoston in debt to the corporation; the society's profits continued to languish, and in 1866
Haraszthy himself was forced out. He contracted to produce
brandy for the firm of Kohler & Frohling, but his still blew up
and he was injured trying to escape from a second-floor window.
The colonel's California sojourn appeared to have reached a
conclusive end. In 1868 he emigrated to Nicaragua, where he
and a new group of investors proposed to distill spirits from
sugarcane.

On July 6, 1869, Haraszthy went to meet a business associate
on the banks of a Nicaraguan river. He never returned. His
footprints were found leading to a tree whose limbs reached
across the river; one of the branches, broken off in the middle,
was presumed to have snapped as Haraszthy tried to cross the
stream on it. A few days earlier at the same spot a crocodile had
killed a cow, and to this day Agoston Haraszthy is assumed to
have followed that unlucky bovine into the jaws of oblivion.

Zinfandel, however, marched on. Throughout the years of Haraszthy's troubles at Buena Vista, the grape had been rising in
popularity and stature—it was found to prosper in almost every
winegrowing region of the state and to improve dramatically
the quality of Mission wine when the two were blended. In 1866
the *Alta California* noted that in Sonoma "a grape called Zinfindal
is declared to be best for producing . . . claret mixed with the
native [Mission]; consequently there has been a very great demand for the cuttings." It spread from the Sacramento area into

the Sierra foothills, and in Napa Valley Jacob Schram surmised that the "Zenfenthal" might be the best red wine grape for California. By 1869, the year of Haraszthy's death, wine made from Zinfandel grapes was bringing seventy-five cents per gallon, compared with forty for Mission.

By that time Sonoma County boasted more than three million grapevines, a direct legacy of Haraszthy's evangelism. The following decade the state's wine industry received a backhanded boost from the phylloxera louse ("the unconquerable worm," as Robert Louis Stevenson called it in *The Silverado Squatters*),which ravaged vineyards throughout the world.* Among European immigrants on the East Coast the result was a sudden demand for California wine. After an economic depression had thinned the roster of wineries in the 1870s, a record ten million gallons were produced in 1880, and Northern California pulled permanently ahead of the south. A new grape-planting boom swept the state. This time, however, the most widely sought grape was no longer the Mission. By 1884 two-fifths of the grapevines in California were Zinfandel.

After resigning from Buena Vista, Árpád Haraszthy moved to San Francisco, where he finally succeeded in producing California's first commercial champagne. Made largely from Zinfandel grapes, it was christened Eclipse. (The name was thrice removed from its astronomical inspiration—Árpád named the wine after a popular cigar that itself had been named after an English racehorse.) Árpád, however, apparently lacked his father's flair for entrepreneurship as well as skill in domestic relations—he and his wife, Jovita, moved from one shanty to another, and in 1877 General Vallejo himself had to come to town to dissuade his daughter from divorce.

*The infestation was controlled only when native North American rootstocks were found to be invulnerable to it. The phylloxera also threatened California until West Coast vineyardists switched to these Midwestern rootstocks, which by that time had to be imported from France. Most of the venerable vineyards of Europe now nourish their esteemed products on roots originally transplanted from Missouri.

The following year Jovita died after childbirth. Charles Sullivan writes: "Research into the psychology of familial recollection indicates that Árpád Haraszthy's manufacture of the myth regarding the introduction of the Zinfandel may have been an honest error. Such apparent falsifications are not uncommon, particularly by family members under stress, as Árpád was during the mid-1880s." It is also understandable that Árpád should have sought some credit for his departed father, who had been effectively exiled after doing so much for the state's fledgling wine industry. The upshot was that in 1886 Árpád penned a four-page statement for the California historian Hubert Howe Bancroft in which he (Árpád) claimed that, in 1853 and 1854 at his Crystal Springs nursery, his father had "laid out . . . a large number of vines that were all imported by him from the East and from Europe through the late General L. Mészáros, former Minister of War of Hungary. . . . It was in this importation of vines that the first Zinfandel grape vine reached California, and ever after it was his pride to recommend its plantation as the best grape for red wine and claret." Thereafter it was generally accepted that Zinfandel was a Hungarian grape, perhaps the Kadarka (a notion helped along by Chief Viticultural Officer Wetmore, a good friend of Árpád Haraszthy's, who observed that it was "generally Hungarian in character"). Gradually the legend grew up that the grape's name tag had become muddled on its trip around the Horn or that the colonel had confused it with a tag for the German Zierfahndler.

In his article for the *Vinifera Wine Growers Journal*, Charles Sullivan exhaustively discredits Árpád's claim. He points out (1) that Árpád was studying in the East and in Europe at the time when he claims his father imported the Zinfandel; (2) that the name Zinfandel was not included on the list of 156 grape varieties that Agoston imported in 1861; (3) that in 1860 the Agricultural Section of the U.S. Patents Office published a list of twenty-four Hungarian grapes for distribution without once mentioning the Zinfandel; and (4) that while Árpád said his father transplanted the grape from Crystal Springs to Sonoma between the spring of 1856 and May 1857, "we do not hear of a vintage from

Sonoma Zinfandel for at least five years, a surprising circumstance, since the Zinfandel can easily give a small crop in its third year."

In his study of nineteenth-century editions of the *San Francisco Evening Bulletin*, Sullivan discovered a letter written by Robert A. Thompson, a well-known historian and journalist, in May 1885. "I would not deprive Col. Haraszthy of a moiety of the credit due him as the first among the first grape culturists of this State," Thompson wrote, "but an investigation of the subject forces the conclusion, that the glory of having introduced [the Zinfandel] into the State is not among the laurels he won." Thompson traced the grape to its cultivation under glass by New England nurserymen, who, for the delectation of Boston Brahmins, compiled a selection of exotic table grapes, including the Golden Chasselas, the Muscat of Alexandria, the White and Grizzly Frontignan, the Black St. Peter's, and occasionally the "Zinfindal." After the gold rush got under way, these collections were commonly brought around Cape Horn to California by ship. "To who [*sic*] is the honor of [Zinfandel's] introduction due?" Thompson asked. "To an enterprising pioneer merchant of San Francisco, the late Captain F. W. Macondray, who raised the first Zinfindal vine grown in California in a grapery at his residence, on the corner of Stockton and Washington streets, San Francisco."

It stood perfectly to reason. As mentioned earlier, Macondray had been a merchant sea captain as well as a member of the Massachusetts Horticultural Society. Thompson documented a meeting of the society on June 13, 1846—the day before the Bear Flag was raised at Sonoma, as he pointed out—at which the "Zinfindal" grape was displayed by one J. Fiske Allen of Salem, Massachusetts, and said that it commonly appeared at the society's weekly exhibitions for years thereafter. In 1848 Macondray exhibited "some thirty varieties of pears, a number of grapes and took the first premium for the best display of vegetables of all kinds" at the society's annual festival, where Allen again showed the "Zinfindal"; the following year Macondray emigrated to San Francisco and exhibited the "Zinfindal" at the Mechanics Institute Fair in 1857. According to Thompson, Zinfandel first entered Sonoma County on the wagon bed of one William Boggs, who bought it in 1859 from Napa's J. W. Osborne, who had gotten it from Macondray. Boggs in turn bestowed cuttings upon Vallejo's winemaker, Dr. Faure, who "pronounced it the best claret wine grape he had seen." In a subsequent letter to the *St. Helena Star*, Boggs himself said that Árpád was "mainly indebted to his own vivid imagination" for the idea that his father had introduced the Zinfandel grape; Boggs declared that he had been present when Agoston replanted his Crystal Springs cuttings at Buena Vista, "and there was no foreign vines shipped to Sonoma with these fruit trees." As a matter of fact, prior to his own purchase from Osborne, "there was no foreign vines introduced into Sonoma, excepting one or two varieties of the table grape, Black Hamburg and another grape that resembled the Zinfandel, called . . . Black St. Peter's."

Black St. Peter's: the grape from which Antoine Delmas had made his prizewinning wine in 1858. Sure enough, Delmas now came forward to announce that *he* had imported the Zinfandel in 1852—under the name Black St. Peter's. Furthermore, he claimed that he had sent cuttings to Vallejo two years later—in other words, two years before Haraszthy purchased his Buena Vista property. Of the "table grapes" from which Delmas made his 1858 red wine, Charles Sullivan concludes: "They were Zinfandel."

"And if Zinfandel is the Black St. Peter's, there are lots of connections with English gardeners," Sullivan said to me. "The West St. Peter's and the Black Lombardy were the same grape; it came here and became known as Zinfandel. By the end of the 1860s all the Black St. Peter's vines had magically disappeared. Haraszthy did plant Zinfandel in different vineyards in the 1860s; he may even have imported it in one of the standard New England collections during the 1850s. But there is not one instance where Agoston Haraszthy ever used the word *Zinfandel* in print."

. . .

The case, it seemed, was closed—or at least the question of whether Haraszthy had introduced Zinfandel to California. Sullivan and his wife, Roz, invited me to stay for dinner; after I accepted, they asked if I wanted to try a bottle of old Zinfandel. I responded with a rhetorical question regarding the religious affiliation of the pope, and Sullivan escorted me into his backyard, where we ascended the steps of a gazebo. He shoved aside a wrought-iron table and reached downward, whereupon I noticed the presence of a trapdoor in the floor. He pulled it open and we descended into a cellar, where we were surrounded by hundreds of bottles.

"What are you interested in?" Sullivan asked. "Claret style? Or do you want your head taken off?" Steering a middle course, he selected a '76 Rutherford Ranch, and we clambered back out onto the lawn.

We drank the wine with lamb stew. It was a fine aged Zinfandel—smooth but spicy, rich and round, not especially "old." Later that evening, for purposes of comparison, Sullivan resubmerged for the same winery's '77, which was hotter and less ready to drink even at ten years of age. For proper perspective we also polished off a bottle that Sullivan said he'd started on with Dave Bennion the night before—a '78 Ridge, the vintage upon which Paul Draper had said he'd "learned his lesson."

I asked Sullivan how Ridge wines had changed since Draper had come along. "They didn't make as many *crazy* wines after that," said Sullivan. "Paul came in with a sound understanding of how to avoid mistakes. But Roz says she could never get passionately attached to any of their later wines, whereas Dave's '64 and '68 were really something special."

"Do you ever talk to Bennion about it?"

"Nah!" said Sullivan. "All Dave and I ever do is get drunk and throw up on each other."

During my hour-and-a-quarter drive home on the mercifully

deserted Nimitz, I had ample opportunity to muse on the Haraszthy legend. Sullivan had constructed a strong case, but there were still a few openings in the framework. Besides keeping a grapery in his house in San Francisco, Captain Macondray had also owned a nursery south of the city, near San Mateo. One of his neighbors there, at Crystal Springs Reservoir in 1853 and 1854, was none other than Agoston Haraszthy—Charles Sullivan himself had mentioned a time when Haraszthy and Macondray's son, Frederick Jr., met there while riding. If one entertained the possibility that Macondray got Zinfandel cuttings from Haraszthy around then, the captain would have had sufficient time to raise the vines to maturity and exhibit the grapes in 1857, as indeed he had at the Mechanics Institute Fair. As for Árpád's absence when he claimed that his father received Zinfandel cuttings from General Mészáros (the former Hungarian minister of war), Árpád was indeed living on the East Coast at the time—in Plainfield, New Jersey, where Mészáros had settled in exile and Árpád was going to school. Such proximity could have given Árpád even closer knowledge of the vines shipped by Mészáros than Agoston enjoyed upon receiving them—especially if the ID tag was muddled or confused on its trip around Cape Horn, as the traditional story had long maintained.

It seemed there was still room for legend in the Haraszthy saga. However, having participated in that vertical Zinfandel tasting earlier in the evening, by the time I reached Oakland I was in no condition to contemplate the matter further. As a matter of fact, I was in no condition to drive any farther either. I exited the freeway near the Oakland Coliseum and pulled into the parking lot of a Holiday Inn, temporarily overcome by Zinfandel mystique.

After the initial rush of grape harvesting that took place in late August and early September, things cooled off for a couple of weeks as fogs and the pall of forest fires imposed a moratorium on the grape-ripening process. John Kemble left Ravenswood temporarily to fight a fire in Tuolumne Country, where his family owned a cabin in the Sierra Nevada foothills. Given the short '87 crop, when Joel wasn't working at Sonoma Valley Hospital, he spent much of his time in his car, looking for grapes. "I keep discovering vineyards in places where I never expected them to be and getting good grapes from people I never expected to be interested in quality," he said. He found several patches of Zinfandel in semi-residential neighborhoods around Sonoma and worked out distinctive deals entitling him to a certain percentage of these small vineyards, provided the owner's mother got another percentage, the grandfather another. He bought three and a half tons from somebody in Napa whose father had recently died, preventing the family from making wine that year; some from a vineyard that usually went to Rosenblum Cellars but wouldn't fit onto its truck; some second-crop from a Caymus vineyard on the Oakville Cross Road in Napa Valley; some from a vineyard where Gundlach-Bundschu usually took a ton but this year decided to take only half that. At Ravenswood the crew established a "Chianti vat," into which was crushed each small batch of grapes as it came in, drawing out the fermentation with the successive additions, as is traditionally done in Tuscany. All of it would eventually end up in the Ravenswood Vintner's Blend, the Zinfandel that Joel releases young and sells cheap ("Chateau Cash Flow," in the winery's specialized vernacular).

On Saturday, September 6, the manager of a Napa Valley vineyard with whom Joel had contracted for Zinfandel told him that he wanted to pick his grapes the following day (a Sunday). Joel told him that he had no space in the winery for the grapes— all of Ravenswood's fermentors were full of wine from other vineyards that had come in earlier. To make room for a lot of unpicked grapes that were pushing the limits of acceptable ripeness, Joel had already pressed one tank of Lyeth Zinfandel off its skins earlier than he wanted (to compensate, he would let the other two Lyeth tanks macerate on the skins longer than normal). "I can take grapes anywhere between twenty-two-point-five and twenty-three-point-five," Joel said. "I'd been watching these Napa grapes; they were at twenty-two-seven. I thought they'd probably hold for another four days, which was the next time they told me they could pick."

On Monday morning Joel arrived at the winery and found a message on his answering machine informing him that the grapes were being picked that day. Apparently the grower had decided that they wouldn't hold for another four. His preexisting agreement with Joel had been that he (the grower) would, under his own label, market some of the wine that Ravenswood made from his grapes. "They didn't want the alcohol to be too high, so they decided to go ahead and pick," said Joel. "They sent the grapes to a winery that doesn't even have a Zinfandel program. I called and told them to stop picking right now, and they said they'd already crushed six tons. Now we're trying to get them to pay for it and ship it to us. If that doesn't work, we'll take legal action."

Under the bottlenecked circumstances, Joel had arranged to have his Dickerson Zinfandel grapes custom-crushed and fermented at Buena Vista Vineyards, five miles from Ravenswood. In late September I went there with him when the wine was being pressed.

The spectacularly picturesque ivy-covered tasting room that Buena Vista maintains on the spot where Haraszthy founded the winery is something of a ruse: The actual modern-day two hundred-thousand-case fortress is hidden away in the Carneros hills, several miles to the south. As we drove toward it through the windswept landscape, the Bay Area's major landmarks— Mount Diablo in Contra Costa County, Mount Tamalpais in Marin, the shining bay itself—all were featured in a wide screen picture; undulant rows of grapevines graced the hills as far as the eye could see. (Haraszthy, resting on the bed of a Nicaraguan river, would have been gratified—to a wine lover, the scene truly constituted *una buena vista*.)

At the winery the requisitely rubber-booted throngs were driving tractors to and fro beneath gigantic overhead cranes and hosing down cement floors that supported some fifty stainless-steel tanks. Buena Vista's smallest fermentors were roughly the size of Ravenswood's standard ones—thirteen hundred gallons. The largest were more than ten times as big. Near the entrance to the building an enormous hydraulic press was raining purple wine: the '87 Dickerson Zinfandel. Joel got a glass and dipped some out; when he raised it to his nose, his hand was covered with pink sediment. As he sniffed and sipped, he narrowed his eyes and peered into the distance, thinking hard. He looked like a raptorial bird.

"That's about what I expected," he said, handing the glass to me. "Real nice Dickerson fruit; intense raspberry-citrus nose; pronounced mint-eucalyptus quality. Plus a hint of Rutherford dust—like what it smells like in an old book room. The acid's a little sharp. When the grapes first came in, the acid tested out at point-seventy-seven grams per liter; depending on the grapes, you generally want it to be at least point-eighty-five. So we bumped it up a bit, and the next test went all the way to one-point-zero. Clearly, the first test was wrong—it was probably point-eighty-five initially."

We left the wine and went upstairs. When we passed the empty office of Jill Davis, the Buena Vista winemaker, Joel placed a bottle of 1985 Old Hill Zinfandel on her desk as a present. "That'll intimidate her," he said with a chuckle reflecting the spirit of giving. (Unlike other commercial arts, the nice thing about the wine business is how little ego plays into it.)

We climbed a ladder onto a catwalk that ran among scores of closed-top fermentors. An air lock on one spit and fumed with the force of thousands of gallons of fermenting wine. The Dickerson Zinfandel had been housed in a ten-thousand-gallon tank, even though the wine itself amounted to only a fourth that much. "Ordinarily I would have fermented it in smaller tanks," said Joel, "but Jill needed her small tanks for Chardonnay and Sauvignon Blanc. This winery is so cold, the wine this year probably won't be as rich. I've never fermented in jacketed stainless steel before. For small-lot fermentation, wood has the thermodynamic properties I need—I can keep the temperature up longer and get the kinds of flavors I'm looking for without getting into trouble. But Jill let me do everything else the way I wanted, with the exception of adding stems. Her assistant tasted our wine four days out and said there was something awful, like rubbing alcohol, in it. There wasn't anything wrong with it—he was just so sure that there was going to be a problem with the wild yeast, he was determined to smell something bad, no matter what. Generally people who operate wineries like this have been trained in high tech methods, and their thought patterns don't vary from the norm. Depending on how this turns out, I might change my attitude toward wood fermentation. It's interesting to play with this equipment; it gives me a different perspective on how I do things, what I might do to make life easier. My methods probably make me just as myopic as theirs make them. As you know, mine are pretty hard on the body."

Downstairs Joel ran into Jill Davis, a pleasant woman in her thirties, wearing a white lab coat. "We were talking about swapping some of your Zinfandel with some of ours if you didn't come around for a while," she said to Joel. "We didn't think you'd notice. Ours isn't that good; Carneros doesn't grow good Zinfandel. It just doesn't. It rots. '81 was the last time we made a good one. Yours got a good write-up somewhere recently, didn't it?"

"Well," said Joel, "in Parker. . . ." (Robert M. Parker, Jr., had recently compared the Dickerson Zinfandel with the '59 Mouton Rothschild.)

"Right," said Davis. "I'm just glad I didn't get slammed by him. When he doesn't care for something, he's not even polite. I'd rather he didn't say anything about me at all."

We departed and drove back to Ravenswood, where various wines had completed fermentation but continued to macerate in their redwood tanks. In the absence of carbon dioxide, the cap of grape skins on the wines had sunk to the bottom, and only a few seeds still floated on the surface of the still, dark liquid—a situation that would give most winemakers a profound case of the heebie-jeebies. Out back, Cabernet Sauvignon was being crushed and pumped through one hose while Old Hill Zinfandel was pressed and pumped through another.

Joel dipped his glass into the Old Hill. "Taste the difference between that and the Dickerson?" he said, offering the glass to me. "Dickerson is more in the raspberry vein; this is more the deep black pepper."

We peered down into the Cabernet tank, where the rampant smell of green peppers floated up from a mountain of must. "Lots of skins," Joel observed. "Not much juice."

"Why is that?"

Joel shrugged. "Cabernet."

About a month and a half later we returned to Buena Vista. Apparently because of its high acid and low pH, the Dickerson Zinfandel was refusing to undergo malolactic fermentation (the transformation of malic to lactic acid, which creates a softer, more complex wine). Joel intended to solve the problem by adding calcium carbonate to the wine, where it would precipitate the tartaric acid out as cream of tartar and raise the pH. When we arrived at Buena Vista, we went upstairs and entered the laboratory, a hospitallike room whose shelves were full of sodium oxalate, calcium chloride, capric sulfate, potassium permanganate, hoses, beakers, bottles, and wineglasses. "This is a real winery, with a real laboratory," Joel said as we entered. "They even have real people working in it." The people were performing tests for alcohol, acidity, sugar, pH, and, by the looks of it, that most elusive of sciences, the matching of food and drink: One of the lab workers was eating a piece of cheesecake while drinking a Diet Pepsi.

Back downstairs we passed Jill Davis's empty office. On her desk stood the bottle of Old Hill Zinfandel that Joel had left there six weeks earlier. Hardly any of it had been drunk.

I checked Joel's face for disgruntlement as we went on to the fermentation room. When we got there, he opened a spigot on the Dickerson tank and sprayed some wine into his glass. When he tasted it, all traces of disgruntlement disappeared.

"Just like Mouton, huh?" he said, handing the glass to me.

In 1985, in his comment in the *Vinifera Wine Growers Journal* about the BATF's decision to outlaw the importation of Italian "Zinfandel," Charles Sullivan reiterated his finding that Zinfandel came to California in the 1850s from New England, where it had been grown as a table grape since the 1830s. In fact, in his letter, he went even further, saying that the grape had come to New England from a nursery on Long Island, New York, where it was brought in the 1820s— "probably from the Imperial collection at the Schönbrunn in Vienna." The source point of Sullivan's theories, apparently, was one William Robert Prince, "a nurseryman from Long Island whose Linnaean Botanic Gardens in the 1830s contained an extraordinary collection of wine and table grapes. His Catalogue, published in 1830 as part of his Treatise on the Vine, contained most of the major wine grapes we know today from Europe. Under a category of foreign varieties 'the most of which are of recent introduction' he included the 'Black Zinfardel, of Hungary.' "

In the late nineteenth century, Árpád Haraszthy and his friend Charles Wetmore, California's viticultural commissioner, frequently cited Prince in their attempts to prove the Hungarian origins of Zinfandel, thus supporting the contention that Colonel Haraszthy had introduced the grape to California. Wetmore explained its absence from Hungarian ampelographies by surmising that it "was probably also known in Hungary under other more popular names." Today no red Zinfandel-like grape grows under any name in Hungary, and no "Zinfandel" or "Zinfardel" name appears in any European ampelography, historical or contemporary. The mystery of Zinfandel's origins, then, is etymological as well as biological: The question of how the grape got its name complicates the question of where it came from.

New light as well as new confusion was thrown on these questions in 1967, when Austin Goheen, a U.S. Department of Agriculture plant pathologist, discovered the Primitivo grape growing in the vineyards of Puglia in southeastern Italy. Goheen, who has since retired, still maintains an office at the University of California at Davis, and I went to visit him there on a warm weekday in the fall. Goheen turned out to be a true agricultural-college-style professor, friendly and unpretentious in a denim jacket and jeans, sufficiently relaxed in retirement to have forgotten about our appointment. From his office I called him at home to remind him, then occupied myself by reading up on Zinfandel in the library until he arrived.

Leaning back behind his desk, Goheen related how, in the fall of 1967, he'd attended a conference in Germany on the subject of viral plant diseases. "My project has been to identify viral diseases in grapes and develop sources that don't carry them," he told me. "On the way home I stopped in Puglia to visit Giovanni Martelli, a plant pathologist who had been at Davis. Up until that time all our contacts at Davis had been with northern Italians; after World War II the Italian government had made Conegliano, near Venice, the center of its viticultural research, so all the money and ampelographies were there. The northern Italians didn't get along with the southern Italians, so there wasn't much communication back and forth. But Martelli was studying viral diseases in Puglia, and I wanted to see the situation in the vineyards there. So I was the first Californian scientist to visit southern Italy.

"Bari is an ancient city of a hundred or two hundred thousand people. My plane got in at about six o'clock in the evening, and by the time I got to my hotel it was dark. Martelli and I went out to a local restaurant, and he ordered a wine with dinner that tasted very familiar to me. It had a fruity raspberry flavor, and it was high in alcohol. I said, 'You don't grow Zinfandel here, do you?' and he said, 'No, this is the wine of the district. It's called Primitivo.' I told him I wanted to look at the vines first thing in the morning.

"The next day he took me about fifteen miles southwest to Gioia, a smaller town of flat-roofed stucco and brick buildings. The area is similar to our south coast—there are the undulating foothills of the Apennines, fishing and agriculture, citrus fruits, table grapes. Gioia is purely a grape town—they had thirty thousand hectares of Primitivo there. As soon as I looked at the vines, I knew what I'd found. Zinfandel has a lyre leaf shape, lots of shot berries, and a spot on the fertilization end of the grape called a stylar scar. The Primitivo was identical to it. I had Martelli send some cuttings here. The vines are still growing; they look more like Zinfandel than the Zinfandel does."

"Where are they?"

"Over on the west side of the campus."

"Do you think I could look at them?"

"I don't see why not."

We left the building and drove to the foundation plant sciences area, where, behind the barrackslike buildings and alongside a row of olive trees, acres and acres of green grapevines were growing in the sun. Goheen had brought along a coded set of diagrams that revealed the locations of different varietal plantings in the vineyard; after negotiating a network of dirt access roads, we parked in the shade of the olive trees and marched out into the sun among the rows of vines. Goheen stopped and started periodically, studying the sheets and the plants. Finally he said, "Here we are."

The Zinfandel and Primitivo vines were planted right next to each other, but even after studying them closely, I still couldn't tell which was which. The bunches on both showed uneven ripening from green berries to wrinkled raisins; the black berries of both tasted the same, each exhibiting a tiny brown spot on the ends; the leaves were identically shaped, with deep "vaginations" and hair on the back. Goheen said that in 1976 a UC Davis scientist named Wade Wolfe had performed isozyme fingerprint tests on the vines: Enzymes were extracted from the grapes, placed in a starchy paste, and subjected to an electric current. Given such treatment, the different enzymes in the grape move toward a positive or negative pole, always in a consistent pattern unique to the type of grape. Wolfe found the isozyme patterns of Zinfandel and Primitivo to be identical. As Hugh Johnson wrote at the time: "The news [of Primitivo] is going to ruin a day for all those Haraszthyian romantics who could smell the volcanic soils of Hungary in every sip of Zinfandel." With regard to the origin of the grape, however, there was still a problem. Italian growers apparently refer to Primitivo as an "imported" variety; historic Italian ampelographies note its presence no earlier than 1860. If Zinfandel was indeed growing on Long Island as early as 1830, the vine could conceivably have come to Italy from *America*. Zinfandel and Primitivo might well be the same grape, but the ancestral roots of the varietal still apparently lay somewhere else.

Considering this question, Goheen told me that the leaves of Zinfandel/Primitivo are "bigger and thinner than vines from France. They're more like the grapes of eastern Europe—the Plavac Mali of Yugoslavia, the Kadarka of Hungary, or the Tokay, which originally came from North Africa." He offered the possibility that, recorded or not, the Primitivo might have been brought to Italy from North Africa by the armies of Napoleon or, going back considerably further, that it might have been introduced by the Greeks, who invaded southern Italy before the time of Christ. Indeed, several southern Italian grapes—the Greco di Tufa, for example—boast Hellenic nomenclature, and many Puglians reportedly hold this to be the origin of the Primitivo.

In an article entitled "On the Trail of the Zinfandel" in the *Journal of Gastronomy* in 1986, Miles Lambert-Gocs had this to say about the Primitivo/Greece hypothesis:

> . . . of more likely significance to a search for the source of the Apulian [Puglian] tradition would be the Greek and Albanian refugees from Ottoman rule, who settled in Apulia and other parts of southern Italy during the fifteenth and sixteenth centuries. . . . Southern Italians tended to call all Orthodox Christian refugees "Greeks."
> . . . Many grape varieties now grown along the eastern Adriatic (that is, the Greek Ionian area, Albania, and Dalmatia in Yugoslavia) no doubt came from the eastern Mediterranean area, or possibly the Black Sea area, where the characteristics noted in their varieties . . . are yet more common. The eastern Adriatic coastal area had been in commercial contact with the eastern Mediterranean area and Black Sea areas since antiquity, and there is reason to suppose that vines were brought from the east.

Because of its similarity and geographical proximity to Primitivo, the Plavac Mali grape—which grows directly across the Adriatic from Puglia, in the Yugoslavian province of Dalmatia—has frequently been named as a suspect in the Zinfandel case. Its cousin the Plavina, owing to its large crop load, is sometimes even called *Pagadebiti* (debt payer), which happens to be precisely what early Italian California growers called the Zinfandel. But Goheen told me flatly that Plavac Mali had been planted at Davis and was "not the same."

We returned to the campus. After I said goodbye to Goheen, I walked from the plant pathology building to the viticulture and enology department, where I had an appointment to see Harold Olmo, the plant geneticist known in the industry as the "Burbank of the grape." Olmo's lifelong project at Davis had been the crossbreeding of grape varieties especially for California; his first successes had been the Emerald Riesling and Ruby Cabernet, the latter a cross between Carignane and Cabernet Sauvignon designed to provide balanced acidity in the oven of the Central Valley. On a Guggenheim Fellowship in the late 1940s, Olmo had gone looking for the original home of the *vinifera* grapevine growing wild near the Caspian Sea. He took a bus from Peshawar, Pakistan, over the Khyber Pass to Kabul, Afghanistan, where he combed through the local bazaars, looking for fruits and inquiring where they'd come from. From a North American oil company he bought a customized Chevrolet with high ground clearance and drove it into the Iranian desert, buying gasoline and meeting local mayoral figures through a letter he had from the shah. When he stopped in remote villages, the local citizens would expropriate from the car anything that moved—mirrors, gas caps, nuts, bolts—so Olmo welded the bumpers and headlights to the chassis. Since the primitive roads were innocent of signs, he followed produce trucks through the desert, sometimes waiting for days for one to come along. Eventually he hired a guide, who drove the Chevy into a gorge and later disappeared with his food and blankets. Luckily nearby was a tribe of nomads who, employing camel hair ropes and stopping periodically to pray, took three days to extricate Olmo's car from the gorge.

In the desert villages Olmo found fruit trees and grapevines growing inside walled compounds. He collected cuttings and lined the boxes with sphagnum moss to keep them moist, but he was away from civilization for so long that the vines began growing, and he lost them. One day, passing through a small town in northern Iran, south of the Caspian Sea, Olmo saw some grapes growing wild near a stream; when he climbed down the ledge to collect some of their seeds, he noticed that the vines had some of the same qualities as wine grapes cultivated in the West. The berries were black, for example, and smaller than normal for Middle Eastern grapes. *Unlike* most European varieties, however, which contain both sexes on one vine, these were divided into male and female plants.

Olmo brought the seeds home and planted them at Davis. As the vines matured, he noted that the flowering clusters on the male plants were similar to those of European *vinifera* grapes and that the male vines sometimes produced berries in addition to pollen. From this he deduced that modern wine grapes descended from these wild male vines and that our table grapes—which are not very cold-tolerant—developed near the Caspian Sea or perhaps in more southerly latitudes where the climate was even warmer. Contrary to what had been previously thought, it appeared that modern wine grapes had evolved not from a single vine but rather from a complex group of *vinifera* plants in Persia.

Like Goheen, Olmo was now retired. Also like Goheen, he had forgotten about our appointment. I sat outside his locked door for some time before he came along with a friend, each of them carrying a bottle of red wine. They explained that they were just returning from a party celebrating the fortieth birthday of Ruby Cabernet; I noted that the atmosphere around them had an appropriately enological air.

After a few minutes the friend departed. Olmo—a big man with close-cropped hair and tinted eyeglasses, wearing a tweed sports jacket and a pair of work boots—ushered me into his office. His shelves were full of file folders with names like Fertilization, Flowering and Fruiting, New Varieties, French Hybrids, Ampelography, and Propagation (Seeds, Cuttings, Rootings, Budding, Grafting). I asked him how he'd gotten started in the work he'd done at Davis.

"After Prohibition the state's industry wasn't really geared to go back into grape growing and winemaking," Olmo said in an accent that evoked the Bronx (though he was born and grew up in San Francisco). "There'd been a long period of inactivity, and the composition of the vineyards had changed. A lot of people had switched to varieties like the Alicante-Bouschet that could be shipped east for home winemaking. When Prohibition ended, people collecting fruit didn't know one grape from another, so my job was to identify varieties. I started by studying the seeds, which are less variable than berries. The grape is quite a bit different from other fruit plants; there's a lot of variation within what we call a variety. Characteristics may vary even though the enzymes are the same—for example, some clones of Zinfandel set tight clusters, and some are loose. Some have hairy leaves, and some don't. To this day, people bring me Zinfandel, and I can identify it; but I can't tell you all the reasons why. It's like you identifying your brother."

I asked if isozyme fingerprinting offered a foolproof method of identifying grape varieties.

"Identical enzymes indicate that varieties are at least descended from the same parent," Olmo said. "If many types are descended from one, their genes should be the same. But it's hard to work with genes—very few have been identified and located in the grapevine. There are hundreds of enzymes, but in isozyme fingerprinting we work with only about eight. So our knowledge is limited."

"What does that mean about Primitivo and Zinfandel?"

"From the standpoint of fingerprinting," Olmo said, "if Zinfandel and Primitivo aren't the same, they're very closely related. But you know, Martelli's shipment to Goheen contained three different vines; two were black varieties, and one was white. Only one was like Zinfandel. There are several different types of Primitivo scattered around southern Italy—there's a Primitivo di Gioia, a Primitivo di Manduria, and another type of Primitivo up along the Adriatic. They're populations rather than single clones—composites rather than derivations of one vine—and they differ among themselves."

In between statements Olmo shut his eyes and sniffed spasmodically and repeatedly. I wondered if he had hay fever or asthma, but when he resumed talking, he seemed fine.

"Identifying grapes is more difficult in Italy than anywhere else," he went on, folding his fingers together across his chest. "It's a long peninsula with a favorable climate for grape growing, and a crossroads or melting pot for grapes from the Middle

East and Europe. Winemaking and grape growing originally developed in the Middle East; the cultivated varieties went from there to places like Italy, where they crossed spontaneously with wild vines, which gave rise to even more variation. The Italian seldom pulls anything out of the ground—if a seedling comes up, he'll put a stick on it and wait to see what it does. There are probably two thousand different varieties of wine grapes in Italy now. In different regions of the country, the same variety will get different names. *Lambrusco* means 'wild vine,' and *Lambrusco salamina* is a vine with clusters shaped like a salami; but in Sardinia they call it *Lambrusco sarda*. On the other hand, some varieties end up with the same name when actually they're different."

The development of modern grapes is at least as complicated as Eurasian history. Archaeologists have uncovered primitive grape presses, fermentation tanks, and treading platforms—antedating Christ by millennia—in roughly the region that Olmo explored: the Caucasus between the Black and Caspian seas. From there it's fair to say that, wherever Caucasians went, they took grapevines with them. From what we now call Syria and Lebanon, the Phoenicians distributed grapes throughout the Mediterranean. So did their successors, the Greeks, who, upon first being exposed to Italy, called it the Land of Vines—the same thing that the Vikings said about North America two thousand years later, when confronted with the profusion of *Vitis labrusca*. The *vinifera* is only one of about forty indigenous grape species in the world, almost all of which are deciduous, highly susceptible to fungi and parasites, needful of considerable heat and sunlight, and—perhaps most important—able to crossbreed spontaneously. The original group of wild vines native to western Europe was called *Vitis sylvestris*—"grape of the forests." Its fruit is thought to have been gathered and utilized by prehistoric people, but the groundwork for the great vineyards of Europe was laid mainly by the Romans, who brought wines and vines with them as the moved up the Rhône from Provence into Burgundy, into the valleys of the Moselle and the Rhine, and westward to Bordeaux and the Loire. The Middle Eastern *vinifera* varieties, marching up from the Mediterranean, weren't well suited to northern climes; but where they encountered *V. sylvestris*—which had already adapted itself naturally into different ecological groupings in different regions—members of the species interbred, and some of their progeny, uniquely suited to the regions where they arose, combined the best qualities of each parent. Over the succeeding centuries, the most felicitous (i.e., most flavorful as well as most hardy) offshoots of this orgy of interbreeding were selected and cultivated by the local populace, each one becoming, through mankind's contributions (i.e., culture and agriculture), a kind of distilled essence of the place where it evolved. In time some of these strains developed into today's "noble" European varieties: the Cabernet Sauvignon in Bordeaux; the Pinot Noir and Chardonnay in Burgundy; the late-ripening, cold-resistant Riesling in Germany. Then there were the dozens of other grapes that, if not afforded the status of royalty, still found ideal homes and flourished: Syrah in the Rhône; Gewürztraminer in Alsace; Sangiovese and Nebbiolo in Italy; Zinfandel in California.

Olmo described eastern European grapes to me as a cross between the large-berried table grapes of the eastern "Adriatic side" and the European varieties, which have smaller berries and clusters and higher sugar and acidity. As Goheen had pointed out, Zinfandel perfectly fits this crossover description—a fact that naturally returns one to ruminations about Hungary, which serves as a kind of geographical way station. In Haraszthy's heyday, another grape Goheen had mentioned—the Kadarka of Hungary—was commonly offered as Zinfandel's Old World counterpart, a theory that persisted until somebody placed the grapes side by side and saw that they bore no resemblance to each other. For obvious reasons, the search for a central European forebear has long cast suspicion upon the German name Zierfahndler; but Zierfahndler is a known synonym for Sylvaner, and since Sylvaner is a white wine grape, the name sheds little light on the etymological origins of Zinfandel. Unless, of course, the Zierfahndler was confused with another grape en route to America, in exactly the manner that the Haraszthy legend claimed.

Miles Lambert-Gocs writes:

The "Zierfahndler" name enjoyed its greatest popularity in the area where Hungary (at Sopron), Slovakia (at Bratislava), and Austria (at Rust), came together. The dominant grape variety for red wine throughout the area . . . has been the blue/black variety known in Hungary as "Kékfrankos" [also known in Slovakia as Frankovka and in Austria as Blaufrankisch]. . . . In 1841, the Austrian ampelographer Franz Trummer indicated that at Sopron . . . people knew the Kékfrankos as "Blauer Zierfahnler." . . . Furthermore, some contemporary Slovakian ampelographies . . . have continued to list the name "Cierny Zierfandler" [sic], or "black" Zierfahndler, as a synonym for Frankovka (a.k.a. Kékfrankos).

Lambert-Gocs surmises that when the Long Island nurseryman William Robert Prince received the "Black Zinfardel, from Hungary" in the 1820s, "he in all probability had received the Kékfrankos." The same goes for J. Fiske Allen's New England "Zinfindal." Thus, according to Lambert-Gocs, "we are brought back to the Haraszthy family story. There is nothing fantastical about an identification tag on a bunch of vines being in poor condition after a long journey. . . . [Furthermore,] Haraszthy's failure to recognize the 'Zinfandel'-like name on the tag is not so surprising. Although involved with viti-viniculture in Hungary before leaving there, Haraszthy's lands were far from the area where the Zierfahndler synonym was in use."

In fact, Haraszthy's lands (which during the time of the Hapsburg dynasty were part of that great shifting mass known as the Austro-Hungarian Empire) today lie within the borders of Yugoslavia. Lambert-Gocs raises the possibility that "the Zinfandel/Primitivo procured for Haraszthy [by General Mészáros, the Hungarian minister of war] reached Poszony [then the capital of Hungary] via Dalmatia (whether or not the variety is identical with that region's Plavac Mali). In the time of Haraszthy and Mészáros, Dalmatia belonged to the Kingdom of Hungary. It would have been easy to procure vines from there." Charles Sullivan himself had pointed out to me that during the Byzantine era a continuous connection existed among Asia Minor, the Black Sea, the Balkans, and southern Italy, making rather likely the general distribution of a Primitivo type of grape, if one existed anywhere in the region at the time. Lambert-Gocs's point is entirely consistent with Sullivan's observation that "in 1820, the Austrian Empire was a unit. There was, as yet, no autonomous Hungary, so that the entire collection [of so-called Austro-Hungarian grapevines] would be centered in Vienna until the late 1860s."

When I'd spoken with him, Sullivan was trying to persuade the Schönbrunn archive in Vienna to unearth its records of grape shipments from the early nineteenth century, which might actually reveal whether a *blauer Zierfahndler*—aka Kékfrankos—was sent to Prince on Long Island or whether any grapes at all were ever sent to Haraszthy's supposed supplier, General Mészáros in New Jersey. Harold Olmo, for one, was still prepared to recognize the possibility.

"Haraszthy has been defamed, but on faulty grounds," Olmo said. "If we find two or three other varieties in Yugoslavia with characteristics similar to Zinfandel, maybe we'll call that the origin. I'd like to visit Haraszthy's old village in Yugoslavia and see what I turn up."

Sullivan had told me that *he* had gone to Haraszthy's village, studied the tombstones in the local cemetery, and found nothing Magyar (i.e., Hungarian) in the inscriptions there. Nevertheless, the colonel's figurative grave appeared to remain unquiet.

"Who knows?" Olmo said as I got up to go. "In the end Haraszthy may turn out to have been right."

In early November I drove to Ridge for a production tasting of 1986 Zinfandels. The reds and golds of autumn had arrived, both in the vineyards and in the canopy of trees that overarched Monte Bello Road. I found Draper on a hillside behind the winery, conferring with his vineyard manager, Fred Peterson; the Santa Clara Valley, Santa Cruz Mountains, and Pacific Ocean stretched away below the broad clay-brown slopes of the vineyard, whose rows gracefully followed the contours of the hill. It would be hard for Monte Bello wines not to be transcendent, considering their view. Holding a white Samoyed on a long retractable leash, conferring with an adviser high above the kingdoms of the earth, Paul Draper struck me as some sort of duke or grandee.

In the background bulldozers were ripping out vines while tractors disked the newly exposed earth. "This is one way that our new ownership has really helped matters when it comes to decision-making," Draper said. "We're removing nine acres of heavily virused old Chardonnay and some Cabernet that hasn't made the Monte Bello cut for the last three years. Some of our original owners couldn't see the point of tearing out the vines they had so lovingly planted in the sixties—they had this idea that you planted vines for life. I'd been accepting those blocks of Cabernet, but they weren't my favorite; they really weren't giving us the quality we needed to make one of the great wines of the world. In this poor soil, with very wide spacing between rows—the California ideal back then—the vine roots weren't filling up the space, and our yields were only one to one and a half tons per acre. We found that, with closer replanting and cane instead of cordon pruning, we could get three times as many vines per acre. Even with each plant yielding less than the widely spaced ones, we should move up toward three tons per acre.

"We're going to experiment with four strips of different grapes. This whole swale will be Merlot, beyond the olive trees will be Petit Verdot, and here we'll have two clones of Cabernet with an avenue down the middle. The primary Cabernet will be the La Questa clone, which has been growing in the Santa Cruz Mountains for over a hundred years. A guy named Rixford brought it here from France in the 1800s and planted it near Woodside at a place called La Questa, which became one of the most famous small Cabernet vineyards between 1880 and 1940. In 1941 Frank Schoonmaker wrote that the finest California Cabernet Sauvignon came from 'the hills west of San Francisco Bay,' and I'm sure what he meant by that was La Questa. Martin Ray planted some of the cuttings at Mount Eden, where Fred used to work as winemaker and vineyard manager. We just made some Cabernet from Fred's young La Questa vines, and we were bowled over by its complex, developed character.

"It's surprising how exciting a destruction can be," said Draper, surveying the scene. "It's a little traumatic to undergo our first replanting in twenty-five years, but when you start to work the open land, you can really see the potential."

A breeze stirred the leaves of some aspens and poplars bordering the vineyard. Draper craned his neck around to investigate the noise. "Whenever I hear leaves rustling, I immediately turn around," he explained with the low chuckle that indicated trepidation and delight. "It sounds like running liquid. You could be emptying a tank of Cabernet onto the ground!"

We made our way to the upper winery and into the laboratory, a room with vertical redwood siding and a white Formica-topped table. David Noyes was pouring red wine from plastic beakers into twenty glasses on the table. At Draper's place there was also a pint carton of half-and-half.

"It coats my stomach and keeps the alcohol from changing my perception," he explained. "Olive oil is good, too—it's a wonderful version of cod-liver oil—but boy, it burns." This precaution was necessary, of course, only if one swallowed the wine—a rare habit among serious wine tasters, but one that Draper employs. "If you're in the fine wine business, I think one of your top tasters making decisions has to swallow. Otherwise you don't truly get a technical judgment on the finish—you won't pick up on a harshness or burn that's there in one out of four wines. Swallowing very little is the key. I don't go around talking in the industry about how I swallow; the first requirement of English wine merchants is that they learn how to spit. But I learned to love wine by drinking it, and I have no desire to change."

We were joined by Otsuka's apprentice winemaker, Hiro Oguri, a tall, thin young man with a strong jaw who, instead of half-and-half, kept a Japanese-English dictionary by his side. Noyes had poured out five different wines, identified only by the letters *A* through *E*. These barrel samples of Ridge's five national-release Zinfandels all shone a beautiful cherry red against the white Formica. The three men sniffed the wines while making notes on yellow pads; only after they had smelled all the samples in succession did they begin to sip and taste. The bald, stocky turtlenecked Noyes leaned forward with his arms on the table, sucking wine through his teeth, taking notes steadily as if they were being dictated through a tiny speaker in his ear. Oguri sat ramrod-straight and occasionally consulted his dictionary. Both men spit their wine into plastic beakers after tasting it. Draper, by contrast, leaned back, hung one arm over his chair, and swirled his glass leisurely with his wrist, tossing the wine gracefully back and forth, describing ellipses rather than circles, and sniffing in short, rapid-fire bursts while exhaling air through his mouth between sniffs, and closing his eyes while tasting. Occasionally he chuckled to himself and shook his head.

The men evaluated the wines comparatively, distributing grades of two pluses, two minuses, and a neutral zero among the five samples. After about ten minutes they handed their votes to Noyes.

I didn't vote, but wrote in my notebook:

A. Slight turnip quality to nose—VA? Good flavor, but not as much finish as flavor
B. Good fruity nose, slightly oaky—alive in the mouth
C. Slightly flatter—losing interest with each minute— not much taste at all
D. Mellow nose—good bite in mouth—good tannin and acid
E. Very nice wine—not a fruity nose, but good, sharp, full flavor

The results of the vote, in order of collective preference, were:

1. E—Lytton Springs (near Dry Creek Valley) 13.9 percent alcohol
2. B—Geyserville (Alexander Valley in Sonoma County) 13.4 percent
3. D—York Creek (at two thousand feet on Spring Mountain, west of Napa Valley) 13.9 percent
4. C—Howell Mountain (fourteen hundred feet, east of Napa Valley) 13.4 percent
5. A—Paso Robles (in the Coast Range, far to the south) 13.3 percent

The identities of the vineyards were not revealed until after a full discussion of the wines. I've taken the liberty of revealing them now and inserting their names into the following discussion in order to save the reader the chore of matching letters with the vineyard names. For example, while Paul Draper actually began the discussion by saying, "Okay! Should we start with Wine A?," I'm pretending that he said, "Okay! Should we start with the Paso Robles?"

"Very dramatic Zin," said Noyes. "Black pepper. What I like about it is the straightforward Zinfandel berry up front, which offsets the tannic finish. But the feel in the mouth is not quite as rich. It's a little tough."

"I get new oak," said Draper. "There's a sweetness there, almost a viscosity. It's very ripe. I think it's *almost* enough to balance the tannin, but I found myself asking, 'Is it as fine a wine?' I went back and forth between the Howell Mountain and the Paso Robles; at one point I said the Paso Robles was 'a little ordinary.' Then later I said, 'Developed . . . slightly broad feel . . . somewhat tough . . . a little simple."

"I like the sweet cherry quality, but it's not top class," said Noyes.

"I liked the Howell Mountain," said Oguri. "Good acid. Good balance." He looked at his dictionary. "Flowery."

"I thought it had a similar toughness to the Paso Robles," said Noyes.

"It's not as harsh, but it's very dry," said Draper. "The nose is sort of steely. And yet a lot of people are going to take that nose and say, 'Ah! That's nice.' It's a lovely wine, but it's slightly out of balance. We're going to have to help it along and pull that tannin down a bit with fining, though fining is never a total solution when a wine is this tannic.

"The York Creek has tannin, too, but not as much grape tannin as Howell Mountain—more oak tannin. It's a full wine, not a *thin* tannic wine." Turning to me, Draper said, "The York Creek this year is a triumph of the winemaking art. It was the only Zinfandel not picked before the rains in the last week of September; we had wanted to pick before the rain, but the vineyard manager wasn't cooperative. We picked on the first and second of October, and we ended up getting some rot. In Cabernet we don't worry about that because the bunches are loose and the berries are tough. But the York Creek Zinfandel had less color this year because of the Botrytis."

"Berries make tannin in response to Botrytis," Noyes explained. "But I find this very soft despite the tannin. There is wood, but it's very delicate. I had 'a little oaky Zin fruit,' 'ripe,' 'hot.' I actually gave the center on this one a minus because it didn't seem as interesting to me as some of the others. There isn't as much fruit there."

"I had 'delicate, intriguing fruit/oak,' " said Draper. "In the mouth I thought it was quite round without being huge. But certainly richer than the Howell Mountain—the tannins are more in balance. It's a lovely, well-balanced Zin without waving its flag—a good food wine, a good normal wine. Not an overpowering monster that you've got to build a meal around. With that balance and elegance, we could almost bottle it next month.

"The Geyserville is also well balanced, but not as ripe as the York Creek. York Creek is drier; Geyserville is livelier in the mouth."

"The Geyserville has oak, but nice berry flavors in the middle despite the oak," said Noyes. "It's very complex; it's got a milky feel in the mouth. I got a strong quality in the nose that I called 'phenolic smells'—sort of a Plasticine or plastic bandage smell that's a little bit off-putting. I don't think it's typical of the wine, so I'm discounting it."

"It's hard to judge because of that," Draper agreed. "I tasted this wine the other day, and it didn't have that smell; I think it's a temporary artifact. Coming back to it separately, I really like that richness. And the smell is clearing up now, I think. I actually ranked the Geyserville first and the York Creek second; they're the two most elegant. Lytton Springs I had third."

"Lytton Springs has the most Zinfandel berry fruit in the mouth," said Noyes. "I wrote 'strong berries—*extravagant* berries!' For me it's that green, wild-berry Zinfandel quality."

"I thought it was a little hot, but with good body and tannin and so on," said Draper. "I find it almost slightly medicinal in the good sense of the word—a high, penetrating, volatile, concentrated quality. When we see that early on, it always develops positively."

"I was thinking," said Noyes. "We always say that Lytton Springs has the most Zinfandel fruit. But it's the combination of different varieties that makes the wine so fruity. Think of a fruit salad; it's always fruitier than the individual fruit."

"Lytton Springs has the most mixed varietals of any of our vineyards," Draper explained. "It has Zinfandel, Grenache, Carignane. . . ."

"And a little bit of God knows what," said Noyes.

"Lytton Springs and Geyserville are our two most famous Zinfandels," said Draper. "They're perceived by wine writers and by our market as the epitome of Zinfandel style, but in fact, they're only about seventy-five percent Zinfandel. Of course, if we go back a hundred years, that's how Zinfandels were made; traditionally there was never a pure Zinfandel. I read recently where somebody called the idea of blending varietals 'the new thing' in California. It's the *old* thing; we're just getting back to it."

I asked why, if he thought that blending was so fortuitous, Draper insisted on keeping the grapes from his different Zinfandel vineyards separate.

"It's very smart to cherry-pick a lot of vineyards and blend them together," he said, "but that approach doesn't interest us. What interests us is seeing what a single vineyard will produce, how it will express the characteristics of its soil and climate— its 'earth,' as the French say. We find that Napa Zinfandels are more spicy and austere, while Sonoma Zinfandels are richer, more berrylike, and fuller-bodied. For many years I tried to make the Paso Robles vineyard into York Creek—we'd go longer on the skins and add more Petite Sirah for tannin—but it just wouldn't do it. Eventually I learned that you've got to allow the vineyard to be itself. It's like a person: He may go through some bad times, lose his job, or go through a divorce, but he'll retain the same basic characteristics. You just have to make a decision as to whether that vineyard is going to give you the kind of wine you're looking for and then help it, through your practices in the winery, to express its basic character as clearly as possible. Good old Zinfandel to a great degree is going to make itself, but only so far; you need to correct certain tendencies with longer or shorter fermentations, more or less barrel age. For example, we want full extraction in our Geyserville Zinfandel; we've yet to see it overextracted. But only in some years will our Howell Mountain vineyard produce grapes full and rich enough to match its tannins. It just demands different treatment. We found that we were making Howell Mountain Zinfandel that might age twenty to thirty years, but never in those twenty to thirty years would it give much sensual pleasure. This year we did a series of experiments on it—submerged cap with extensive pumpover, submerged cap with limited pumpover, floating cap with various cutoff times for pumping over, different press fractions, and some whole clusters—which worked out quite well. In the future we think we'll be able to make a wine from Howell Mountain that's richer, rounder, and less tannic to start with, whereas the Geyserville grapes are in better balance naturally."

During the tasting a sandy-haired man in his late thirties, wearing blue jeans and hiking boots, came in and out of the room, printing out data on a computer. This was Leo McCloskey, biochemist and formerly winemaker at Felton-Empire, farther south in the Santa Cruz Mountains. He was conducting a research project that I had seen written up in *Newsweek*, of all places. When the tasting ended, I followed McCloskey next door, where he was racing between his computers and racks of test tubes.

"This is a madcap time of year for me," McCloskey acknowledged as I peered at his equipment. "I have one chance at getting a chemical snapshot of the wines while they're new, and we want flavor histograms of a hundred of them. This device is a high-performance liquid chromatograph, which cracks wine into its flavor and pigment components. I inject a drop of wine into the machine, and the flavors and pigments stick to the top a column of sand that's coated with wax. Alcohol is used to wash them off, and as they leave the column, a scanning spectrometer takes a color picture of them. It comes out looking like a bar graph, indicating the levels of flavor and pigment in the wine. The amounts vary from year to year, but some varietals have more flavors and pigments to start with. For example, Cabernet has nine pigments; Pinot Noir has four. Zinfandel has eight.

"Now that the pressure is on Ridge to produce wines of high quality consistently, we're using this to try to make better wine more consistently," McCloskey explained. "We're investigating the link between wine's chemicals, sensory, and economic values. Fine wine is basically a synthesis of chemical flavors from the skin, pulp, and seeds of the grape into a very rare fine-food flavor. It's a group of molecules—you can measure it, and you can tell during harvest whether the grapes that year are going to have high levels of it. Take the '73 Geyserville Zinfandel, a legendary wine within the winery. Why are other wines not up to that par? If you have a Frenchman, an Australian, and an American in the same room, they'll all attribute success to 'good years.' There's certainly something to be said for the notion that California has no 'bad' years—a Frenchman would love to have one of our bad years—but the French make more top wines. Why? We need more chemical information on what makes wines 'good' or 'bad.' Winemakers remember the type of barrels and the crushing dates, but with this research we're trying to pinpoint the conditions chemically and objectively. We want everything to be like the best conditions we ever had.

"The biggest gap in knowledge is between the primary and secondary chemistry of the wine. The science of wine chemistry now involves alcohol, sugar, pH, volatile acidity, tartaric and malic acid—all primary chemicals. This was a forefront area a hundred years ago; Louis Pasteur may be the reason the French wine industry got off the ground before the Spanish and the Italians. UC Davis, in trying to bring California up from a backwater in the world wine industry, also focused on primary chemistry and chemical engineering problems. But if you measure the primary chemicals in wines from good and bad years—

or, say, in Ridge Cabernet versus some jug Cabernet from the Central Valley—they're very similar. So the puzzle remains: What is 'good' about one and 'bad' about the other?

"A plant systemacist knows that certain plants make only certain chemicals. Grapes, for example, make only one or two major classes of flavonoids. If winemakers were schooled in tea or cocoa, they'd be more familiar with this sort of chemistry. Three Nobel Prizes were given for secondary plant chemistry before World War II, and those scientists got some of their chemicals from grapes. But secondary plant chemists tend to be attracted to private industry and pharmaceutical firms, which are more high-powered than universities; UC Davis can't be funded by the federal government, for example. So nobody really knows what makes red wine tick.

"We're trying to measure, for the first time in California, the secondary chemicals that are in red wine. We believe we've found the class of compounds that distinguish wines in good years and bad years. We've figured out the chemistry that makes wine brown as it ages—it's flavonoid chemistry, which is very valuable to understand because brown wine won't be good wine. It's extremely exciting research—like being Sherlock Holmes. If we can increase this kind of knowledge, the consumer's going to benefit and maybe more wine will be drunk.

"Ultimately my interest is in linking the chemical compounds to the economic value of the wine. In Chianti versus Bordeaux, for example: The wine laws for Chianti are very stiff—they have to use Sangiovese grapes in all of their wines. But what if those grapes don't have the basic building blocks to make great wine? Grapes like Barbera, Grenache, and Petit Verdot are all missing one of the basic building blocks. Zinfandel? In a great year I think Cabernet from the same vineyard will always outrace Zinfandel. Cabernet has higher levels of the building blocks that make great wine. But it also has the building blocks to make poor wine in a *bad* year—it can be outright bad, green-tobacco-smelly. Zinfandel is somewhere in the middle.

"We find that wine writers are very unnerved by this research because they're going to have to tune up this level. The idea

110

that we would even *attempt* to analyze scientifically what makes great wine! They think we're taking the romance out of it, but I'm sure people thought Pasteur was taking the romance out a hundred years ago, too. The craft side will always be there. A winemaker is like a painter: He knows what he likes and what he doesn't like, and he continues to stir the pot with decisions that affect the final product. And I'm only working on taste and pigment, not odor—as wine gets older, the nose plays more of a role. I bet Paul would say that sixty percent of wine quality is in the odor. That's the connoisseur's position.

"We don't want to get off on the wrong track—synthetic winemaking or anything like that. And we do want to see if humans can detect the same differences that the computer shows. In 1986 the machine corroborated our tasters' opinions on nine out of ten lots of Monte Bello Cabernet. The '84, '85, and '86 Monte Bellos have all been products of this kind of thinking. The reason it's so compelling is that it shows that great wine actually exists. You can build a three-D model of a molecule of it. It's not just that somebody *thinks* it's great."

At a winery that claimed to be so old-fashioned, McCloskey's talk sounded awfully modern. As I returned to Draper's office, Silicon Valley seemed nearer to Ridge than ever before.

"The majority of my original partners here were scientists," Draper acknowledged as I sat down beside his dusty Latour bottles. "They were very interested in why traditional methods worked the way they did. We like to say that we do high tech research on our low tech winemaking. Basically, what Leo's research gives us is a question mark to consider. It might trigger something like 'Aha, this wine is low in tannin though it doesn't seem so now; will it need Petite Sirah?' What journalists want us to say, of course, is that we can synthesize the chemicals— like the vanilla bean—put them in jug wine, and get Château Latour. But even Leo wouldn't say that his research could replace tasting. Tasting is what the consumer and connoisseur are most concerned with. Tasting, in the end, is absolute."

When I told Joel Peterson about Ridge's research, he didn't react very well. As a matter of fact, he sounded like one of the wine writers that Leo McCloskey had described. "They're trying to apply a precise scale to an imprecise thing," Joel protested. "They're making an assumption that there's a universal taste, that everybody likes the same thing. Unless you're manufacturing a product that's the same year after year, somebody's still got to make a decision about what the data represent and what they mean. Grape flavonoids come from lots of places, and you can do various things to increase them: adding stems, increasing skin time, aging in wood. That sort of thing should be the winemaker's job."

Of course, Draper and McCloskey had said the same thing: that the winemaker continues to "stir the pot." But Joel was inconsolable.

"Paul Draper is the only guy I know who carries a clipboard with him everywhere he goes," Joel laughed, speculating on the possible roots of Ridge's research. "If Paul finds a kind of sausage he likes, he'll write down its name and find out where it's from. I suspect that he has a very significant filing-and-retrieval system. As a winemaker, you might say that he operates more from his head, whereas I operate more from my heart."

This was a self-aggrandizing analysis, of course; people who "operate from the heart" get the sentimental inside track—a position that Joel often seems to enjoy. At times he can be downright maudlin in his efforts to garner a listener's sympathy, and his shamelessly romantic attitude toward wine borders on the histrionic. "Wine is a shared experience, and very few things are as comforting as a shared experience," he once told me. "It's thrilling to drink a good bottle of wine—there's something immortal about it. The grape is very transitory; it perishes quickly. But put it in a bottle and it gets better with time—you can watch it grow and mature. In a way it parallels the ideal human life."

Joel's own life began in Point Richmond, California, a surprisingly charming community at the bottom of the uncharming chain of oil refineries that line San Pablo Bay. His father, Walter Peterson, worked for Shell Development as a chemist, developing solid rocket propellants and high-temperature bearing greases from special clays. His mother, Frances, was also a chemist, but when World War II ended, she found it hard to compete with returning veterans for jobs; she went to work in Shell's chemical library, which was where she met Walter. A renowned cook, Frances taught Joel from an early age why egg whites got stiff when they were beaten (protein linkage through oxygen addition) and why bread rose when yeast was added (carbon dioxide gas released by fermentation). Walter, for his part, spent his spare time pondering the esters and aldehydes that made wine smell like apples, bananas, or dirty socks. Wine accompanied dinner every evening, and Joel grew up assuming that his friends also drank Lafite, Pétrus, and La Tâche with their meals. In addition to serving as a wine judge at the California State Fair, Walter headed the San Francisco Wine Sampling Club, which met twice weekly at his home to taste wines from all over the world; he spent his nonworking hours searching out wines for the group to sample, and each year the club bought the best Bordeaux that had been released.

Joel's first experience of wine came from a tasting of pre-

1900 Latours. Awakened by the enthusiasm of the group, he waited until all the tasters had gone home, then went down to the kitchen and raised one of the bottles to his lips. All that remained was sediment, and he "couldn't imagine why anybody would want to drink such disgusting stuff." For a time Walter tried to sell wine, accompanied by detailed tasting notes, through the mail—a plan in which he was frustrated by the BATF and the licensing division of the Alcoholic Beverage Control Commission, which required that he obtain a retail liquor seller's license. To judge by the volumes he left behind, it was the potential subscribers' loss. Walter Peterson provided introductory tasting instructions defining the nature of aroma, bouquet, flavor, mouth feel, and finish, along with a list of common adjectives—astringent, dry, flat, round, soft, steely, et al.—in addition to exhaustive information on individual wines. For example, in his entry on "Aged Red Bordeaux," he described how French clarets are classified by growth and by region, how the wines age, how their methods of production have changed, how those changes have affected the wines' character, the importance and appearance of corkage and sediment, and how to select old wines for purchase. He then furnished notes on selected vintages of Château Latour and Château Rouget from 1904 to 1961 (ranging from "mediocre" to "very great") and finally supplied a step-by-step guide to the serving and "examination" of a wine chosen for distribution:

> The wine distributed, a 1945 vintage Ch. [Château] Rouget from the Bordeaux District of Pomerol, is an excellent example of a bottle-aged wine that is near maturity. This wine *requires and merits special handling.* The wine has sediment, as an old wine should. It is a healthy, compact, rather granular sediment that stirs up with difficulty. The wine should be allowed to rest at least two weeks undisturbed, on its side, label up, in a dark cool place, and then carefully set upright the day before serving in the kitchen or dining room. This treatment will

allow the sediment to drop to the bottom of the bottle and bring the wine to room temperature.

On removing the lead foil capsule, inspect the cork. Note that the top is moist, dark, and covered with mold. When the cork is pulled, the brand "Ch. Rouget—Pomerol—1945—Mis en Bouteilles au Château" can be read. Observe the deep stain on the inner end of the cork and how the cork retains its compressed shape, barely expanding beyond the diameter of the bottle. This wine has probably never been recorked and the cork bears evidence of its long stay in the bottle by its stained and compressed condition. (Note: Six bottles were examined and one was found with a partially decomposed cork but the decomposition had not penetrated far enough to harm the wine.)

Decant the wine just before serving or use a cradle that keeps the bottle tilted on its side. The sediment may stir up, so pour with a minimum of motion and be sure the label is up. Pouring the wine directly off the sediment into the glass helps preserve an old wine by slowing the rate at which it acquires an oxidized character through contact with air. Some wines, when served directly off the sediment, undergo a marked deepening in color soon after the wine is in the glass. When first poured, the color is often a light orange red and during a period of about five minutes the color will deepen to a dark red. The 1945 Rouget is so dark in color that increase in color on air contact is unnoticed. If the decanting is successful, the wine will be clear, limpid, bright and without haze-causing solids to muddy the wine's appearance and taste. Smell and taste the wine soon after it is poured so as to observe the changes that occur in bouquet and flavor as it absorbs oxygen from the air (breathes). To the nose the wine is at first all bottle bouquet. It has a slight acetic character which is expected in an old wine; it adds complexity and seems to intensify other odors. The odor is generous, pervasive and winey—like the smell of a clean winery. It has an aged, almost musty odor that is a complex blend of vaguely distinguishable scents, such as a slight mushroom effluvium, the suggestion of emanations from blue cheese, a faint toasty fragrance, and a whisper of the bouquet of clean earth freshly turned in the spring sunshine. As it airs, the odor grows and attains increased complexity in fragrances that suggest the rich fruitiness of cooking plums and floral perfumes that elude definition but are both violet-like and suggestive of slightly spicy eucalyptus scent. The floral fragrances are the more dominant. The complexity, richness, amplitude and generosity of the bouquet are delightful and produce a mouth-watering reaction.

On sipping the wine, note the smoothness and the full, round sensation produced on the tongue, as well as the increased intensity of the bouquet and floral perfumes. The floral fragrances are at first somewhat masked by the rich bouquet but intensify as the wine "breathes." With a larger mouthful, a rather piney-tar-like pungency (reminiscent of sailing ship's rigging) and a phenolic flavor can be noticed. Now the wonder of the round, soft, aged characteristics of the wine become fully apparent. The wine is luscious with a fair amount of sugar and medium amount of acidity. The acidity lends a freshness to the big substance and full body of the wine.

After swallowing, complex flavors linger long and suggest age, truffles, and multiple fragrances that are gossamery, fleeting and tantalizing. The strength of these flavors and the appreciable sugar content mask the bitterness of a considerable amount of tannin. The tannin indicates that the wine has not fully matured. These residual tastes in the finish have the long-lingering and pleasant satisfying qualities that are the hallmarks of a *Great Wine*.

In summary, this is a very big wine, fully worthy of its very great vintage year and one that has aged well. It is beautifully balanced and unusually fragrant with a complex bottle-age bouquet. The wine is near maturity; its tannin content suggests it can age longer, but the acetic flavor may become too prominent in another five years. It is a great wine and a fine example of the quality that bottle aging adds to the flavor of a Red Bordeaux. The privilege of drinking a wine such as this can only be enjoyed by a relatively small number of wine drinkers.

When he was nine years old, Joel was allowed to begin sitting in on his father's club tastings. "We had wines I'll never, ever be able to taste again," he remembers. "Old ports, red Burgundies, white Burgundies, Sauternes, German Beerenausleses, Rhône wines, Italian wines, Chilean and California wines. Every other week we'd have exhaustive tastings of first-growth Bordeaux, wines that would cost sixty to a hundred dollars a bottle now. A lot of doctors and dentists were members, as well as people like the jazz musician Denny Zeitlin and Darrell Corti from the Corti Brothers Grocers in Sacramento. But I didn't know what anybody did; in the group everybody was on the same level. The only criterion was whether you could taste wine or not. I'd call the atmosphere semicompetitive." Walter Peterson's enological advice to his son was simple: "Shut up and spit." He measured the samples that Joel was given and measured the amount in Joel's spittoon at the end. If they didn't match, says Joel, "there was hell to pay."

By the time he left home for college in Oregon, Joel possessed a sophisticated working knowledge of French wine, so as an undergraduate he selflessly endeavored to catch up on domestic varieties that his father's group had missed—labels such as Boone's Farm, Ripple, and the lesser-known but very considerable Annie Green Springs. He hewed to the family path academically, majoring in biochemistry and microbiology and eventually becoming a research immunologist at Mount Zion Hospital in San Francisco. He also began writing about wine while consulting for retail stores. As a result, he was caught in a building storm: the Bay Area gourmet hurricane. He went out to tastings every night and sometimes on his lunch hour—trade tastings given by brokers and distributors, by the Sherry Institute, by the Burgundy Institute, by individuals hosting dinners that featured old wines. On average, he tasted about five hundred wines per week. At one point he resolved not to buy himself a meal or a bottle of wine for a month; at the end of that month he had gained ten pounds. ("It's amazing how much food and wine you can get if your name is on the right lists," he says.) He was also meeting with the Basque brown-bag tasting group every week, and at about this time—1972—the San Francisco Vintner's Club was formed along the lines of his father's group. Each week a different flight of twelve wines was offered; members would gather after work at a hotel where glasses were prepoured, numbered, and set out on white linen. The tasters scored and ranked the wines on a twenty-point scale before discussing them. Joel, who arrived by motorcycle, bound his chest-length hair in a ponytail in order to keep it out of the wine.

"At the Vintner's Club you learned a lot about people's tastes," he says. "What they perceived as oak or alcohol, as volatility, as bulk-wine character—and whether or not they were right. When people talk about wine, they bring in a lot of associations, and those with a broad range of experience—cultural literacy, for want of a better expression—provide the most interesting associations. One of the most interesting was Paul Draper. He brought information from his experiences in Chile and Bordeaux, and he studied things very carefully. He tended to like wines that were complex, but not overly big. He didn't like alcoholic wines. More than anything else, he was an *appreciator* of wines. As a nonwinemaker I was less tolerant of defects and flaws in a vintage. Paul understood that if it had rained, acids might be low and pHs high. I would just say, 'God, why'd they do *that*?' "

Still, Joel was one of the Vintner's Club tasters whom Draper most enjoyed sitting next to. Indeed, ponytail, motorcycle, and all, Joel was a Vintner's Club star. Reed Foster, the club's co-founder who collected the notes and compiled the scores, found

Joel to be the most accurate, consistent, and perceptive taster in the entire group. He could frequently identify a wine, who made it, when, where, and from what vineyard. "Joel had palate memory, which is very rare," Foster says. One memorable day the club conducted a "pairs" tasting in which an array of unidentified wines from unidentified countries were supposed to be matched by varietal: a French Burgundy with a California Pinot Noir, say, or an Australian Cabernet with a French Bordeaux, or a late-harvest Washington Riesling with a Beerenauslese from the Rhine. Joel guessed every wine correctly and identified each one not only by varietal but by origin. "You have to be 'on' to do that sort of thing," he says now. "You have to be training on a regular basis and then have a hot day. It's sort of like running a four-minute mile."

In his other life, Joel was running a cancer research laboratory, growing tumors and lymphocytes, using white blood cells and tubercular bacteria to build up human immune systems that chemotherapy and radiation wore down. "Cancer research and immunology are very demanding and not very rewarding," he says. "The field is quite competitive, so people don't share their information; you get the impression that not all is being done that could be done to save lives. I was dealing mostly with melanoma and breast cancer patients, so I got to be good friends with a lot of people who died. It was like living in a war zone— you never knew who would go through the trauma of the next disaster. It seemed to me that there must be a happier side to life; I'd seen enough sadness and sorrow.

"If I were going to pursue wine, I had two choices. I could become a full-time writer and consultant—I was already making as much money doing that as I was in research—but then I would just be a businessman and writing hack. When I was growing up, I'd never had any inkling that I'd be a winemaker; I always thought I'd go into medicine or chemistry. But the pieces just fell into place. This was at the end of the sixties, and the idea of growing things and being close to the earth appealed to me. Winemaking reconciled aspects of my upbringing—it incorporated my interest in science, even in sociology and an-

119

thropology. And it seemed to be more on the positive side of people's emotional lives."

Joel had no track record, of course. He had made wine at home from Cabernet grapes and from blackberries and apricots that grew in his yard in Berkeley, but as he says, "There's a lot of difference between sixty gallons at home and twenty thousand gallons in a winery." Needing to learn how to make wine in quantity, he looked around for someone to teach him. As he remembers it, "One person's name kept popping up, a guy who I thought was making fascinating, high-caliber wines." That name was Joseph Swan.

Joe Swan was a retired airline pilot who had a one-man winery near Forestville in Sonoma County. He made fewer than two thousand cases of wine per year, but his Zinfandels dominated the Vintner's Club tastings, where in the early seventies they consistently beat out Ridge for first place. As Charles Sullivan said, "Ridge taught people that Zinfandel could be outstanding. Swan taught them that it could be magnificent." The roots of Joel's fascination can be perceived by a perusal of old Vintner's Club tasting notes, where the most persistently recurring adjectives for Swan wines are "dark," "robust," "intense," "tannic," "rich," "full-bodied," "complex," "spicy," "fruity," and "deep"—a veritable thesaurus for Ravenswood wines of the 1980s.

Swan had grown up during the Depression on a cattle-and-grain homestead in South Dakota. His parents were Methodist teetotalers, but as a boy Joe had read a reference to "velvet-red Burgundy" in a novel that steered him down a different path. As a teenager he brought chemistry equipment home from school (where his father happened to be the principal) and set up a still in a chicken coop behind the house, concealing the entire operation from his parents. Using a potato masher, he crushed some rhubarb and chokecherries, added sugar and yeast, and fermented the fruit in a lard bucket. When the time came to press the wine, he employed the wringer on his mother's washing machine. He had gotten his lard bucket from a quartet of brothers who owned a bakery in town as well as a single-engine, water-cooled Eagle Rock OX5 airplane. Swan helped the flying baker brothers maintain their plane, and in return they taught him how to fly. He soloed over the wheat fields of South Dakota when he was seventeen.

After graduating from high school, Swan studied art in Minneapolis and won a scholarship to the University of Iowa, where he was one of three students selected to paint a farming mural designed by Grant Wood. He continued to paint seriously for several years, but when World War II came, he joined the army as an aviation instructor. When the war ended, he went to work for Western Airlines. Domiciled in Salt Lake City, Swan actually made his first Zinfandel in Utah from grapes planted on the ancient wave terraces of prehistoric Lake Bonneville. He bought the fruit for five cents a pound, crushed it in a kettle, fermented it in a crock on top of the refrigerator, and called the finished product José's Rosé: an early white Zinfandel.

In 1948 Swan was transferred to Los Angeles, where an appropriately named old friend—Johnny Bliss—introduced him to fine wine. On his days off from piloting, Swan paid visits to the viticulture and enology department at the University of California. Judging by the evidence, one supposes he found little there to influence his later winemaking style. UC Davis, funded largely by massive Central Valley bulk wineries, had fostered an agribusiness approach to winemaking that favored production and consistency over character, nuance, or ageability; after the repeal of Prohibition the school had led the state's wine industry back to solvency through science, promoting such clinical practices as primary chemistry, tightly controlled fermentation, vigorous vine production, meticulous sanitation, and heavy filtration. As a result, California had the highest standard of cheap, homogeneous jug wine in the world—the enological equivalent of the tasteless, ubiquitous supermarket tomato.

At Davis Swan met a pair of Maynards who would greatly influence his life, if not specifically his technique. One was a graduate student named Monaghan; the other was a Professor

Amerine, who with Albert Winkler had developed the now institutionalized system of classifying California wine regions by their average daily temperatures during the growing season (Region I, Region II, etc.). On his vacation from Western in 1949, Swan helped Amerine pick grapes all around the state. Soon after, Monaghan went to work for Beaulieu Vineyards, where he lived in a little house behind the BV estate in Napa Valley. Swan visited him there often, and frequently André Tchelistcheff would drop by in the morning for tea. The intense, diminutive Tchelistcheff—an expatriate Russian who had served as an officer in the Crimea, studied agronomy in Czechoslovakia, and learned enology in Paris—had been the winemaker at Beaulieu for a dozen years; employing traditional European methods, he was making the most highly regarded Cabernet Sauvignon in California. For all intents and purposes, varietally labeled Zinfandel was the exclusive domain of Louis Martini, whose top product came from the old Monte Rosso Vineyard in the Mayacamas Mountains. It therefore came as a revelation one evening when, in a restaurant, Swan and Monaghan ordered a 1937 Fountain Grove Zinfandel and were bowled over by its balance, color, and bouquet. Later they returned with Amerine, who, forced to taste the wine from a bag, guessed that it was Bordeaux.

Swan became a full airline captain in 1951. For years he had been looking for vineyard land—he'd gone so far as to plant Pinot Noir at five thousand feet in the Sierra Nevada, from cuttings purported to have originated at Romanée-Conti in Burgundy—but he continued to buy most of his grapes for home winemaking in Napa Valley, driving them in a station wagon four hundred miles south to L.A. In 1967, when Western Airlines opened an office in San Francisco, Swan—who by that time had acquired seniority—entered his name at the top of the list and promptly bought thirteen acres of rolling hills a mile and a half from the Russian River. The property contained a farmhouse and a barn, but most important, it also had a cellar and a vineyard containing the classic California mix: Carignane, Petite Sirah, and Zinfandel. Still harboring his memory of the

'37 Fountain Grove, which had been made from a vineyard not far away, Swan produced his first Sonoma County Zinfandel in 1968. Soon thereafter, helped along by a Roy Brady review that "blew his cover," he vaulted to the forefront of the budding boutique winery movement.

In 1974, when he reached the mandatory retirement age for airline pilots, Swan was given a membership in the San Francisco Vintner's Club. There he met a young, confident biochemist who had "a very good palate and a gift for descriptive words and phrases."

"Joe came to the club to learn tasting," Joel Peterson recalls. "He knew what he liked, but he didn't know how to analyze or describe it. I started going to his house for dinner, and eventually I offered him a deal: I'd give him information I had about tasting—words connected with flavors and so forth—and he could utilize me as a boy Friday." So it came to pass that in 1976 Joel spent all of his vacations and most of his weekends helping Swan put up a building, harvest grapes, punch down tanks, and rack wine.

Among other things, Joel learned that Swan picked his grapes by taste, rather than strictly by their sugar level. Contrary to the UC Davis catechism, he insisted on old vines and low tonnage, aged his wine in French oak, and fermented it longer and warmer than almost anyone else in California. (As Joel continues to do today, Swan allowed the must to approach ninety degrees Fahrenheit and didn't press it until after the cap sank.) "He tended his fermenting wine as if it were a newborn child," says Joel. "He was so meticulous. He smelled every barrel in the winery, made sure everything was clean to his nose; he never rushed, never did anything unconsciously. Everything was thought out and planned—in the same way, I suspect, that it takes to be a pilot. Joe always said there's no such thing as an accident; only people who allow accidents to happen."

Joel made his first vintage—the 1976—at Swan's, using the older man's pumps and crusher and his own redwood fermentors. He had already decided that he would concentrate on Zinfandel. "It was virgin territory," he explains. "Outside of Swan and Ridge, nobody was exploiting it, even though Zinfandel had the best old, low-tonnage grapes available. People thought it didn't age, but that's because most people didn't make it to age. One of the best wines I'd ever tasted was an 1898 Inglenook Zinfandel; it had such power and perfume, it was so vibrant and alive, it was like an elegant old Bordeaux. It was as good as any wine I've ever drunk. Clearly Zinfandel had some place to go, and I saw that if I wanted to avoid getting lost in the shuffle of two or three hundred Cabernets and Chardonnays, Zinfandel was the way to do it."

The Zinfandel vines on Swan's property were so old and shy-bearing that after his first vintage, he'd ripped them out and replaced them with Pinot Noir. Most of his early Zinfandel grapes came from Dry Creek Valley, and he suggested that Joel go there for his fruit, too. Chiefly by making a nuisance of himself, Joel contracted for eight tons of grapes from two growers who customarily sold to Gallo. When the time came to pick the grapes, Joel did it by himself. All day clouds gathered over the valley from the west; late in the afternoon it began to rain as rare California lightning licked at the clefts of the hills. As Joel lifted tub after fifty-pound tub of grapes onto the truck, two ravens stationed themselves in a nearby tree to harass him. At the time Joel was reading Sir Walter Scott's *The Bride of Lammermoor*, a gothic novel whose hero, Lord Ravenswood, falls off a bridge and drowns in quicksand while coming to the rescue of his sweetheart. Under the circumstances, it seemed to Joel that such a plot might also describe the start of a small winery. As he drove away from Dry Creek Valley with his first load of grapes, the setting sun squeezed beneath the clouds, igniting the landscape a surreal orange and painting two rainbows on the charcoal sky. In Joel's mind, Sir Walter Scott receded and Native Americans appeared, as he recalled an Indian legend wherein man is discovered in a pod, and instructed in the arts of survival, by a raven.

From his eight tons of Dry Creek grapes Joel made six hundred cases of Zinfandel. The following year Swan expanded and needed more space, so Joel moved his fermentors a couple of miles away to Mark West Vineyards. The year after that he moved them again, and again the year after that. Partly because of his peripatetic path, he made red wine exclusively: "Everybody told me I should make white for cash flow, so I'd have something I could release in a year. But I knew I was going to be moving a lot, and white wine is much more delicate than red. Besides, the wines that I liked best were red. Somebody once said that every great white is really trying to be a red—in other words, not so much crisp, clean, and fruity, but more intense, flavorful, and complex." All the while he continued to work as a medical technologist on the graveyard shift at Sonoma Valley Hospital, doing bacteriology, hematology, urinalysis, cell differentiation, and blood tests. In 1978 the two founders of the Vintner's Club—Reed Foster and Jerry Draper, a real estate broker and wine seller—were sufficiently impressed by Joel's early results to back him with a few thousand dollars' seed money and form a limited partnership. John Kemble, a former member of Foster's Boy Scout troop, signed on as Joel's assistant after completing enological studies at UC Davis.

Joel released his first vintage in 1979. Reed Foster subsequently arranged a private tasting where twenty people could sample a selection of 1976 Zinfandels. Thirteen wines were offered, including Joe Swan's and the Ridge Lytton Springs. When the tasters' scores were compiled, Swan and Ridge were neck and neck as usual, with Swan pulling slightly ahead. That is to say, Ridge finished eighth and Swan seventh. Sixth was the Zinfandel from Burgess Winery; fifth was a late-harvest Zinfandel made by Merry Edwards at Mount Eden Vineyards; fourth was a dark horse from Stony Ridge; third was a well-pedigreed Zinfandel from Mike Grgich, who had left Chateau Montelena to form his own winery, Grgich Hills.

The top two wines were produced by the same winemaker, though the grapes had come from two different vineyards in Dry Creek Valley. The label on the bottles bore a circular pattern of three ravens joined at the talons, and the name of the new winery was Ravenswood.

Once fermentation finally began, the Young Gentlemen's Big Zinfandel took nine days to reach zero degrees Brix. In thirty-gallon plastic garbage cans, the fermentation wasn't terribly intense; the temperature never rose above seventy-five degrees Fahrenheit. Joel said that this would give us a fruitier wine, but one that was less "deep." We had hoped to emulate Ravenswood and wait until the cap sank before pressing the wine, but our schedules permitted us to work with it only on the weekends, so we were faced with a choice of leaving it on the skins for two or three full weeks. Contemplating this question, Paul Draper told me: "If you want more extraction, you'll be getting it now because of the alcohol. But you run the risk that the alcohol might also begin to work on the seeds, which could give you some bitterness. Plus, if there's any acetic element on top when you press it, you might be adding a vinegar starter to the wine. We like a certain amount of volatile acidity, but if it gets to the point where you can smell the acetic acid, it's not a fine wine. A good trick is to hold a match to it; you can tell the carbon dioxide level by when the match goes out. If you can hold it right to the surface and it stays lit, then you'd better press the wine."

I did as Draper said; the match stayed lit. Respecting the honor of our maiden vintage, we erred on the side of restraint and pressed the wine after two weeks. We rented an old-fashioned basket press from a winemaking supply store, whooped for joy as the raspberry-red liquid began running into white buckets, and funneled the wine into an old French château–style sixty-gallon barrel, the kind with willow hoops on the heads. In fact, it was one of the barrels that John Kemble and I had picked up from Joseph Phelps on that beautiful fall day three years previous.

We'd pressed our ten-gallon nouveau-style batch earlier, at ten degrees Brix. Stored in five-gallon glass carboys, it continued fizzing for weeks thereafter, completing its primary fermentation, but also the malolactic (for which we had inoculated it, in order to avoid a spontaneous occurrence in the bottle). To our surprise, the earlier-pressed nouveau wine was deeper in color, and more tannic, than the Big Zin; the stems on the whole clusters had given it a clear taste of wood in the finish, though it had never seen any wood. From the beginning it was delicious, intensely fruity wine—partly the result of the cool fermentation, but also the gift of the superb Dry Creek grapes.

After a few weeks the nouveau began to smell like rotten eggs. Joel said this was hydrogen sulfide, which sometimes develops from bacterial action on the elemental sulfur on grapes in the vineyard. He said we should go to the supermarket, buy a copper kitchen scrubber, place it in a funnel, and pour the wine through it. We did so; the sulfur bonded with the copper ions, precipitated out as copper sulfide, and the rotten-egg smell disappeared.

In mid-November I took samples of both wines to Ravenswood for Joel to taste. He stood in the office running them through his teeth, staring hard as usual, and periodically going outside to spit the wine onto the ground.

"Nice nouveau!" he announced on returning. "Strawberries, raspberries, a hint of rhubarb. Good acid, good brightness—everything a nouveau should have."

I went into the winery to siphon out a glass of Ravenswood's '87 Dry Creek Zinfandel—harvested from the same vineyard, on the same day, at the same ripeness as ours. We tasted it side by side with the Young Gentlemen's so-called Big Zin: an unfortunate idea. The character and quality of the fruit were the same, but the Ravenswood wine was pepperier in the nose, fuller and richer in the mouth, and more tannic in the finish. It simply possessed more—and more intense—flavors. After the glasses had stood for an hour, the difference became depressingly wide; the Ravenswood wine still smelled fruity and tasted round and full, while ours had turned flat and hard.

"It's because there was more in ours to begin with," Joel said. "It has more extract in the middle of it. Yours definitely needed more heat—you didn't get the center. It'll be okay; it'll need some barrel time."

So much for '87.

In early December I took two bottles of Young Gentlemen's nouveau to Chez Panisse on the first night of the New Zinfandel Festival. Every year Joseph Phelps Winery makes a nouveau Zinfandel from the grapes of that vintage, and the restaurant serves it as a counterpart to the Beaujolais celebrations of France. As Chez Panisse is commonly credited with creating "California cuisine," the apparent intention is to toast the new vintage with California's native wine. A sucker for all things seasonal, I cultivate the habit of attending, even though the hip-but-privileged movieland atmosphere of Chez Panisse makes me about as comfortable as a snake being poked with a stick.

This time, before visiting the restaurant, I returned to the scene of my earlier epiphanies—Joseph Phelps—to talk to the winemaker, Craig Williams, about the nouveau Zinfandel he makes for the restaurant. His office was on the winery's third floor in a pleasant, sunlit room with a view of the vineyards and a "Fifth Annual Chez Panisse Golf Tournament" poster on its walls (which were covered with—see if you can guess—redwood siding). Williams was a friendly, if slightly tense, fortyish guy with dark hair and a mustache. He said that the Chez Panisse

New Zinfandel tradition had begun through the winery's "family association" with the restaurant.

"We make the Chez Panisse house wine, which is also a Zinfandel," Williams told me. "The nouveau is made by the *macération carbonique* technique, which was developed in France sixty years ago as an antidote to high acidity. It consists completely of whole berries; they're placed in a tank which is purged of oxygen and filled with carbon dioxide. So it's an anaerobic fermentation which occurs not from yeasts but from enzymes within the grape. It produces ethyl alcohol, which decomposes the berries; the tartaric and malic acids are respired. After about two months, when we open the tank and press the wine, the berries have shriveled and broken down and lost their liquid and color—they're light pink, not dark blue. With this method you extract the color of the grape but not the tannin, so you get the fruity flavor without any of the astringency. It gives a characteristic aroma to the wine, a distinctive cherry-berry-soda-pop quality. Any young wine has exotic, short-lived fermentation smells, but this one doesn't have any of the estery banana qualities associated with yeasts. It retains that candied nose for only a short time, and to capture it, you must drink it young. The key is its immediate appeal in the glass. What's great about it is that it goes with everything. We send it down to the restaurant in stainless-steel tanks, and they put it in an ice bucket about ten minutes before serving, so it's slightly cooler than room temperature—about sixty-five degrees. We used to make about twelve hundred cases and sell the rest of it around the country, but we found that it was still sitting in warehouses a year later. It isn't made to be drunk that way—it should be consumed soon after the harvest. Now we only make about five hundred gallons, and what Chez Panisse doesn't use gets blended into our Napa Valley Zinfandel."

I asked him why they'd chosen Zinfandel for a domestic version of the Beaujolais tradition.

"Zinfandel is part of our heritage and what makes us unique," Williams said. "Pinot Noir will make the same sort of wine, but we wanted to do something that other countries don't do. Zinfandel is thought of as an American variety—it stands for variety and the spice of life, sort of like the restaurant. Chez Panisse works with materials from its own backyard, taking traditional methods and applying them to local ingredients, which is what we do with the wine. It seemed like a perfect match."

An acquaintance of mine has a theory of morals that prevents him from dining out on Monday or Tuesday—in his Judeo-Christian cosmos, the early part of the week is for suffering, which may be rewarded only from Wednesday on. His system isn't being observed at Chez Panisse. On Monday night—opening night of the New Zinfandel Festival—the place was jammed. A four-piece blues band was playing in the upstairs café, and fashionable people were streaming in from all over the world: blonde women with Eurasian men whose hair was tied in tiny ponytails; women wearing black lipstick and long black overcoats; redheaded women in leopard-skin dresses and fringed black leather jackets.

As the throngs surged toward the flower-bedecked bar, they were greeted by a host who was wearing a bow tie, a baggy forties suit, and tiny round-framed eyeglasses. The good-looking green-eyed young black bartender was dressed in various shades of gray: gray cashmere turtleneck, charcoal wool trousers, anthracite suspenders, and midnight black beret pushed to the back of the skull, imparting a royal African look. The new Zinfandel, transferred from its stainless-steel kegs on the back porch, stood on the bar in pitchers whose sides were coated with condensation. I ordered a glass, swirled, sniffed, and detected a strong note of baseball cards.

Next to me, a man I recognized as a nuclear physicist stood at the bar with a gray-haired lady. Looking at the nouveau Zinfandel, the lady said, "Ugh. That stuff gives me a headache."

The physicist explained that the wine was made by carbonic maceration.

"Sounds wonderful," said the lady. "Do you do it alone or in groups?"

A handsome young Italian came up the stairs with his girlfriend and mother in tow. He announced that his mother "just got off the boat." Then he ordered a glass of nouveau and turned to the physicist. "What do you think of this wine?" he asked.

The physicist said he didn't like it.

"Nobody has to like it," said the Italian. "That's what's great about it." He turned away and started necking with his girlfriend.

I made my way toward the open kitchen, where the chefs were carving up rare pork legs and rolling out pizza dough. Almond-and-pear polenta tarts and bowls of blood oranges in caramel sauce sat in glass bowls on the counter; Zinfandel sauces simmered on the stove. One chef poured some onto a plate, then added roast rib eye slices, shoestring potatoes, and watercress. I glanced at one of the cards that had been placed on each dining table; it said:

13TH ANNUAL NEW ZINFANDEL FESTIVAL

Nouveau-style Zinfandel from Joseph Phelps Vineyards
Cassoulet—grilled radicchio with pancetta—
wood-oven roasted birds—rosemary fougasse—garlic soufflé—
sausages—chicory garlic salad—squid and leeks in Zinfandel—
confits—persimmon pudding—fig tarts

I asked one of the chefs whether, as advertised, the restaurant structured the week's menu around the nouveau. "No," he said. "It's too light."

A moment later Alice Waters came in, dressed in black pants and a knee-length black sports coat that made her look like Charlie Chaplin. She wasn't much over five feet tall, but she sped around like a ball of fire, kissing and hugging her employees and saying, *"Ça va?"* She took one chef gently aside by the arm and told him to put more pasta on a plate; when she walked away, he shook his head and said with a French accent, "First less, now more." When Waters returned, I introduced myself and asked her how the festival had started.

"I always wanted a house wine," she said. "Fourteen years ago I heard that a friend in Amador County had some extra Zinfandel grapes. Joe Phelps had been coming to the restaurant since the beginning, so I asked him to crush the grapes for us. We decided to do it in a nouveau style; it's meant to be drunk young and to have the same qualities as Beaujolais—full of berries and fruit, with a little spritz."

I asked if she liked Zinfandel—personally, I mean.

"I always had a soft spot for Zinfandel because of Ridge and Swan," she said. "I think it should be made in a distinctive way, with a distinctive taste." I dutifully wrote this down, feeling like a sportswriter talking to a major-league manager who was trying his best to be accommodating and think of something to say. "I can't say I'd want Zinfandel every night with everything," Waters went on. "Actually, I don't drink much Zinfandel anymore, for the same reason that I don't drink many California wines. You can get good wines at a better price from Italy and the south of France."

Waters got a glass of the new Zinfandel and took a sip. Then she put it down and said, "This really needs to be drunk with food." I thanked her and gave her a bottle of the Young Gentlemen's nouveau. Then I took the other bottle to a table where I'd spied the Phelps winemaker, Craig Williams.

I complimented Williams on his nouveau and poured him a glass of ours. He swirled, sniffed, and took a sip.

"Is this fruit available?" he asked.

Over the next several months I spent a considerable amount of time with Paul Draper—accompanying him to tastings, observing his appearances at public events, or simply having lunch or dinner with him when he was in town. In due course, I assembled a rough understanding of his modus operandi. From the start he struck me as a gentleman in the traditional sense of the term: unfailingly helpful and polite, well mannered, well spoken, and well schooled. He was a paragon of the liberal arts education: Fascinated by all manner of subjects, he could discuss history, geology, music, psychology, literature, and meteorology with equal ease, and observations about world culture from the British to the Japanese rolled effortlessly from his tongue. For all these reasons, it was hard for a writer not to like him; however, for a writer whose subject was ostensibly Zinfandel, a problem soon presented itself. Though Draper was widely renowned as the guru of the "mystery grape," it soon became clear that his favorite child wasn't Zinfandel at all, but rather the Monte Bello Cabernet. Draper exposed this prejudice in ways that were both forthright and sly. One day I attended a vertical tasting of Ridge wines, arranged at the request of the English wine writer Jancis Robinson, who was then in the midst of researching her book *Vintage*

Timecharts, in which she offers aging advice on wines from the world's great vineyards. As it happened, I'd been standing outside Draper's office when Robinson called to suggest the tasting, so I knew that her first request had been to taste the Ridge Geyserville Zinfandel—the only Zinfandel, as a matter of fact, that she planned to include in her book. Draper agreed, of course, but he also suggested that "since we don't control the vineyard"—Ridge's Geyserville Zinfandel grapes are grown by Leo Trentadue—she also taste the Monte Bello Cabernet (which she had, in fact, previously included in her *Great Wine Book*, an examination of thirty-six famous vineyards). When the day of Robinson's visit arrived, the Monte Bello was poured first and scrutinized exhaustively in the morning; after that we all repaired to Draper's house, with its view of the Santa Cruz Mountains and the Pacific, for lunch. The Geyserville tasting was assigned to the afternoon, by which time Robinson had another appointment pressing. Thus the Zinfandel—Robinson's original request—ended up receiving only slightly more than half as much attention as the Monte Bello Cabernets.

Still, Draper was quite capable of lecturing at length on the preeminent qualities of the lesser wine for which his winery was best known, even as he admitted (to the sommeliers, for example) that he made it primarily to generate income. In other words, he was aware of which side of his bread was buttered, but he tirelessly buttered up the other side whenever he saw a chance. Sometimes Draper's comportment in this regard was so smooth that it could be termed slick; he frequently worked both sides of an adversarial fence, making a strong assertion for one side of an issue and then immediately qualifying it with a statement supporting the other. In this context, Draper seemed to be not only a gentleman, a scholar, a poet, and a philosopher, but a diplomat—though some, less sympathetic, might say a politician.

Paul Draper grew up on a farm near Barrington, Illinois, where his father, a Christian Scientist, moved after leaving a position as an investment banker in Chicago and going broke during the Depression. On the farm (which he leased) Draper's father aspired to total self-sufficiency, raising fruits, vegetables, cattle, hogs, sheep, chickens, and ducks; during World War II he plowed with a team of Belgian horses in order to conserve gasoline for his Buick Roadmaster. Paul's job was to take care of the horses and the half-acre vegetable garden, through which he remembers his father walking, picking ripe tomatoes, and tearing into them with his teeth. "He was a sensualist, though he never would have admitted it," says Draper. "Christian Scientists don't like to deal with the dark side, the shadow. Christians in general don't see both darkness and light in God—they want to put evil out there on the Russians or somebody. It's a major problem in Christianity."

Paul remembers his father as a man in whom "the feminine was very well developed, although he himself was afraid of women." The elder Draper didn't marry until his fifties; the woman he eventually wed was Dorothy Higbie, an accomplished horsewoman, a world-class golfer, and a Presbyterian. Paul therefore grew up going to two churches and as a result "was a relativist from about age seven." Like a good Christian Scientist, however, he attributes his teenage asthma to the "unspoken Victorian tension" between his parents.

Paul wanted to be an engineer when he grew up—he liked building things with his hands, dams most of all. "My God!" he remembers. "To change the course of that water when it was running in the spring!" When he reached adolescence, his parents sent him east to the Choate School, where he got good grades in English and history and came close to failing physics. "It was so boring to work with tables and formulas," he says. "It made me realize I wouldn't be able to make it as an engineer." He preferred reading "everything Aldous Huxley ever wrote," Greek mythology, Latin poetry, and European novels, all of which included wine as "a central issue."

Draper had a roommate at Choate, one George Erlanger, who came from the Upper East Side of New York. Paul often stayed with the family in the city, where they went to the Alpine Club (Mrs. Erlanger was a mountain climber of Swiss-French ancestry) and Broadway plays like *Can-Can*, which brought Paris into the cross hairs of Paul's attention. The family had wine with dinner every night, from which Draper "developed an image of wine as part of the good life and the sophisticated life. It seemed like a corrective to my Victorian, northern European upbringing. The Erlangers' table was much more joyful and humorous than ours had ever been. When I was growing up, my father had wine only on special occasions."

One weekend, when the other Erlangers were away, Paul and George downed a fifth of scotch and went out to a ballroom in Manhattan. There they bought another fifth and drank it at a table in the middle of the crowd. The year was 1951; a big jazz band was playing; Draper, whose dancing experience had been limited to lessons in the fox-trot, found himself jitterbugging on the table by the end of the evening. "Moving to music by myself like that was a connection with something I'd never known. It took a fifth of scotch to make it happen, but it's been an important part of my life ever since. Just last year I learned to experience Beethoven, not only with my ears but with my hands and my whole body."

In his senior year at Choate Draper applied to Princeton and Stanford. His sister had a boyfriend at the latter institution; he told Paul that in California " 'people don't ask what your father does.' He said it was the opposite of the East, where you're out until you prove yourself worthy of being in." Princeton made the choice easy by rejecting him for admission, so Draper enrolled at Stanford in the fall. Upon arriving, he was "shocked" by California's lack of water and the commercial trashiness of El Camino Real, the main drag that runs north and south on the San Francisco peninsula. He began making forays into the hills, to San Francisco, and along the coast. "In my early years here California to me was the coast," he says. "It became a major part of my life. I began to feel that I would never want to leave that connection with water that touches other continents." (Dam builder Draper, who once confided to me that his astrological sign was Pisces—the fishes—often makes references to the power of water.) "I remember when I was in the Colombian rain forest, how oppressive was the isolation from the coast. But how liberating was the river! It was the only place in the jungle where you could see the sky. It meant you weren't cut off; you could get in a dugout canoe and go a hundred, or five hundred, or a thousand miles away."

One day at a Stanford student hangout called the Cellar, Draper met a fellow undergraduate who had grown up in Iowa, gone to Deerfield Academy in Massachusetts, and stood to inherit a share of the Maytag washing machine fortune. Today Fritz Maytag owns and runs the Anchor Steam brewery on Potrero Hill in San Francisco, and one day in early 1988 I visited him there to talk about his early days with Draper. The brewery's upstairs office had a tasting bar with a half dozen taps, a polished brass footrail, and antique oak furniture—rocking chairs, rolltop desks, a piano—in view of enormous German copper fermentors and maturation tanks, among which men were walking in spotless white jumpsuits and high rubber boots. "Wine starts with sugar, but beer starts with starch," Maytag explained as I sat down in his office. "You start making beer by cooking—you go through a very complicated process to get to the equivalent point of grape juice for wine. Wine is like an oil painting: Come February, if you don't like it, you can fix it. But beer is more like a Chinese ink painting: You can't make any mistakes. It's all done in a matter of a few days or weeks." With his square jaw, close-cropped hair, Oxford cloth shirt, tweed jacket, and tie, Maytag cut a figure that suited his reputation as a fervent neoconservative, though as an undergraduate at Stanford he had worked on the antinuclear-testing boat *Everyman* and protested the arms race by carrying bomb casings around the campus.

Recalling his college years, Maytag said: "Stanford was full of bright, lovely, uneducated high school presidents and football quarterbacks wearing clothes and laughing in a way that was different from anything Paul and I had ever seen before. People from eastern prep schools were rare enough that we could spot each other two hundred yards away. The giveaway was the combination of blue jeans and tweed sports jacket. We'd both grown up in the Midwest in families that combined the best of liberal and conservative, European and American values. Paul had an outgoing, physical way of life similar to mine, and we got to be friends. We'd ride our motorcycles up to Berkeley to hear Alan Watts or into the mountains where we'd make a campfire and sleep out under the stars and discuss Chinese poetry and Plato. There are very few people I'd rather talk to about almost anything of importance. Paul has a sense of the magic and amazing quality of life but also a seriousness and willingness to think and ponder. We certainly had some amazingly deep ideas. We were nice young men; we were so sincere and decent. And not smug. We didn't consider ourselves superior; we hoped to *become* superior."

When Draper's father died, Paul inherited two thousand dollars. At that point he "saw that for me to ever have a lot of money would take single-minded dedication, and I'd still never reach the level of my friends. My father had given me his full trust when I was fifteen; most young men then were still pressured to go into their family business, but he had told me just to let him know why I decided to do whatever I did. I'd grown up around wealthy people, and I'd seen that wealth doesn't make you happy. My father taught me that what was more important was how you lived your life."

While most of his friends from Barrington and Choate "went into subjects that would advance them in business," Draper decided to major in philosophy, in order to "find out what it was all about." He didn't particularly enjoy it. "I remember reading that John Wisdom, who taught at Oxford, had described his life by saying, 'I play violin, I love my wife, and I do philosophy.' It was emblematic of this idea that analytical philosophy was something you do, not something you live. I said,

'Forget it.' " Instead, he concentrated his philosophy studies in Stanford's Value Theory program, which incorporated elements of ethics, aesthetics, political theory, German and Romance literature, and existentialism—Nietzsche, Sartre, Dostoyevsky. "*That* had to do with life," he says. He was especially interested in Nietzsche "because he let the chaos in. He was a reaction to Hegel's tidy 'thesis, antithesis,' boom-boom-boom."

Before Draper came to the West Coast, he had never tasted California wine. But he took his clipboard with him to Italian restaurants and took notes on the available vintages of BV, Inglenook, Charles Krug, Wente Brothers, and Louis Martini. "In those days you could count on two hands the number of people trying to make good wine in California," says Fritz Maytag. "But part of the excitement of the fifties was bringing the good stuff of Europe to America. We considered it mature, romantic, and life-affirming to have a bottle of wine with dinner; to us, it meant the values of southern Europe. It was an affirmation of the Dionysian principle that said yes to everything."

As it happened, one of Draper's roommates had grown up in Dry Creek Valley. One year he invited Paul home with him at Thanksgiving. "It was Indian summer—beautiful football weather. The leaves had all turned color," Draper remembers. "They lived in a simple farmhouse much like the one I'd grown up in. For Thanksgiving they had one long trestle table that started on the front porch, went through the living room into the hall, through the kitchen, and onto the back porch. It was loaded with turkey, ham, lamb, and roast beef. Every few feet were bottles of wine made from vines around the house. There were about fifty people there, spanning four generations. I sat there thinking: My God, this is what I want—this has to be part of my life. It had the connection to the soil I had grown up with, but also the Latin-Mediterranean side which hadn't been part of my English-German bloodline. The northern Europeans need the Mediterranean so much; it's the other side of their character. But I thought that to be a winemaker, you had to be trained and to have money. I never thought I could make it happen for myself."

In spring of his junior year Draper visited Europe. He sailed from New York to Italy on a Greek passenger ship, and after docking in Naples—where he noticed people spooning so much sugar into their coffee that it overflowed—he went into a motorcycle shop where no one spoke English and came out with a Moto Guzzi, which he promptly pointed toward the Amalfi coast. He had seen Fellini's *La Strada* a half dozen times at Stanford; his goal now was to retrace the steps of Anthony Quinn. He bought himself a World War II aviator jacket with a sheepskin collar and passed through Praiano, Positano, and Calabria, acquainting himself along the way with the vaunted southern European character. In Sicily, when he suggested that a shopkeeper had miscut a piece of rope, the merchant became so irate that his wife had to restrain him as Draper backed out of the store. In the mountains near Nicosia he came upon a horse fair to which Sicilians had brought steeds from all over the island; Draper had ridden his motorcycle all day to reach the place, and his fingers were so cold that he couldn't move them. That night a hostelkeeper served him what he remembers as "the best meal of my life": a cup of hot tea and a slab of bread dipped in virgin olive oil. Despite having grown up on a dairy farm, Draper had never cared for cheese—he would get sick if his sister ate a grilled cheese sandwich—but in Parma he found the aroma wafting from wheels of *parmigiano* so seductive that he bought a hunk, put it in his pocket, and ate it all day while riding his bike.

Draper refers to himself as "a natural imitator." When he got to Harry's Bar in Venice, he ordered a meal in English— with an Italian accent. The waiter responded: "*Per favore, signore, Lei non deve parlare inglese con mi* [Please, sir, you don't have to speak English with me]." Because of the French reputation for intolerance, he circled Europe for six months, delaying a visit to Paris; when he finally summoned the courage to go, he went into a shop and, standing in line at the counter to buy food, watched the storekeeper rake a nonfluent German over the coals.

There were four other people in line ahead of him, so Draper studied their pronunciation intently, and when his turn came, he gave his order in impeccable French. "The shopkeeper never even looked up," he says. "It was a triumph."

Draper stayed in the Sixth Arrondissement for a couple of weeks, seldom venturing from a sector six blocks square. When he returned to Italy, riding down the Rhône Valley and through the Val d'Susa, he noticed upon crossing the border that things immediately became "much less tense. A lady with a bunch of little kids waved as I passed, and when I finished a meal and wiped my face, I felt olive oil there instead of dry white skin." Just as at Thanksgiving in Dry Creek Valley, the Anglo-Saxon Draper felt he'd come home to the Mediterranean—which perhaps explains why, upon graduating from Stanford, he arranged to return under the auspices of the U.S. Army.

When Draper finished college in 1958, the Korean War was over, but the cold war was just getting started, and the draft was still going strong. Not desirous of a doctorate in philosophy—and therefore assuming that military service loomed immediately in his fate—Draper sounded out recent army dischargees about the most expeditious assignments. Operating on information thus obtained, he volunteered for army intelligence and, as a consequence, was sent to the Defense Language Institute in Monterey, a notorious training ground for spies (rumored, at about this same time, to have numbered Lee Harvey Oswald among its students of Russian). In classes with army security forces personnel, officers assigned to Mediterranean posts, and "FBI agents boning up to break the Cosa Nostra," Draper studied intensive conversational Italian in Monterey for six months. He was subsequently sent to Venice, where he was assigned to the 163d Intelligence Battalion out of Verona.

Italy's northeastern border with Yugoslavia is a broad, essentially indefensible plain. The core mission of Draper's divison was to provide nuclear artillery support there for the Italian army; Draper's job was to act as a liaison between Italian and American officers and civilian authorities, expediting joint maneuvers and making sure that sensitive areas—those housing missiles or documents—were secure. Draper would sometimes enter military encampments unannounced, if not exactly unauthorized, to see whether or not he'd be challenged; in view of the strong influence of the Communist party in Italy, he studied all the daily newspapers to stay abreast of political developments and cultivated the *carabinieri* (police) to obtain background information on local citizens who applied for jobs at strategic sites. Under such circumstances, a high martial profile was obviously inadvisable, so the army cloaked Draper in the trappings of a civilian: He worked weekdays from eight to five and—for reasons that apparently were not entirely military in inspiration—"tried to be Italian in every way I knew." When in Venice, Draper reasoned, do as the Venetians do: He dressed in custom-made Italian suits and—forging his surveillance skills with the local customs—upon entering a restaurant would scan the room for its most attractive female diner and position himself at a table where he could spy on her throughout the meal. ("In Italy I became rather amoral where women were concerned," he says.) He lived in a five-hundred-year-old twenty-five-room villa near Vicenza in the Colli Berici, where a maid did all the cleaning and cooking ("simple things like polenta, rigatoni, and osso buco") while her husband took care of the grounds. In the local tradition, Draper drank wine with all his meals—soft Soaves and simple reds from Conegliano and the Colli Berici, sturdy Brolio Chiantis with lunch, and big, tough Barolos with dinner. "My stay in Italy really changed my eating and drinking habits," he says. "It brought me by leaps and bounds into the sensual life." Increasingly intrigued by winemaking, he befriended local vintners, bought their wines for twenty-five cents a bottle, and began casually to observe their methods. "Paul's real smart at figuring out what the good deal is," Fritz Maytag says in summation of Draper's Italian military career. "He knows what to order, he knows the right people, and he knows how to manipulate and maneuver them to get what he wants."

When Draper was finally discharged from the army after three years, he immediately moved to Paris, where he studied French at the Sorbonne and made friends "who enjoyed showing me what excellent French food and wine were." Lacking sufficient funds for a proper Parisian lifestyle, he asked one of his acquaintances, who happened to have a part-time job with the U.S. embassy, for an introduction. When Draper told the embassy that he had studied political theory, served in army intelligence, and could speak both French and Italian, someone from the "political section" said there might be a job for him. The assignment—for which Draper was paid by the hour—was to report on international political meetings, most of which had a Marxist bent. Draper says he wasn't required to do anything more than sit in the audience and take notes, but at one meeting he found himself functioning as a translator for the French and Italian Communist party delegations. His employers in the "political section" were sufficiently pleased with his performance that when Draper's studies at the Sorbonne were finished, they asked him if he'd next like to learn Spanish. When he said that he would, they sent him back to Stanford and paid for his tuition.

Living in the hills near Skylonda while he studied Spanish at Stanford, Draper reunited with Fritz Maytag, who was studying Japanese. The scion of Iowa home hygiene, resisting the temptations of his family legacy, was now supporting himself with a paper route. Another friend who was doing the same thing was Sam Armstrong, a recent graduate of the Stanford Business School who—with help from an acquaintance who'd made a fortune importing monkeys for use in medical experiments— had recently started a wholesale pharmaceutical company. Armstrong bought antibiotics directly from the manufacturers, repackaged them in prescription sizes, and sold them to doctors who provided them to poor patients, bypassing the markup imposed by pharmacists. When the drug manufacturers got wind of this, they quit selling Armstrong their products. In retaliation, Armstrong prepared an antitrust lawsuit, but it was soon derailed by his major stockholder: the monkey importer, who, it turned out, enjoyed a good deal of animal trade with the pharmaceutical manufacturers. The monkey monger bought out Armstrong, and the saddened but wizened M.B.A. retreated to the hills above Stanford, where he delivered the *Palo Alto Times* with Maytag while outlining out a novel that criticized the U.S. economic system.

Armstrong subsequently volunteered for the Peace Corps. Maytag went to Japan. Honoring his arrangement with the people who had paid for his postgraduate education, Draper went to work in New York for a company that "published in foreign and political affairs." Specifically, it published in several languages and circulated in developing countries a newsletter promoting "a democratic alternative to the Marxist viewpoint." Draper prefers not to name the publication, since its funding, similar to that of his Spanish studies, "was undoubtedly coming either partly or wholly from the CIA."

Looking back at this time in his life, Draper says he "felt confident that nothing I ever did caused someone to be detained or arrested or to lose a job. I wasn't an operative who paid or otherwise got anybody to do anything; I was just interviewing people to find out what they thought was necessary to improve the situation in their countries. I was liberal, but I wasn't Marxist; I had simply seen enough situations that I thought the Russian solution wasn't it. To me the question was, How can you involve the people of a country in decisions made about their country? And what can we foster, aside from a dictatorship of the military or of the extreme left? My group was trying to talk to primary sources for the sake of the accuracy and objectivity of information that reached the president and the State Department. My job was to travel and meet with aspiring political leadership in Central and South America, so that if a crisis occurred, someone could fly down there and have a dialogue. I'd

145

like to think this same sort of thing is being done today, but I fear that it isn't—certainly not under the Reagan administration, or they wouldn't have had this miscalculation with Noriega, or this *shit* with Nicaragua. I mean, who on the grass-roots level is getting to know these guys today? We should have said to the Sandinistas: 'Hey, guys, you're in our sphere of influence. We'd rather not have to do what the Russians did in Hungary and Czechoslovakia, so we'll support you as long as you don't go to Russia for your advisers. You can go to Scandinavia, or France, or India. It doesn't have to be us. Just don't go to the Eastern bloc.' It's preventive medicine, but nobody wants to pay for it. There's a fine line between being naive and forcing the world to behave honestly. I think this country needs to act a little more creatively in that area."

Today Draper acknowledges that this era "carried over into mistakes like Vietnam. When Johnson sent paratroopers into Santo Domingo, even though everybody I knew in the State Department and the CIA had advised him not to, I said, 'Fuck it.' I figured that with Fritz, I could continue what I'd been trying to do without someone as dense as Johnson in charge."

With Maytag and Sam Armstrong, Draper formed a non-profit corporation called Pacific Development International (PDI for short). At the time, the U.S. government was funding all manner of development projects in the third world; Kennedy's Alliance for Progress was spending millions of dollars throughout Latin America, partly to answer Fidel Castro's charge that industrialized nations weren't contributing to third world countries whose resources they razed and largely to counteract what it perceived as the Communist threat. PDI's money, however, came exclusively from Maytag; its motto was "Idealism Without Illusions." As Draper describes it, "We studied what different foundations and agencies like Ford, Rockfeller, or USAID [the U.S. Agency for International Development] were doing and found that the majority of them didn't dovetail. We thought a small organization could fill in the gaps in agriculture and family planning." According to Armstrong, who still works as a fi-

nancial consultant to farmers, ranchers, agricultural coopera-
tives, and occasionally third world governments, PDI operated
according to an oil can theory of development: If people doing
work they deemed constructive got stuck for lack of funds,
Maytag's money would be introduced as a lubricant. In PDI's
first foray into Mexico, it bought a truck for a rural doctor so
that he could expand his rounds, and it donated money to Be-
nedictine monks to be distributed among peasant farmers.

As Fritz Maytag says: "The third world was full of smartass
people riding around in Land Rovers thinking up ideas. One
guy we talked to at the UN told us he had a whole roomful of
ideas, but to have any effect, we'd have to move down there."
The first place PDI had targeted for attention was Peru, which
had a progressive political administration, a high birthrate, and
a low standard of living. The native Indians, however, spoke
little Spanish, much less English. Radio messages in the Quechua
language were being broadcast by Communist China, which
was vying with the Americans, Cubans, and Russians for influence in the area. The entire region was rife with guerrilla activity,
and as Draper and Armstrong traveled together in the mountains
and the cities, Draper pointed out undercover agents and explained the machinations of their activities to Armstrong. For
his part, Armstrong wasn't completely convinced that Draper
had severed all his connections with them. He found Draper to
be rather inscrutable, not to mention something of a dandy. No
matter how primitive the surroundings, for example, Draper
always took time to press his jeans. "Paul insisted on wearing
contact lenses, even though we were traveling mostly on dusty
roads," Armstrong told me. "He had to stop and clean them in
some of the *damnedest* places."

U.S. aid to Peru was terminated when the Peruvian government made the misstep of buying Mirage jets from France
rather than F-86 fighters from the United States. In the face of
a mounting confluence of frustrations, Armstrong was moved
to suggest that Pacific Development International switch its
focus from Peru to Chile. When Draper went along without a

hitch, Armstrong concluded that he was clean—not just sartorially but politically.

Fritz Maytag says that PDI chose to work in Chile "for selfish reasons. It was beautiful—like Europe in California. Also, we wanted to work in a country that had a true democracy." Armstrong adds that "one thing Paul, Fritz, and I agreed upon was that population was a problem, and Chile was the only country in Latin America where birth control was legal." Nevertheless, half the hospital beds in the country were occupied by women recovering from the effects of crude abortions. U.S. agencies were distributing family planning films, but, says Draper, "most of the films were made in Puerto Rico, and South American dialects are very different from Puerto Rican Spanish. It was like a New Englander being told how to run his life by a guy with a heavy Oklahoma accent. Worse than that; the Chileans would feel insulted and condescended to, certainly not inspired to take the advice. We found one good film that had been made by Chileans for Chileans, but it was having trouble getting distribution. So we assisted them."

Agriculturally, Armstrong endeavored to introduce soybeans. The Chileans had been famous for their "chili" beans since the eighteenth century, but some of the beans had to be cooked for twelve hours. "Chile's climate is the equivalent of something stretching from Acapulco to British Columbia," says Draper. "Some sections are inaccessible during the rainy season, and vast areas of the country are desert. As the population grew, there was insufficient firewood for people to cook their beans, and the protein level in their diet had seriously diminished." To imitate the middle class, poor people were giving a mixture of flour, sugar, and water to their babies instead of breast-feeding them. To attack the problem, Armstrong imported various North American soybean varieties, from which oil, bean curd, infant formula, and animal feed could be derived. In deference to the country's diverse geography, he selected several types of beans that had proved successful from Winnipeg to New Orleans. Then he spent night after night sitting on hay bales, trying to foist these foreign plants on feudal farmers who still flailed their wheat to separate it from chaff.

"My parents asked me why we didn't do good in Mississippi instead," says Maytag. "They were right, of course. It's a vicious, evil thing to do good to some poor bastard. We committed the sin of hubris—of condescending superiority. I'm now convinced, for example, that people give themselves enough children to support them in their old age. Family planning was frowned upon in most of the places we went. There was an underground railroad mentality about it; we'd meet with rather high people in the government who said they didn't want it known that they were involved."

Eventually Maytag decided that PDI's task should be to "seek out business opportunities. By definition, a business is a helpful thing that requires self-discipline; it would make clear that we weren't there just to tell other people how to live. But it would be a business with a hidden agenda. We had the model of a dairy farm in mind—something from which health, research, medicine, and feed advice would be logical outgrowths. It was Paul who recommended that we make wine. Vineyards were already the number one crop in Chile, and we thought that by making better wine and packaging and marketing it to the latest standards of the U.S. market, we could create foreign exchange and a valuable export product. Exporting wine for hard currency would have been fantastic for a Chilean winery, and with luck we thought the effects might ripple throughout the industry."

Chile had a winemaking tradition that dated from the sixteenth century—in fact, it was the only temperate wine region in the world that had escaped the incursions of the phylloxera louse. Bordeaux-style wine grapes—Merlot, Sémillon, Cabernet Sauvignon—do very well there. "I had tasted some Chilean wines, and I thought they were good," says Draper. "They were selling for low prices, so they were considered cheap. But the microclimates suitable for fine grape growing were at least as extensive as California's. For a hundred years, Chile had grown far more Cabernet than California had. With proper methods, I thought the country had the potential to produce some of the greatest wines in the world."

Chile's major winegrowing region is the Valle Central, which runs hundreds of miles south from Santiago between the Andes and the coast. The most prestigious estates are on the valley floor, but Draper had already formed his belief that the world's best wine grapes come from unirrigated hillsides, so he began investigating the sparsely populated coastal hills. "It was like seeing the California of an earlier era," he says. "The climate was Mediterranean, the trees were oak and eucalyptus, and the rural areas were still using the agriculture and transportation methods of a hundred years ago. The majority of people still made their own tools, rode horses, and moved their goods and families by oxcart." Through a connection in California, Draper contacted a Swiss-Chilean family that was growing Cabernet Sauvignon near the village of San Ignacio de Palomares, in the Itata River valley. On the property was an abandoned adobe winery that the family agreed to lease to Draper and Maytag, in addition to providing them with grapes. Draper collected and resurrected a ratchet-driven basket press, a fifty-year-old crusher, and the sixty-year-old cellar master who had previously worked at the winery. He found the old *bodeguero* more than willing to accommodate his penchant for traditional techniques: fermentation on natural yeasts; punching down the cap by hand; eschewing filtration; aging in small oak. Chilean wine quality had been widely compromised by storage in a native wood named *rauli* (because of prohibitive import duties, no new oak barrels had arrived in the country since the 1930s), and Draper therefore commissioned a cooper to make barrels from air-dried European oak that was being grown locally for use in furniture and flooring. He and Maytag visited a bottle factory and, upon picking out a style from the various shapes they saw there, were told that only one style was being manufactured—the variation, it seemed, was unintentional. So Draper designed his own mold, persuaded the company to make the glass a darker green than usual, and then had to have the corks cut by hand.

"We were trying to set standards and create for Chile a label with the clout of a first-growth Cabernet," says Draper. "The wines we made were stable and complex—one of our '67s later won a blind tasting over Petrus and Cheval Blanc. Recently I pulled out one of our old bottles, and the Ridge marketing director thought it was Monte Bello. It isn't all that surprising; both wines were made from Coast Range grapes, and they have more in common with each other than they do with other wines from Chile or California.

"Our problem was how to publicize the wine. The normal channels of distribution are very cynical; after all, it's hard even for California to convince the eastern U.S. We couldn't talk North American wholesalers into buying our wine at a price that made the enterprise worthwhile. For a while we set up our own importation company, and we selected some good Chilean Cabernets. But when we redesigned the labels to give more information and asked some of these wealthy old producers to do things like fine their wines less, they just resented it."

Another foreigner who shared Draper's frustration was Philippe Dourthe, a Bordelais who, to fulfill a quasi-military commitment to his country, was acting as an adviser to the Chilean wine industry through the French embassy. Dourthe's family owned several small châteaux, and when his tour of duty expired, he invited Draper to visit him in Bordeaux. As a consequence, Draper spent the 1968 harvest observing and discussing the practices of Châteaux Latour, Lafite, Mouton-Rothschild, Margaux, Montrose, and Calon-Ségur.

" '68 was a terrible vintage in Bordeaux, so I saw the worst conditions possible," Draper says. His day at Calon-Ségur was cut short, for example, when a cellar worker slit his throat on a picking bin. As Draper was driving away, he noticed a tour bus turning in at Latour; he had an appointment there the next day, but since he now had nothing to do, he followed the bus and filed in with the tourists. As they were receiving the standard lecture, Draper wandered off by himself and noticed an elderly man tending a pump among the fermentors. Draper asked some intelligent questions, so the man began to show him around. That night, back at Dourthe's, Draper described the encounter and was told that the old man's nickname was Maître—short for *maître de chai*. The next day Draper returned for his appointment and spent the entire day with this man, the cellar master responsible for the most famous wines of Château Latour.

"One thing I found out in Bordeaux was that their reasons for doing things weren't scientific," Draper says. "They were empirical. They'd simply tried different things and found out what worked; the process wasn't highly mysterious. What actually turned these grapes into a fine bottle of Latour or Lafite was mysterious, but the *methods* were very straightforward. At Lafite I'd climbed up on top of a fermentor and gotten a big hit of vinegar. When I asked about it, they said they just skimmed the vinegary skins off the top and threw them out before pressing the wine. Here they had an active acetic culture going, and they weren't worried about it in the slightest. It made me realize that if you have things basically under control, you can afford to take risks like that. I felt everything they were doing was within the realm of possibility for me to achieve; ultimately the only variable would be the grapes themselves."

Meanwhile, the politics of Chile were undergoing a change. The term of the Christian Democratic president Eduardo Frei was nearing its end, and with the center and the right ending their coalition, the Marxist Salvador Allende was gaining strength despite the best efforts of the U.S. State Department. As for PDI, Draper says: "It was becoming increasingly difficult for us to make a capital investment in Chile. The Socialists were interested in what we were trying to do, but even under the centrist government our profits were being taxed away. We saw little hope of ever being able to make the business self-sufficient."

"We were growing up, in a way," says Fritz Maytag. "Paul

was feeling strong career urges; I'd turned thirty, gotten married, and I'd bought this brewery before we'd even gone to South America. Finances were no longer available to do whatever I wanted." Armstrong had married a woman whose father was soon to become commander in chief of the Chilean army. Despite this liaison with the upper class, Armstrong—who in the course of his Chilean experiences came into frequent contact with starving children—had shifted politically to the left, whereas Maytag—dispenser of the money—had moved to the right. Draper stood somewhere in the middle, and Armstrong wasn't much charmed by the way Paul functioned there.

"Paul and I occasionally disagreed with Fritz about things," Armstrong remembers, "but Paul admired Fritz greatly, so when Fritz showed up, Paul would shift his position to be more in line with Fritz's, and I'd end up as the odd man out. I suppose it's what any good corporate infighter does, but I don't know if it's properly called admiration or ass kissing." As far as the winery was concerned, Armstrong flatly considered it frivolous: "Gourmands are people with disposable incomes, and grapes occupied a lot of good land in Chile. Alcoholism was a major problem there." As a result of all the above, Maytag decided to terminate Pacific Development International—and with it the winery—before he and Draper had bottled their first vintage.

In fall of 1970 Allende was elected president of Chile, and three years later he was killed in a right-wing military coup believed to have been carried out with U.S. support. A year before Allende entered office, Draper sent thirty cases of wine home from Chile and sold the rest off in bulk. By the time the U.S. government perfected its efforts to "make the Chilean economy scream" under the Marxist leadership, and long before the coup that terminated Allende's life, Paul Draper had returned permanently to California.

On the day before Christmas I descended into the delirium of Telegraph Avenue in Berkeley, where, among the legions of jewelry artisans and tie-dye auteurs, an array of last-minute gifts can be amassed in under an hour. I tempered the taxations of this mission with a ritual stop at Moe's, the venerable antique bookshop where, on Christmas Eve, the employees stash stimulating refreshments behind the counter. Soon after I arrived, my friend Laura, who works there, poured me a glass of something that, to my surprise, *filled my mouth with lush berry fruit on a background of subtle oak* while stimulating the rain from my tastebuds that I'm always on the lookout for, winewise. Searching out the bottle below the shelf, I found a 1985 Dry Creek Valley Zinfandel; the red and gold label said "Nalle."

A couple of weeks later I attended a Zinfandel tasting at the San Francisco Vintner's Club. As tradition dictates, it was held at four-thirty on a Thursday afternoon in the dining room of the Hotel Bedford, just up Post Street from Union Square. The tables were lined with white linen and white middle-aged men in ties; at each place was a water glass, a plastic spittoon, some breadsticks, a scorecard, and a dozen glasses of red wine labeled *A* through *L*. Each wine was to be rated according to instructions on the card: 0–2 points for appearance or clarity, 0–2 for color, 0–4 for aroma and bouquet, 0–2 for acidity, 0–2 for asescence (the more objectionable the volatile acidity, the fewer points), 0–1 for appropriate sugar, 0–1 for body, 0–2 for flavor, 0–2 for astringency (or tannin—same scoring as for asescence), and 0–2 for overall quality. A perfect score, then, would by 20. Each taster was to score the wines, rank them, and give his results to an official who would compile the group consensus.

As I sat down, a man across the table from me was refilling his water glass. "Water isn't sufficient," he said.

"Maybe Drano," agreed the guy next to him. Apparently they were having trouble washing away the tannins.

"I guess this goes to show that there's no such thing as a Zinfandel style," the first speaker concluded—and indeed, the twelve wines on the table, if not fully representative of the whole Zinfandel spectrum from soda pop to port, still ranged far and wide from big-dark-purple-tannic to light-red-moderate-reserved.

As I tasted, I inwardly picked out one of the former entries as a Ravenswood. Another well-balanced, more claretlike wine I guessed to be a Ridge. I was wrong on both counts. My "Ravenswood" turned out to be the '85 Lytton Springs, the wine that finished fourth in the overall standings. In third place was the actual '85 Ravenswood Old Hill, the most tannic entry on the table; second was Hop Kiln's so-called Primitivo (the winery had trademarked the name for use in the United States, though the wine had been made from Zinfandel grapes grown in California). The winner was the wine that I'd guessed to be a Ridge, which turned out to be—surprise!—the 1985 Nalle.

As it happened, the guest speaker at the tasting was none other than the winemaker, Doug Nalle—a boyish, freckle-faced, young (i.e., fortyish) guy wearing wire-rimmed glasses and coat and tie, who looked as if he might be more comfortable in a sweatshirt and baseball cap. Nalle had been sitting unidentified at my table during the tasting; after we'd handed in our scores (but before the wines were unveiled) he had correctly picked out his own wine by its nose and the Ravenswood by its abundance of mint. Of the Ravenswood he said, "I'd tell a customer to lay that wine down for ten years and hope for the best. But regardless of whether you like the style, it's very good wine."

Regarding the wide variety of wines present, Nalle opined that five years earlier the styles would have been even more widespread. "This is reined in," he said, noting that the main difference between the wines was in the "use of oak and type of oak." Discussing Zinfandel's different microclimates, he revealed that over the years he had worked for several different wineries in Alexander and Dry Creek valleys, and he described the way "the heat changes" as you drive up and down U.S. 101. "Dry Creek cools off earlier in the day than Alexander Valley or Napa Valley north of Oakville," he said. "It gives the Dry Creek grapes better acid without any manipulation. Napa's is a *softer* Zin."

At this point I can report that over the course of the next couple of years, Nalle's wines won him wide acclaim, garnering 90-plus scores and "Highly Recommended" notations in many wine publications. At this writing he is the hot Zinfandel guy of the hour—especially among people who don't cotton to Ravenswood. The *Wine Spectator*, for example, included the '86 Nalle among the best hundred wines in the world released in 1988 (accompanied by no Ravenswoods and by only one other Zinfandel—the '86 A. Rafanelli, also from Dry Creek Valley).

A couple of weeks after the Vintner's Club tasting, I drove up 101—carefully noting changes in the air temperature—to talk to Nalle. I found him at the tasteful, modern, expensive-looking Quivira winery, where he was employed as winemaker. As I soon learned, the label that bore his own name was a small (two thousand cases per year) operation that Nalle had begun with financial help from a well-known venture capitalist named Bill Hambrecht, who also owned the Belvedere winery, where Paul Draper served as a consultant. In 1984 Draper had arranged for Nalle to tour Bordeaux in the same fashion that Draper himself had enjoyed twenty years earlier—as a guest of the Dourthe family in the Médoc.

Despite his recent enological achievements, Nalle said that

he hadn't by any means followed a concrete path toward this career. "I was a history major at the University of Redlands," he told me, leaning back in his lab chair among the beakers and half-full bottles and now wearing the sweatshirt instead of the coat and tie. "When I graduated in 1969, my draft number was eleven. I joined the Peace Corps and went to Kenya for a while; when I came back, I moved to Oregon and took agriculture courses at Oregon State. For a brief time during the summer, I pitched for a semi-pro baseball team. Then I remet an old girlfriend from Redlands, got engaged, and went to work as a bank trainee in L.A. Six months later the engagement ended, and I wanted to get the hell out of Southern California. I didn't know where I was going or what I was going to do next. I thought Southern California weather was boring, but Oregon's was tiresome in the winter. I didn't want to work in a bank, but my eyes weren't good enough to be a pilot. But I could always smell and taste real well—I was the one in my family who always knew when the milk was about to go bad.

"At my lowest point of indirection it suddenly hit me that for where I wanted to live and what I was equipped to do, winemaking was ideal. When I'd gotten out of high school, my parents had taken me to Italy, where we drank wine with all our meals. It got me out of my rum-and-Coke stage—I saw that wine was not just a way to get drunk. I used to drive five hundred miles up to Napa Valley from Redlands with a buddy to visit Beringer, Inglenook, Krug, BV, and Mondavi.

"I wanted to go to Davis, but I only had a two-point-five average in college, with no chemistry or statistics. In sheer desperation I came up here and started knocking on doors. When Pillsbury bought Souverain and opened its new winery in 1973 (in the middle of Ridge's old Trentadue vineyard at Geyserville), I got hired as the first cellar worker. They paid good wages and attracted some smart guys—we pulled that cellar together pretty fast. Meanwhile, I was taking chemistry at the local junior college; Davis told me I could come there on a 'concurrent' basis, and only if there was room in the classes. I went there Monday through Friday and came back to Healdsburg on the weekends.

I applied to the master's program three times; I was so mad at them that it drove me.

"In '77 Jordan hired me to work the crush. I planned to stay there even if it was only as assistant winemaker. If you've ever been there, you know why—in 1977 the place was like the Taj Mahal. The technology was state-of-the-art, and André Tchelistcheff was the consulting enologist. *That* was when I finally got into the master's program at Davis. So that winter I went back to school and got my master's degree in a year and a half. When I got out, I helped design the Balverne winery, where John Kongsgaard and I made eleven different varieties. By the time I met Bill Hambrecht, I had helped design three different wineries, so I was getting pretty good at deciding how high the tanks should be. He and I had an agreement to make forty thousand cases of Zinfandel at a winery on Lytton Springs Road, but it fell through at the last minute. As a compromise, we set up this partnership."

Nalle rolled his chair over to his lab counter and from his beakers and bottles poured me his not-yet-released '86 and '87 Zinfandels. He watched me intently as I tasted them; I felt as if I were at a sneak preview of a film whose director was sitting in the seat next to mine. I liked the full, grapy '87 best; its taste-bud-rainmaking device was solidly in place. Nalle, however, was of the opinion that the '86 was the finest Zinfandel he'd made. He considered the much-lauded '85 too high in VA. "Don't get me wrong," he said. "I think it's a stunning wine. But its beauty is sort of like Meryl Streep's—slightly flawed."

When I asked why he'd chosen Zinfandel as the varietal for his own label, he answered that it was mostly a matter of convenience: His winery was located in Dry Creek Valley. "When I set up a business plan," he said, swiveling back around in his chair, "I needed cash flow. I couldn't afford to make a wine that nobody could drink for three or four years. I knew that the majority of Zinfandels I'd tasted and made hadn't aged very well; they have great, up-front fruit right away, but usually the tannin outlives it and you end up with a dumb red wine. I think Zinfandel is genetically inferior to Cabernet and Pinot Noir—

it's a number two hitter, whereas Cabernet is your cleanup guy. The grape would probably do well in southern France, Tuscany, or Algeria. The reason it didn't do well in the cooler areas of Europe is that it has too much acid. It was planted widely in California because it could survive the heat and retain enough acid to make a balanced wine. But I think the Italians saw that it lacked a little something, which is why they combined it with Carignane and Petite Sirah.

"The reason Zinfandel isn't appreciated all over the world is that it's difficult to produce a wine that has depth, flavor, and richness without its being too alcoholic. The old Italians *wanted* alcohol, but there's a difference between ripeness and maturity. I think Zinfandel is really hard to make, and the hardest thing about it is knowing when to pick the grapes. I follow pH and taste as much as I follow degrees Brix now. I leave Zinfandel on the skins for seven to fourteen days; I have to question the amount of time that other people leave it on the skins—the structure of the grape just doesn't warrant it.

"Zinfandel is really complicated because there are so many different ways to approach it," Nalle said. "This isn't like the Médoc, where everybody's making Cabernet pretty much the same way. I think the mistakes that most people make with Zinfandel are leaving it on the skins too long, picking it too ripe, and not using Petite Sirah or French oak. I could save ten thousand dollars a year by using American oak, but it has a rough, coarse finish that I don't like. Ridge is one of the few wineries that don't *abuse* American oak; they integrate it with the fruit structure of the wine and use it to brighten the berry tones. I always look forward to Ravenswood wines at the Harvest Fair because they're such statements. I may not agree with their style, but they're intentionally made that way—it's not an accident. All I can gather from tasting them is that Joel Peterson likes more tannic wines than I do. He's trying to build his with ageability; I'm not. I'm trying to make world-class wines, but I want them to be at their peak in three to four years.

"I think Zinfandel is coming back to its pre-overextraction era—a sophisticated, mature middle ground. Cabernet and

Chardonnay drinkers are growing weary of paying twelve to fifteen dollars for a bottle. One thing I've learned in the last few years is what a hype this business is. It's all subject to the critics, and price and quality don't go together—an era just accepts a certain genre as best. What continues to get me up in the morning is the smells and the creativity of putting things together. Being a winemaker is like being a potter, or maybe a carpenter who owns his own forest and quarry—you're going right from the ground base, pruning the vines and watching them grow, to picking and crushing and all the decisions that go into the bottle. To bring all those things together in one job is rare. But it's still too egocentric. You listen to some winemakers talk, and you realize that they *really think they're God*! I see guys ten years younger than me who think they're so hot—I think: 'Just wait, you'll blow it.' And they do! *I've* blown it! I have to keep telling myself not to get cocky. There are too many things that control your destiny—you've got to have the right grapes, the right people. To have a winning thoroughbred, you know, you need a good jockey *and* a good horse. The winemaker is the jockey, but the grapes are the horse."

After leaving Nalle, I drove half a mile down the road to visit A. Rafanelli. As I entered the winery's driveway, I saw a license plate that said "RAF ZIN." The barn was decorated with bleached white antlers, the fences with silver abalone shells. Inside the rustic but spotless winery, rows of varnished oak barrels shone softly under spotlights.

"I like things to look nice," admitted Dave Rafanelli, the dark-haired, clean-shaven, short but strong-looking owner and winemaker. The *A* in the winery's name stands for Americo— Rafanelli's father, who had died the previous year. The son was now carrying on the family tradition, making a relatively small amount of Zinfandel, Cabernet, Chardonnay, and Gamay Beaujolais—though "Zinfandel was all Dad ever drank," Rafanelli said as I tasted his rich, delicious '86.

"Dad always said this is the place to grow Zinfandel," Rafanelli said. "We've got the right soil and the right climate. In the early seventies, UC Davis said, 'Dry Creek is Region Two. So plant Cabernet.' What a mistake! Even in this one valley you get unevenness of soil. Seventy percent of Dry Creek is the valley floor; only about fifteen percent is hillsides, which have the well-drained gravel with some clay. The upper end of the valley is much warmer than the bottom, and the east side is warmer than the west. In cool years I have to clip the leaves on the east side of the vines, but I never touch the leaves on the west, 'cause that's where we get hot afternoon sun."

Rafanelli leaned back and folded his forearms across his chest. He was wearing a navy blue sweatshirt and work boots. "Dad didn't have a lot of formal training," he told me. "His father was an Italian immigrant; his mother's family made wine near Florence. She was the one who was really the farmer. My mother died when I was two; I was raised by my grandparents, and I can tell you, those old Italians were serious drinkers—they'd have three or four glasses of wine with lunch. And it was high in alcohol, too. Every year they made their two or three or four hundred gallons. The old-timers liked Zinfandel because it could be drunk young, but also because it lent itself to a few years of aging if they didn't finish the barrel. When my grandparents gave me water, they'd pour a little color into it. I do that now with my daughter; I think kids who are shielded from alcohol are the ones who'll abuse it later on. And I used to hate it when my father dragged me into the vineyard, but now I do the same thing with my kids.

"The old-timers usually mixed Zinfandel with Petite Sirah and Carignane, but we've always kept ours a hundred percent Zinfandel. On average, it stays on the skins for eight or nine days, and I age it for two years in oak. I lose a case and a half in evaporation from each barrel in those two years, but it's worth it to me in quality. My wife does all the selling and delivering. The phone rings off the hook all the time here now; people who've had good Zinfandel know what it is. But I won't raise our prices more than twenty-five or forty cents a year. Dad instilled in me the philosophy that wine should be drunk. You figure out what it costs you to grow it and make it and what it costs you to live, and that's what the wine should cost. You don't raise your prices just because you know you can get 'em now. You don't want to alienate your customers, 'cause your old customers got you where you're at. The industry today is too hyper; it's all press. To get ahead, you're supposed to kiss this and that wine writer's butt. That isn't us; we're *farmers*. We're custodians—washers and scrubbers. We're not really making the wine. If you've got good grapes, the wine makes itself."

I departed after tasting Rafanelli's '86 Cabernet, a wine that would soon be adding to his acclaim. As I drove back down 101, it seemed to me that Rafanelli and Nalle (though united in their belief that the wine business was a hype) represented two distinct sides of the Dry Creek Valley Zinfandel coin. One, seldom straying from the place of his birth, had only his wife and children to help him as he labored to carry on the traditions of his elders. The other, a member of the new breed of baby boomers, had, from among a range of possible careers, settled on winemaking as a suitable outlet for his abilities (spurred to the decision by privileged sojourns overseas), then been bankrolled by financial wizards and tutored by the winemaking elite. This is not meant to discredit Doug Nalle; he had worked hard to prove his talent. In fact, it was undoubtedly more difficult for him to make a name for himself than it had been for Dave Rafanelli, who had, after all, inherited his land, his winery, and his skills. Yet neither is *this* by any means to discredit Rafanelli; he hadn't had to compromise, but to his credit, he hadn't.

The best part was that both men—each of whom seemed thoroughly honest—were producing a product that, by at least one stylistic yardstick, could be placed among the best in the world. It made me realize that if wine is a thing of endless diversity, it also serves as a link: Doug Nalle and Dave Rafanelli—disparate in upbringing, outlook, and temperament—were in the end wedded by geography and by the grape traditionally grown in the place where they'd come to live: Dry Creek Valley in Sonoma County, the hearth and home of Zinfandel.

In February Joel Peterson tasted through the '87 Zinfandels that had been harvested in the fall. To obtain samples of the wines, Clyde Crawford clambered among the stacks of barrels with his plastic thief; as he slapped at the bungs with a wooden hammer, the whole rack shook— you could hear wine sloshing in the barrels from the floor to the ceiling. Clyde covered a plywood table with white butcher paper, lined up fourteen glasses, partially filled each one with wine, and affixed plastic wrap to the tops of the glasses to exclude oxygen and fruit flies. Then, using a felt-tip pen, he labeled the bases of the glasses with initials—DCZ, ABZ, DZ, CKZ, OHZ, MZ, CDZ—denoting the wines from different vineyards.

As Joel tasted from each glass, he spit the wine into a white plastic bucket, hitting it flawlessly from six feet away. Then he commented on what he tasted. First was OHZ—the Old Hill Zinfandel.

"Deep and plummy, with lots of spice and blackberries," Joel said. "Traditional for Old Hill. You can taste it as you breathe *out*—it has enough aromaticity that it fills up your mouth again. There's an almost silky aspect about the nose, a lot of nice things going on in the mouth; there's tannin, but it's so round and smooth that it's a balanced wine."

DZ: "Both Dickerson and Old Hill have an expanded quality to the nose; they have breadth. Dickerson has more raspberries, plus that nice cedar-eucalyptus quality. There's also a woody finish—something that Dickerson always does, no matter where I make it. This year, at Buena Vista, there were no stems; the fermentation was cooler; it was put in closed stainless-steel fermentors, and it was pumped over instead of punched down. As a result, it has less of a center, but more high-toned fruit qualities. Fruit isn't something we usually strive for; we find that the wine develops a more interesting nose without that."

DCZ: "Dry Creek is still very tight. It has a sort of brown edge, but you can really taste the Dry Creek cherries. It's round and dusty, with a little flavor of wood, even though it doesn't have any wood to speak of. It'll be good in the end."

LZ: "Lyeth has a real bright, citruslike quality. It's spicy, complex, multifaceted. It's more lively on the palate than Dry Creek; perhaps a little more astringent. It comes from chalky, gravelly soil with a lot of limestone—the kind of soil Pinot Noir would like. Limestone is one of the things that Pinot Noir mystically thrives on; everybody always looks for the limestone outcroppings."

CPZ, the wine that followed a schizoid path after being picked without Joel's permission, "isn't offering much. These grapes came in very hot—around eighty degrees—and the fermentation took off the next day. We threw our cooling wand in and just barely stayed ahead of it. It's not as rich as I'd like, but it has a lot of Napa Valley cherry-plum quality to it. With oak, it'll make an elegant wine."

CKZ (from a vineyard owned by Charles Cooke): "Cherry-raspberry nose; nice flavors going on; a little bit of a leesy quality; a hint of brininess. That's one of the things wine goes through. It was just racked, and it's pretty stirred up. It'll pass."

ABZ (from a vineyard owned by two people named Ann and Bill): "It has an herbal-spice-anise quality; it's sort of sweet.

This was second crop, and I don't really like it very well. It'll be fine for the Vintner's Blend; I've got no problem with it for that."

DRZ (from a vineyard owned by Ed Durell): "A muted herbal-berry quality. Also, a hint of redwood in the nose that disturbs me. Clyde, is all the wine out of tanks fifteen and sixteen?"

"Durell's still in there," Clyde called from across the warehouse.

"Get it out as soon as you can," said Joel. "It's picking up redwood in the nose." Turning back to me, he said, "Redwood certainly isn't an aroma I like to have in the wine. But that particular wine gets blended enough that you won't be able to pick it up. In time it will change character enough that you won't be able to tell it's redwood."

Last was YGZ: the Young Gentlemen's Zinfandel. As it was lined up beside the less substantial wines, Joel noted that the Young Gentlemen's was "much darker than you think it is. It has a nice brick color; young Zinfandel berry fruit; a good mouth feel. It's spicy and it's clean—you've taken good care of it. You topped it with some your nouveau, right? It has that forward, up-front berry quality. It doesn't have a *lot* of flavor or a long finish, but it has a combination of qualities that will please everybody—especially if you put new oak in it. It won't be around for a long time but will be real nice while it is."

John Kemble came in from outside. "How are they?" he asked.

"Seven-point-five on a scale of ten," said Joel. "Some are in the nine category; some down here are around five or six. But there are no real defects; none of the better wines are short in the finish or thin in flavor. They all have interesting flavors, a multitude of flavors, which ultimately translates into the nose. Most of these are tight in the nose now, which is something I expect at this stage; when wine comes right out of the barrel, the nose tends to be muted. As it develops, the nose becomes more complex.

"Overall, this is a lighter vintage than we've ever made before—I can't remember when we've had wines so low in alcohol. The grapes were picked at the same sugars as last year, but because of the way the weather was this year—consistent and even, with no serious heat wave at the end—there was less raisining. As a result, the wines aren't so burly and intense; they won't need as much heavy, perfumy background, so we'll probably age them in less brand-new oak. All in all, this vintage will be less of a Rhône style—more like a claret. The '87s might just turn out to be Cabernet drinkers' Zinfandels."

Paul Draper's talk about his original partners at Ridge eventually made me realize that I ought to meet them. Dave and Fran Bennion, Hew and Sue Crane, and Charlie and Blanche Rosen still lived on the peninsula south of San Francisco; over the next several months I spoke with all of them.

I interviewed the Cranes and Rosens at the Cranes' house in Portola Valley, where Sue Crane happened to be the mayor. Her husband still worked at Stanford Research Institute, from which Charlie Rosen had retired, though he didn't particularly strike me as the retiring sort. He was an intense, sharp-edged septuagenarian whose combed-back hair leaped stubbornly out at angles from his skull; as he made his points, he repeatedly reached out to touch my arm for emphasis. Crane was his opposite. Quiet and reflective behind a gray beard and tortoiseshell glasses, he said relatively little, though he appeared to be absorbing a good deal.

As we sat in the living room before dinner, Crane poured a rich, golden, buttery wine from out of a brown bag. Rosen, trying to divine its identity, said: "I taste oak; I taste malolactic; I taste an aged wine. I'd guess it's a Chardonnay or a Sauvignon

Blanc." Chardonnay would have been my answer, too. Finally Crane pulled the bottle from the bag: a 1970 Ridge White Zinfandel, made by David Bennion.

When I called Bennion to request an interview, he asked me if I'd heard about him from Paul Draper. I said—truthfully—that I couldn't really remember whether Draper or I had first brought him up. Then I asked why he wanted to know.

"Because Paul Draper doesn't usually mention me at all," he said.

I met Bennion at his house in Menlo Park on a rainy winter afternoon. He was a big, bearded, disheveled man who seemed somewhat scattered but didn't shrink from discussing anything in detail. I expected to stay for an hour or two, but as we talked, Bennion pulled some '64 and '68 Ridge Zinfandels out of his cellar, and I ended up leaving seven hours after I'd arrived. Midway through our conversation, we were joined by Bennion's wife, Fran, a soft-spoken woman with shoulder-length gray hair who sustained the discussion with her own memories and some excellent homemade tacos.

Bennion told me he'd grown up as part of a "rapidly multiplying" Mormon family on a farm in Utah, a state where to this day it is illegal to order wine in a restaurant. His father, who during drives in the country would motion not at mountains and valleys but at scarps, talus, and terminal moraine, steered him toward a career in science. Upon graduating from high school, Dave won a scholarship to Stanford, where, in his freshman physics lab, he met Fran, a budding musician who shared Bennion's love of science, the arts, and the outdoors (on her first Sierra Club trip in 1950, she climbed five fourteen-thousand-foot peaks in seven days). Together they went folk dancing and mushroom hunting near the Stanford campus, where Bennion got his first taste of beer.

Bennion's adviser at Stanford was Frederick Terman, a famous professor of electrical engineering known for persuading his students to become entrepreneurs and thus laying the cornerstones upon which Silicon Valley was built. (It was Terman who suggested to Bill Hewlett and Dave Packard, for example, that they market the audio oscillators they'd been making in their garage.) Terman counseled Dave Bennion to forgo his Mormon missionary work while he was still an undergraduate, and by the time Bennion graduated in 1951 he'd decided to forgo it altogether. He studied nuclear reactor technology at Los Alamos and Oak Ridge for a year, then returned to Palo Alto and, after earning his Ph.D., went to work at Stanford Research Institute in 1956.

SRI, as it is known, is a nonprofit think tank and research and development organization founded by industrialists in the late 1940s to further the aims of both private and public enterprise in the western United States. In the mid-fifties it employed about a thousand scientists pursuing "pure" and applied research in various aspects of chemistry, biology, engineering, medicine, and business. Bennion worked mainly in magnetics, where his mentor was Hew Crane, a product of Jersey City who had worked on the country's first all-electronic computer and soon was to become engaged in studying the engineering aspects of biological systems: vision, hearing, circulation, even the operation of society. Crane's first project at SRI addressed an electronic banking computer system, the circuits of which were designed by Howard Zeidler. After that he teamed up with Dave Bennion, designing "ultrareliable" magnetic devices for use in satellites, missiles, and traffic lights. (The subways of New York City still run on magnetic core computers developed by Bennion and Crane.) The head of SRI's applied physics laboratory was Rosen, a Canadian who, in initiating SRI's artificial intelligence and robotics programs, soon became a legend within the institute. Rosen was known for changing his mind with rapid-fire regularity and for cracking up his colleagues with a delivery that featured expansive mannerisms and mispronounced words. Volatile and intuitive, Rosen reputedly could sell refrigerators to Eskimos, provided that the refrigerators interested him.

In 1958 Rosen, Bennion, Crane, and Zeidler began discussing the idea of buying country property together near Stanford.

Seeing an ad in the local newspaper for "mountain land," Rosen and his wife, Blanche, drove the one-lane dirt road to the top of Monte Bello Ridge. Upon arriving, they learned that the old Italian family who'd advertised the property was interested in selling no less than six hundred acres. When Rosen asked if anything smaller was available in the area, he was directed to another part of the mountain and William Short, a San Francisco broker who, besides bearing a resemblance to Maurice Chevalier, had been a theologian, a chef, a conscientious objector during World War I, and a candidate for governor of California. Ten years earlier, for health reasons, Short's doctor had directed him to Monte Bello Ridge, where among his other activities he planted twenty thousand grapevines on phylloxera-resistant St. George rootstock. At the twenty-three-hundred-foot elevation, however, it was one of the highest vineyards in the world, and in the cool climate the vines were only beginning to bear scant crops. Unsuccessful at repaying his mortgage by selling grapes, Short was now offering his property for sale.

Standing near Short's olive tree on top of Monte Bello Ridge, the Rosens could see all the way from San Jose to San Francisco. Despite the fact that the wind was blowing seventy miles per hour, Charlie said: "This is it." As it happened, two years earlier Dave and Fran Bennion had met William Short while making an unsuccessful bid on some land right across the road—so, bowing to apparent fate, the SRI group put ten thousand dollars down on Short's eighty acres, which came with a house, a barn, the remnants of an old wine cellar, a century-old Mission grapevine, and fifteen acres of mature Chardonnay, Cabernet Sauvignon, Ruby Cabernet, and Pinot Noir.

None of the scientists had previously harbored any ideas about making wine. The lapsed Bennion had begun to develop a taste for the stuff, but he and Fran were unimpressed by California's contributions. "It all seemed thin, hard, and ordinary, contrary to what we'd heard in the media—namely, that all California wines were good," said Bennion. "French wines seemed much more flavorful and interesting, but usually we couldn't afford them; occasionally we'd buy them for the cellar, and California wines to drink right away." At the time, California was selling only one gallon of dry table wine for every three gallons of sweet; white wines were the generic "chablis," "sauternes," and "rhine wine"; reds were "burgundy," "chianti," and "claret." The only common varietal names were Zinfandel and Riesling, but even the so-called Riesling wasn't made from Riesling grapes. When the odd fine-varietal label did turn up, there was no reliable guarantee that the wine contained even 50 percent of the grape named on the bottle, and usually it was difficult to taste the difference between Zinfandel, Cabernet, and Pinot Noir anyway, since the common practice at the time was to combine grapes from everywhere in a single vast batch. The idea that in California "every year is a vintage year" (and correlatively, no year a distinctive year) was enforced by wineries that annually blended their old wines with their new ones to keep the flavor consistent from year to year. Even the rarefied vintages of Beaulieu and Inglenook failed to impress Dave Bennion, who thought that Napa Valley Cabernets, coming as they did from "luscious, rich—almost always too rich—soils, were sweetish and flat and full of off characters."

By contrast, Bennion found the wines of the rugged, thin-soiled Santa Cruz Mountains much more provocative. Monte Bello Ridge was located at the heart of the "Chaîne d'Or"—as Charles Sullivan has described it, the "golden chain of highland wine country." At the northern end of the chain was the long-standing example of the La Questa Cabernet vineyard; on the western slope the Hallcrest Winery (founded in 1941 by a lawyer named Chaffee Hall) was collecting accolades for Cabernet and Johannisberg Riesling; and directly across Stevens Canyon from Monte Bello Ridge, Martin Ray was cutting a swath through the status quo of California enology, endeavoring through varietal bottling and strict adherence to natural techniques to make magnificent wine and—claiming that he was the only person in America doing so—charging correspondingly astronomical prices for it (ten to fifteen dollars a bottle in 1960). When the

SRI group began to entertain the notion of making wine on its new property, Hew Crane called Ray up and—according to Dave Bennion—"got a long chew on the phone about what was wrong with our vineyard." Rosen, for his part, recalls that Ray "promised us we'd never make it." Nevertheless, the lord invited the scientists to his manor, poured them his sparkling wines, served them dinner, and lectured them at length on the importance of oak aging and malolactic fermentation and the evils of sulfur, fining, and filtration.

That fall the scientists harvested six tons of Cabernet and Chardonnay. It was picked on weekends by the families and their friends, who drove up the mountain on Friday night, spread out their sleeping bags on the knoll in front of the barn, and stayed until late Sunday. Some mornings they rose to find themselves marooned in sunlight above a white sea of fog, with only four other islands in sight: Mount Diablo to the north, Mount Hamilton to the east, Mount Umunhum to the south, and Skyline Ridge to the west. During the day the adults toiled in the vineyards while the children played in the mud. The first year most of the grapes were sold to the Gemello Winery in Mountain View; the rest were fermented in a ceramic crock on the Bennions' back porch. Bennion, who had already read up on French techniques, submerged the cap of grape skins with bricks and boards. As far as he was concerned, the 1959 Monte Bello Cabernet was "stupendous—thick, heavy, black, and inky. Our only other exposure to anything like it was Martin Ray wine that had aged for several years." Looking for something immediately consumable, one of Bennion's friends took some of the ink, mixed it with rosé in a one-to-four ratio, and achieved "good drinking material for three or four years."

In 1960 the group made the wine at Rosen's house, in 1961 on Monte Bello Ridge, and in 1962 they rebonded the winery in order to be able to sell the product. The first label actually read "BCRZ Ridge Vineyards"—a combination of the initials of the owners. Initially they had tried to name their winery

Monte Bello Ridge Vineyards, but that name was still owned by the corporate successors to the property's original owner and winemaker: Dr. Osea Perrone, a nineteenth-century Italian immigrant with a medical practice in San Francisco, who needed a place to entertain visiting opera stars. In the 1880s Perrone had terraced the slopes, planted the original vineyard, and built the cellar from local limestone. The cellar, which had no drainage or plumbing, was now full of spider webs, rat dung, and old redwood tanks; the holes in the roof and walls cast rotating constellations of sun flecks on the floor, and the glass in the windowpanes, having flowed earthward for seventy-five years, was thicker at the bottom than at the top. When the scientists' kids played in the house, their balls rolled from one end of a room to the other without external propulsion. Behind the barn was a breeding ground for rattlesnakes, and the rows between grapes in the vineyard were choked with poison oak. The families killed the rattlesnakes, chopped out the poison oak, mowed the grass, put down black plastic to inhibit the weeds, and sprayed the vines with a chemical called Zip to keep away the deer. As soon as they did so, rain generally washed it away, so finally they opted for a fence, which the deer jumped over, burrowed under, and broke through at its weakest points.

Gradually these research scientists were discovering the difference between laboratory conditions and those in a vineyard. That didn't prevent them from experimenting, however. In their early years they concocted such curiosities as white Cabernet, late-harvest Riesling from Botrytised grapes, and a "tawny" Zinfandel "rosé." Rosen served as the winery's chemist; Bennion, known for his attention to detail (his Ph.D. thesis was said to be the thickest in the Stanford electrical engineering department), was the official winemaker. His methods exhibited the primitiveness that, at the time, only a purist would employ. The wines were fermented in small redwood tanks, aged for long periods in small oak barrels, and cleared of sediment solely by racking and settling. Since the owners were able to work at the winery only on weekends, and thus were unable to punch down the cap during fermentation, Bennion devised wooden grates to submerge the grape skins in the tanks, discovering only later that the Picchetti winery down the hill had employed the same technique for decades.

The Ridge owners learned, though, that their seniors in the industry didn't share all their ethics. "People in the wine business were either aloof, conservative members of large corporations or old Italian families who'd inherited the land from their grandparents and were expected to take over the farm," Fran Bennion remembered. "When the Santa Clara Winemakers' Association had their regular dinner meetings, they'd gather in the bar beforehand and drink highballs. I thought it was disgusting. Some of the old country winemakers would come to our place and say, 'This wine's too strong. You should wash out your presses.' They advised us to water down our wine." For their part, the Picchettis thought the scientists were shysters for charging more than $2 a bottle; they asked only $1.50 *a gallon* for their Zinfandel, which they'd been making on Monte Bello Ridge since 1877. The Bennions bought Picchetti Zinfandel in five-gallon jugs, broke it down into fifths, and noticed a marked improvement in quality after a couple of years, by which time the high tannin and acid had practically etched the inside of the bottle. It didn't take them long to realize that the wine was good when it had come from a full barrel, but when the barrel had been half empty, it wasn't so good.

In addition to the products of Souverain and Louis Martini, decent if straightforward Zinfandels were offered at the time by old-time producers like Parducci and J. Pedroncelli. But again the wine that turned the scientists' heads came from the Santa Cruz Mountains. One day a man named Dan Wheeler, who made wine at his home in the hills behind Soquel, poured them a ten-year-old Zinfandel that Rosen, in the classic pattern, mistook for Bordeaux. Bennion thought it tasted like "pure blueberries"; both men immediately agreed that Zinfandel could be a wine for the ages. In October 1964 the families were nearly finished with the Monte Bello harvest when they learned that the Picchettis were giving up the wine business—ordered by the county health officials to put in a concrete floor, the younger generation, insufficiently enamored with winemaking to comply, abandoned plans to pick their grapes. The '64 Monte Bello Cabernet crop had been short, so the Ridge owners leaped into the lurch. They harvested the Picchettis' Zinfandel (at twenty-four degrees Brix, a sugar level that the owners considered overripe) and fermented it according to their traditional methods. "It was so good right from the beginning," Dave Bennion recalled, "that when we needed a wine for dinner, I'd just go get some from the barrel and put it in a flask. Our Cabernet couldn't be quaffed that way. I saw right then that Zinfandel could be our bread and butter."

The Ridge owners promptly fenced the Picchettis' vineyard, and Dave Bennion took it upon himself to begin searching out old Zinfandel vines on unirrigated hillsides around the state. A Los Angeles wine connoisseur named Dick Foster, who'd gotten involved with Ridge after tasting the '59 Monte Bello Cabernet (and parting company with Martin Ray), noticed that many prizewinning wines at the L.A. County Fair came from the Coast Range near Paso Robles, so Bennion drove down there, discovered a wealth of pre-phylloxera vines, and contracted for Zinfandel from a grower named Benito Dusi. Ridge also advanced money to the Jimsomare ranch on Monte Bello Ridge so that the property's Zinfandel vines, which had been neglected since Prohibition, could be resurrected; and in 1966 they arranged to buy Alexander Valley Zinfandel from Leo Trentadue, the owner of the old Perrone building farther up the ridge, who was now growing grapes near Geyserville in Sonoma County.

By the time Trentadue's Zinfandel came ripe that year, all the winery's fermentors were full. The longer the grapes were left on the vines, the more they shriveled; but as Charlie Rosen pointed out, "When they make Sauternes in France, they *want* the grapes to shrivel." The grapes were finally picked as they approached thirty degrees Brix, and fermentation quit at 14.4 percent alcohol with 7.5 percent residual sugar. Ridge subsequently bottled the wine in tenth splits and released it to wide acclaim as a rich, portlike Zinfandel Essence. Bennion repeated the same trick two years later with Zinfandel from the Central Valley, where late-summer heat commonly turns grapes into raisins by September. The '68 Ridge Zinfandel Essence was picked in *November*, by which time the grapes had turned gray with mold, bringing about that rarity, a Botrytised red wine.

Such novelties began to change the way people thought of Zinfandel at the same time that Ridge's other practices were helping change the way people thought of California wine. The Ridge label was something a scientist could love—in contrast with those pervading the shelves, it was pictureless and informative to a fault, as opposed to romantic or nostalgic for an unspecified old country. On each bottle Bennion provided an unprecedented synopsis of salient production details: The vineyard was identified as well as the vintage, the bottling date, and the exact alcohol content. As Bennion later explained, "It was a symbolic thing of being straightforward for the consumer's sake. If age is important, and bottle age is as important as time spent in wood, then the bottling date should be of interest to the buyer. In the cooler areas of France, wine quality is dependent on how ripe you get your grapes, so alcohol content is strictly delimited. But in California you're allowed a one-and-a-half percent deviation, so it was common to say that the alcohol content was twelve-point-five percent, meaning it was anywhere between eleven and fourteen." (Federal excise tax quadrupled when alcohol content exceeded fourteen percent, so Ridge's "symbolic straightforwardness"—combined with its proclivity for ripe grapes—sometimes proved expensive.)

American wine sales had been rising gradually since World War II, and in 1967 sales of dry California table wine exceeded those of sweet for the first time in history. This "millennium" was ushered in by a handful of other small wineries that joined Ridge on the crest of the New Wave. In Sonoma the Hanzell winery (funded by James D. Zellerbach) had been making French-style Chardonnay since roughly the same time that Ridge was founded; in Napa Valley Joseph Heitz was making his first Cabernet Sauvignons, Stony Hill was producing first-rate Riesling and Chardonnay, Mayacamas was crafting Cabernets and Chardonnay meant for long aging, and Robert Mondavi had formed his own enterprise after falling out with his family. As the Ridge founders saw it, the ripeness of the market for top-class table wine was approaching twenty-four degrees Brix. In this case, however, picking was impeded not by full fermentors but by empty coffers: Ridge's revenues in its first four years had been $130, $530, $2,100, and $3,700, as production had gone from 150 to 600 cases—an upward curve, admittedly, but one that, when weighed against the owners' expenditures, merely amounted to a costly hobby. Dave Bennion in particular wanted it to be more than that; in eleven years at SRI, much of his research had gone into government files, never to be seen again, while winemaking and grape growing had become his passions. In view of his obsessiveness, Bennion's passions were forces to be reckoned with. Outwardly simple, Bennion was inwardly labyrinthine, his mind leading him in a maze of directions at any given moment—to him, even backpacking was a science that required exhaustive study and preparation. In the winery he evinced an awesome capacity for concentration on details, with little apparent sense of priorities—when harvest was approaching, he'd spend as much time looking for an antique rolltop desk for the office as he would for wine barrels. "In engineering Dave's attention to detail was positive," said Hew Crane. "In business it's a disaster if you spend as much time on a ten-dollar purchase as you do on a ten-thousand-dollar one." Bennion's case of tunnel vision, however, was corrected by his partners: Where the implosive ex-Mormon complicated everything that he touched, simplification was the forte of the outspoken and emotional Rosen, while model scientist Crane—quiet, rational, objective, and methodical—steered a calm course in between.

When the Ridge founders recognized their need for new investors, the first person they approached was Carl Djerassi, the Stanford chemistry professor who developed the steroid birth control pill. Years earlier the Ridge owners had sold Djerassi some land, and Bennion had impressed him by having an adjacent piece of property logged in such a way that the environment had been positively enhanced. Djerassi was a dynamic perfectionist in the Ridge style, and a mutual respect sprouted between them. When the Ridge founders proposed that Djerassi join them in developing a first-growth château at Monte Bello, Djerassi talked the idea up to his colleague Alejandro Zaffaroni, who not only was president of Syntex U.S.A. but also owned a substantial wine cellar. In 1967 Ridge Vineyards was incorporated: Djerassi, Zaffaroni, and Dick Foster joined on, the bachelor Howard Zeidler bowed out, and Dave Bennion left SRI to become full-time winemaker and president. The group purchased an old vineyard near Scott's Valley and that year tripled its wine production to two thousand cases. It also bought from Leo Trentadue the old four-story Perrone building, which had been in danger of burning down because of vandalism; its cellar was full of frogs, rainwater, old tanks, stoves, and mattress springs, but the eighty-year-old redwood posts and beams were still solid. With the help of an architect named Aaron Green, a Frank Lloyd Wright disciple with a penchant for native materials and natural settings, the group made plans to refurbish the building into a full-scale winery.

Though he was now applying himself to the task full-time, this new level of activity proved too much even for Dave Bennion. For all his unbounded energy, Bennion abhorred selling and was poor at delegating authority. As Hew Crane later said, running both a winery and a vineyard is like running two businesses at once; Bennion was managing more than one vineyard while simultaneously, and somewhat unwillingly, trying to increase production at a winery that was about to be remodeled and moved. He clearly needed help, and one person who was interested in assisting him was George Burtness, a land manager at Stanford who also owned a small winery where he was making Cabernet, Chardonnay, and Zinfandel.

One night Burtness, an aficionado of Coast Range Cabernets, invited Bennion to a tasting at his house. Upon arriving, Bennion discovered that many of the wines were Chilean, and in the course of the evening he met a young man who had made one of them. The two exchanged their enthusiasm for mountain vineyards, and when Bennion described the old-fashioned methods by which Ridge wines were made, the young man said that he employed many of the same techniques. Coincidentally, he had just spent the '68 harvest in Bordeaux, as a guest of the family from whom Ridge was importing French wines in barrel.

Impressed by this articulate young man who seemed to share much of his own philosophy, Bennion asked if he might be interested in helping out at Ridge. The young man responded that he would—he was about to close down his operation in Chile and would soon be returning permanently to California. He said that he could be reached through Fritz Maytag at the Anchor Steam brewery in San Francisco and handed Bennion a slip of paper upon which he'd written his name: Paul Draper.

One evening Joel Peterson chose three Zinfandels for their differences in age, region, and type of oak: an '84 Roudon-Smith from Sonoma County; an '82 Ridge Fiddletown from Amador County; and a '76 Ravenswood (Dry Creek Valley) from Joel's basement.

Following the lengthy selection process in a Sonoma wine shop, where Morgan played hide-and-seek with the clerk while Joel studied the shelves, we took the wines to Joel's house and opened them in the kitchen. In choosing the Ridge and Roudon-Smith, Joel had intended to compare the effects of American and French oak; as soon as he poured and smelled the wines, however, he announced: "I'm afraid we've got two wines in American oak here."

Placing six glasses of wine on the counter—three for him and three for me—he said, "The basic approach to a wine is this. First of all, look at the color. By putting it next to a white surface, you can see the opacity of it—whether it's clear or cloudy. Browning at the edges is a sign of age; younger wines are more purple. Now bring your nose to it, off the glass, to smell the higher tones and perfumes. The Ravenswood has an identifiable cedar-eucalyptus quality. Right away you can tell the difference between the Amador and the Sonoma. The Sonoma wine smells brighter and more raspberrylike; the Amador has more cherries than berries, and a chocolaty, almost cooked quality. The weather in the Sierra foothills is hotter, so the Amador grape skins get thicker and more astringent.

"Next, go deep into the glass and inhale slowly. Get more of the texture, the deep wood-and-fruit character of the wine. If it's low in acid, it will seem dull in the nose; if it's high in acid, it will be sharp in the nose. American oak smells like the inside of an old oak closet. Not even necessarily oak; just wood—wet, dusty wood. In its worst permutation, American oak has a *sour* wood quality; the French oak in the Ravenswood is more of a toasty vanilla. Also, the Ravenswood has no identifiable Zinfandel fruit—it's gone through enough bottle age that the fruit has blended with the oak. You get that fleshy smell, almost like baby fat, in the Roudon-Smith? That's youth versus age.

"At this point you should almost have been able to evaluate the wine completely. Now take a small sip. Balance it on the tip of your tongue, and let it flow back naturally into your mouth. That'll tell you something about the acid balance— whether it's tart or flat—and the astringency, if it makes your mouth pucker or gives you a fuzzy feel behind your front teeth. Now take a bigger sip—a tablespoon, say. Well it behind your teeth and pull air through it. That volatizes it and gives you a sense of its flavors and body characters: the alcohol, the weight of the wine, how dense and complex it is. If the nose is dull but the flavor is full, it's probably a young wine that's going to develop. If the nose is full but the flavor is dull, it's probably an old wine that's about to fall apart.

"Now swallow the wine. Reflect on the residual flavors in your mouth. How long does it last? Does it feel clean and fresh? Or is it heavy, dead, and flat? Does it invite you to take another sip, or does it leave you aghast? Wines have a shape. Try to imagine the spatial representation that it gives you. This Ridge Amador is like a dense, furry ball—it has a brown sugar, slightly baked quality. The Roudon-Smith doesn't have that furry edge. Its surface is smoother.

"Admittedly, language is fairly fragile with regard to these things. It rarely hits the mark when you're trying to describe a sense or an emotion. If I say 'sorrow,' you'll know exactly what I mean only if you've experienced it in the same sense that I have. That's why I think one-man wine reviews are patently absurd—they're trying to communicate a common experience without checking it out with anybody else. I know my nose and palate go off sometimes; in the old days, when I was evaluating a lot of wines, I'd always start by testing myself with a three-blind tasting. I'd put out two glasses of the same wine and one of another, and if I confused them, I'd know I was off. Some days I come in and the wine is absolutely mute. It's because of me. Theoretically you could probably tell what kind of day you're going to have, and what the last twenty-four hours have been like, by the way you react to a wine that you know well. There's an adage that you can tell what a winemaker's life is like by the kind of wine he makes. The only bad wine Joe Swan ever made was in a good year; it just happened to be the year he split up with his wife."

During our tasting Joel as usual had mentioned the cedar-eucalyptus quality in his wine. I, however, had found something else it in, something that I often and unfortunately seem to find in wines that are considered fine—namely, the smell of turnips: the pungent, peppery, vegetal aroma that wafts from my plate about once a year, usually on the fourth Thursday in November. It isn't something I necessarily find appealing in a wine, I have to admit.

I mentioned turnips at Ridge one day. David Noyes politely pointed out that the flavor of turnips is sweet, sharp, and rich. "I sometimes find a blue cheese quality in Zinfandel that I really like," he said encouragingly.

To check myself, on the day following the tasting with Joel,

I took the remains of the '76 Ravenswood to Solano Cellars, a wine shop near my house whose proprietor, a tall, imposing, black-bearded figure named Bill Easton, I knew to possess a good palate. Easton had closed his store before I arrived, but my brown paper bag piqued his curiosity sufficiently for him to let me in.

"Looks like it has some age on it," he said as I poured a few ounces from the bag into his glass. He stood behind the counter in his customary boots and vest, his long hair curling over his ears, looking pensively downward as he swirled the wine and angled the glass out from one side of his nose. "Smells like Zinfandel," he ventured (so much for the absence of identifiable fruit), and after taking a sip he added, "Probably from Sonoma County." He swirled and sniffed and sipped some more. Finally he asked: "Is it Ravenswood?" He didn't mention turnips.

I began to cultivate Easton's company after that performance, becoming a regular at the bistro that he and his wife, Jane O'Riordan, had recently opened in their shop. I learned that Bill had grown up in Sacramento and that we shared an interest in California history and geography, as well as—how shall I say?—offbeat environmental concerns. Bill styles himself a sort of redneck ecological anarchist in the Edward Abbey mold—a curious position for a wine connoisseur, it might seem (though the wine world, like the larger one of which it is a part, takes all kinds). He was also a member in good standing of the so-called Rhône Rangers, a group of California winemakers experimenting with such French grapes as Syrah, Grenache, Mourvèdre, and Cinsault; in partnership with Scott Harvey of the Santino Winery in Amador County, Easton produced and sold a blend of these grapes that he called Domaine de la Terre Rouge. The '86 earned a 90 rating from Robert M. Parker, Jr.

In support of this sideline, Bill and Jane had a cottage in Fiddletown, the Amador County hamlet from which one of the Zinfandels in Joel's lesson had come. As it happens, I myself once lived in Amador County while working as a reporter for the local newspaper, the *Amador Progress News*. Unfortunately, as my period of employment preceded my interest in wine, I'd taken utterly no advantage of the place's Zinfandel legacy. Amador County is in the mother lode country east of Sacramento; its first grapevines were planted during the gold rush, and as a result, the Shenandoah Valley between Plymouth and Fiddletown today boasts some of the oldest Zinfandel vines in existence. As history tells it, the majority of Amador County's original vines disappeared during Prohibition; those that remained after repeal were utilized largely by home winemakers— people willing to pay twice the commercial rate for grapes and able to appreciate the overripeness that resulted from torrid summer heat. In the mid-sixties one such home winemaker, Charlie Myers, an English teacher at Sacramento City College, was looking for Muscat grapes; he was told by an Amador-bred acquaintance that he might find some at the Deaver ranch in Shenandoah Valley. Indeed, Myers did, along with a great many other grapes that the Deavers said were Zinfandel, though they didn't look like Zinfandel to Myers, who was used to the big, tight overwatered bunches from the Central Valley. The Deavers' unirrigated, low-cropped clusters were loose; the berries were small; the skin-to-juice ratio was therefore quite high, and the lush, earthy wine that Myers made from the grapes was nearly black. A Sacramento associate of Myers's, Darrell Corti (head of the wine and spirits department of the Corti Brothers grocery stores) subsequently told Bob Trinchero (winemaker at Sutter Home Winery in St. Helena) about the Zinfandel Myers had made from Amador County. In 1968 Trinchero bought some of the Deavers' grapes, from which he produced a monumental red wine. By '71 Sutter Home was taking the Deavers' entire Zinfandel crop, and by '75 Trinchero had abandoned all other grape varietals, making Sutter Home an exclusively Zinfandel-producing winery.

1968—a warm, early vintage—was also the year that Ridge made its Zinfandel Essence from late-harvest grapes near Lodi. That same fall an ex-stockbroker named Bob Travers, who was crushing his first vintage at Mayacamas Vineyards in the mountains between Napa and Sonoma, found himself in the classic dilemma: His Zinfandel was fully ripe, but his fermentors were full of Chardonnay, Cabernet, and Chenin Blanc. By the time he pressed the other wines and picked the Zinfandel, it was nearing thirty degrees Brix; by the time the wine was dry—two months later—it was 17 percent alcohol. Certain well-known Napa Valley winemakers suggested running a water hose into the tank, but Travers—an exponent of the New Wave—instead printed a label disclosing the accurate alcohol content and calling the wine Late-Harvest Zinfandel. It was rejected by the BATF on the grounds that only wines fortified by spirits could exceed 14 percent alcohol; there seemed to exist a general belief that unfortified wine was incapable of reaching 17 percent since the alcohol would presumably kill the yeast before it got that high. Once again, however, the maverick Zinfandel appeared to constitute an exception: Not only would it ferment to dryness with high alcohol, but it would even retain its famous briary fruit. Not sweet like port, but tremendously tannic, concentrated, and flavorful, the Mayacamas Zinfandel was unlike anything anyone had ever tasted. The director of the San Francisco Wine Institute, Julius Jacobs, found it so fascinating that he personally prevailed upon the BATF to permit its sale. Upon release the '68 Mayacamas created a sensation, ushering in that infamous period of California winemaking known as the era of late-harvest Zinfandel.

Today late-harvest Zinfandel occupies a place similar to that of Nazism in Germany: Few survivors of the era like to acknowledge that they ever condoned such atrocities, much less had a hand in them. The standard contemporary rationale for the wine's past popularity is that new converts to wine—of which there were many in the seventies (and of which the Young Gentlemen stand proudly as examples, albeit ten years later)—need to have their palates assaulted. Doug Nalle had described lovers of late-harvest Zinfandel to me as "scotch drinkers who'd been going to the hungri i, been to Europe once, and heard wine was cool. They liked the burn they got from late-harvest

Zinfandel; after all, it isn't unlike whiskey in a wine package." The enthusiasm was tied up with the emergence of California's fine-wine industry and with Zinfandel's central place in it as the state's "native" varietal; the grape's apparent willingness to ripen forever made it a seemingly ideal vehicle for expressing the bounty of the land and climate. If this was to be our grape, by God, then not only were we going to get everything out of it that it was capable of giving, but we were going to do things with it that nobody had done with grapes before.

A contest atmosphere took over, with winemakers vying to produce the biggest, most alcoholic, most tannic Zinfandel on the market. The grape became the subject of the spotlight— newspaper and magazine articles appeared touting "Good Ol' Zinfandel," "The Flexible Zinfandel," "California's Unique Treasure—Zinfandel," the "Magnificent Ubiquitous Orphan," Zinfandel. For a time the price of Zinfandel exceeded even that of Cabernet Sauvignon. Amador County was the prized source of fruit, and Ridge was considered the consummate practitioner, followed closely by Mayacamas and other occasional upstarts. In 1971, in the Santa Cruz Mountains, one of the Revolution's great experimentalists—Dr. David Bruce—made five different late-harvest Zinfandels ranging in alcohol from 15 to 17½ percent, in style from dry to sweet. Farther south, the Monterey Peninsula winery summed up the unsubtle spirit of the times, tagging its gargantuan Zinfandels "Stomp" and "Big Jim."

Apart from their novelty, the ultimate expectation of these wines was that their massive structure would make them more magnificent with time; it was even hoped that they might rival Bordeaux as penultimate products for long, complex aging. Unfortunately, as the years wore on, their overripe fruit receded, and when it was gone, little but tannin and alcohol were left behind. Most of the wines contained a chemical-medicinal smell that connoisseurs didn't associate with fine wine. As Joel Peterson explains: "What makes port pleasant to drink is that it's sweet and not very tannic. Late-harvest Zinfandel is not that sweet, and very tannic. Once the fruit structure fell apart, the other components fought with each other; the wines tasted cloying, hot, and fuzzy. People had no idea what to serve them with because they didn't qualify either as dessert wine or as table wine. Retailers couldn't be clear with customers about what they were, and after a while they found that they couldn't sell them."

As Paul Draper more succinctly put it, "A guy in New Jersey who'd been drinking cheap Chianti might be told that he should try Zinfandel. So he took a bottle of late-harvest home and said, 'Yuck.' That killed Zinfandel." Indeed, as one wine writer described it at the time, people who expected to spend their retirement drinking transcendent old Zinfandels ended up feeling like the victims of a Florida land fraud. In the course of a mere half dozen years the wine style that created a Zinfandel cult ended up besmirching the name of the varietal; by the end of the seventies, largely because of its schizoid unpredictability, Zinfandel had become *vinifera no grata*: The price of the grape fell back to $150 per ton and growers all over California raced to uproot the oldest vines in the state, replacing them with Cabernet and Chardonnay. Between 1978 and 1983 five thousand acres of Zinfandel disappeared. As white wine began to dominate the marketplace, scores of producers—among them Robert Mondavi and Rutherford Hill—abandoned Zinfandel altogether. Amador County and Mayacamas vineyards, so recently lauded for exciting interest in California's native grape, now were charged with having murdered it.

"California's unique treasure" was on the verge of oblivion. Then, like an anemic foundling rushing in to snatch a wounded knight from the jaws of disaster, salvation appeared on a pale pink horse coming over the horizon. Galloping out of the Central Valley, it soon overran the coast and foothills and all points between, not to mention wine shops and supermarkets across the United States. Amazingly, by the end of the decade this unexpected liberator was to retransform Zinfandel into nothing less than the nation's most popular varietal wine; growers would receive more money for it than they ever had before. Having recognized the error of their ways, they would again endeavor to foster rather than uproot the orphan, which, in the unrelenting face of Cabernet and Chardonnay colonization, would manage to retain its place as California's most widely planted wine grape.

There was only one problem with this saga among the varietal's most devoted followers. They considered the rescuer—white Zinfandel—the villain rather than the hero.

In the early 1980s white Zinfandel was anything but a new idea. Throughout history, blanc de noir wines have been made by separating (i.e., pressing) the juice from black grape skins as soon as the fruit is crushed. The poetic French term for such wines made from Pinot Noir is *oeil de perdrix* because the pale pink color of the wine is said to be like that in the eye of a partridge. (No more or less rarefied a vintner than August Sebastiani had already marketed an Eye of the Swan blush wine in the United States.) In 1888 the California horticulturist George Husmann had written: "There are many locations within this state where [Zinfandel] has been planted, and will not make a first class red wine, where it could be utilized better for white wine"; four years before that the state viticultural commissioner Charles Wetmore had said in a twenty-two-page ampelography that Zinfandel "should be classed as a white wine grape of importance." David Bruce made a white Zinfandel in 1968, and in 1970 Dave Bennion, lacking the tank space to ferment Zinfandel on its skins, did the same at Ridge. In 1972—again at the suggestion of Darrell Corti—Bob Trinchero also produced a white Zinfandel at Sutter Home.

Like Ridge's, the first Sutter Home white Zinfandel was dry, austere, and aged in oak: Zinfandel rendered in the manner of fine Chardonnay. The difference between Bennion and Trinchero was that Trinchero was disturbed when he couldn't sell it. He posited—probably correctly—that people who wanted a Chardonnay-like wine would simply buy Chardonnay instead. Over the course of the next few years Trinchero tinkered with different styles of white Zinfandel: picking the grapes earlier for less color and alcohol; adding filtered grape juice for sweetness; dispensing altogether with oak. As it turned out, the version that did best in his tasting room on Highway 29 in St. Helena was something akin to fermented soda pop: slightly pink, simple and fruity, refreshing on a hot Napa Valley day. Such wine can be bottled and sold quite cheaply within a couple of months of harvest, offering a compelling cash flow incentive if it takes hold in the marketplace. And in the eighties, "take hold" was a mild description of what white Zinfandel did.

In 1980, after building a commercial base for the wine in the late seventies, Bob Trinchero sold 25,000 cases of white Zinfandel. After that his winery began doubling or tripling its production every year. In 1981 the sales rose to 75,000 cases; in 1984, 500,000; in 1985, 1.5 million; in 1987, 2.5 million. By that time sales of varietal wines had outstripped those of jug products for the first time in American history, with white Zinfandel taking by far the largest share (28 percent).* To meet the suddenly burgeoning demand, Trinchero bought an old egg ranch on Zinfandel Lane in St. Helena (across Highway 29 from Ravenswood's Dickerson vineyard) and proceeded to install a series of "largests"—the largest storage tank in Napa Valley, the largest fermentor in Napa Valley, and the largest high-pressure leaf filter in Napa Valley—as well as the fastest bottling line in Napa Valley, capable of turning out 24,000 cases of wine per day. In fact, Sutter Home, which until the mid-seventies had been one of Napa Valley's smallest family-owned wineries, had, in the course of a decade, become the largest winery in Napa Valley. If one applies the standard of cork-finished bottles to the definition, it was now the largest "premium" winery in the United States.

As with the late-harvest era, the explanation for the white Zinfandel craze appears to be sociological. If, in the seventies, late-harvest Zins had won their converts from the jaded ranks

*Chardonnay accounted for 18 percent; Cabernet Sauvignon, 14 percent.

of whiskey drinkers, white Zinfandel appealed to an infinitely vaster class. One dislikes resorting to such terms as *baby boom* or *yuppie*, but the undeniable fact of the matter is that in the early eighties the number of Americans coming of wine-buying age after having had their palates trained throughout their lives by soft drinks amounted to countless multitudes. The ideal introductory wine for them was something inexpensive, slightly sweet, and not very complex or intimidating. Sutter Home was the winery with the right product at the right time.

Of course, to adherents of old-fashioned Zinfandel, this represented a mixed blessing, if not an outright curse. To call white Zinfandel a premium varietal wine was almost like saying the same thing of a corked bottle of 7-Up. In describing how he'd decided to build his 135,000-gallon fermentation tank, Trinchero himself had shed light on an especially obnoxious by-product of the white Zinfandel craze. "A customer came to buy three bottles of Zinfandel," Trinchero told a reporter. "I pushed them across the counter and she pushed them back. 'Zinfandel isn't a red wine,' she said. 'It's white.' That's when I knew I'd better go to my bankers for money to build that big tank."

Though aggravated by this sort of story, the anathema inspired by white Zinfandel among old-time loyalists wasn't solely aesthetic. By 1987 Sutter Home was processing fully one-third of the Zinfandel grapes in California; on top of that, 120 other wineries—among them Beringer, Robert Mondavi, Sebastiani, and Charles Krug—were annually churning out more than five million cases of white Zinfandel. The fact that so many of the state's available grapes were now going into cheap pink wine put the small Zinfandel artisans—for example, Joel Peterson, who was trying to increase production at Ravenswood—in a bind for fruit. Grapes for white Zinfandel can be harvested as low as sixteen degrees Brix, meaning that growers can dispense with ripeness and hang a very heavy crop, which brings them more money at harvest. For the most part, growers willing to limit their production for the sake of fine wine were those rare ones who owned their vineyards outright, loved Zinfandel, and, like the artisan winemakers themselves, considered it a travesty to sacrifice their splendid fruit to an insipid beverage. In the face of white Zinfandel's cash flow machine, locating such arcane individualists now became an important part of a fine vintner's craft.

Yet even for old-fashioned Zinfandel adherents, there was a positive side to the story. Before the advent of the hysteria, a thousand acres of Zinfandel vines had been coming out of the ground each year. Now, with the varietal suddenly in demand, its price began rising sharply. In 1987, when I accompanied Joel Peterson on his rounds of North Coast vineyards, Zinfandel was approaching the unprecedented cost of eight hundred dollars per ton.* Even in the Central Valley, where the price was hundreds of dollars lower, growers had stopped ripping Zinfandel out or grafting it over to other varietals; indeed, other varietals were now being grafted over to Zinfandel. Since a large part of the reason for white Zinfandel's popularity was its price, mass and marginal producers (with the apparent exceptions of Ernest and Julio Gallo) passed on the expensive North Coast grapes, essentially leaving the premium fruit to the best winemakers, who, freed from the task of competing with inferior red wine producers, began to be able to price their wines more in accordance with their quality. In this roundabout way, white Zinfandel not only saved the varietal from oblivion (while introducing its name, albeit illegitimately, to legions of brand-new wine drinkers) but even contributed to an overall improvement in the quality of red Zinfandel on the market. *Quelle ironie!*

Throughout the boom-bust-boom times of late-harvest and white Zinfandel, Amador County abandoned its status as a backwater of California viticulture. Wineries sprouted up like wildflowers in Shenandoah Valley: Where the county had contained only one commercial winery in 1970, by 1986 there were eighteen. In 1987 a claret-style bottle with the word *Amador* embossed on the shoulder began to be offered by several wineries,

*As of this writing, it has gone to a thousand dollars.

signifying the intense regional identification that attached itself to Amador County winemakers. In 1988, my Zinfandel fetish solidly entrenched, I revisited Amador County.

On the way, I stopped in Sacramento to see Darrell Corti, the merchant who, twenty years earlier, had touched off the Amador winemaking revival. Corti's reputation preceded him; he was considered one of California's, if not the world's, most knowledgeable experts on food and wine. He had taught himself French at age seven, was cooking meals for his mother at ten, and now spoke half a dozen languages, which apparently came in handy on his annual buying trips to Europe, where his connections enabled him to procure wines that no other American retailers could. The *Wine Spectator* had called Corti "a scholar-merchant in the British tradition, willing to set aside purely mercantile interests in pursuit of an idea that interests him." It also wrote that he was known "for his erudition and his willingness to display it"—he was considered pedantic and opinionated, sometimes arrogant and even rude, especially with regard to California wine. One vintner had described Corti to me as "one of those people who don't like anything but know everything there is to know about it."

I parked my car in front of the "Cort-yard," a link in the gourmet grocery chain build by Corti's father and uncle in 1947. In the middle of the store a staircase descended into "The Cellar," where a kind of wine museum was located. Next to a tasting bar with a sign listing the "Elements of Wine Tasting" were several glass display cases full of prints, pamphlets, decanters, and old magazine ads:

CALIFORNIA WINE HELPS YOU LIVE BETTER

WINE CHANGES WAR DISHES INTO "FOOD FOR KINGS"

CHARMING MRS. EDGAR RICE BURROUGHS,
WIFE OF THE FAMOUS WRITER, CREATOR OF TARZAN,
SAYS, "I FIND SO MANY OF MY GUESTS
NOW CHOOSE WINE"

Among the Pomerols, St-Émilons, Haut-Brions, Pauillacs, and single-malt scotches in the wine shop, a slight man with horn-rimmed glasses and short, graying hair paced back and forth quickly in a blue lab coat. I asked if his name was Darrell. "Yes."

I introduced myself and said, "Quite a place you've got here."

"Oh," Corti said. "It's a place. Come. Sit you down."

He led me into his glassed office, whose book-laden shelves also contained old caviar tins and ancient, empty bottles of Redwood Empire Burgundy, Napa Chianti by Louis Martini, and a 1906 "California Zinfandel." Adorning the salmon-colored walls were the first contracts for fair trade ever signed by Ridge, Swan, Caymus, Schramsberg, and Chateau Montelena, plus a Chez Panisse menu for the " 'This Ain't No Spring Chicken' [Fortieth] Birthday Dinner for Darrell Corti—April 3, 1979."

Corti sat down behind an enormous desk. In addition to his lab coat, he was wearing a necktie, a purple wristwatch, and tasseled loafers with red socks. "So you were the person who originally connected Sutter Home with Amador County?" I asked.

"Yes!"

"Would you tell me how that came about?"

"Yes!"

Corti placed his fingertips together in front of his nose. "In the mid-sixties Charlie Myers was making wine from Amador County that was very interesting," he said. "Sutter Home had been making our Tosca brand wine for us, and Bob Trinchero had complained that grapes were becoming too expensive. He was paying four hundred dollars a ton for Cabernet in Napa Valley.* At the time I was making wine for one of my grandfathers; both of them had always made Zinfandel from Amador County, and I'd helped them bottle the '55, '57, and '62 vintages. This past Christmas we opened the '62, and it was better than

*It now costs fifteen hundred dollars a ton.

193

two bottles of claret that we had. Amador County grapes were considered very hot by home winemakers."

"Hot?"

"Popular," said Corti.

Thinking he'd meant ripe and alcoholic, I asked if they might not be considered hot in another way as well. Corti stared at me for a second.

"My God!" he exclaimed. "We have a reporter who wants to be a literary savant!" He threw his head back and went on. "At that time Amador County grapes only cost a hundred and fifty dollars a ton. So I asked Bob, 'What if I could show you some more interesting grapes?' In 1968 we drove up to Plymouth for a picnic and met Ken Deaver. He brought some of his '68 grapes down to Sutter Home that fall; they were about twenty-eight Balling [Brix], and the wine Bob made from it was over fifteen percent alcohol. I selected one lot from that, put it in French oak, and bottled two hundred cases as the Corti Brothers Reserve Selection. I continued to do that every year until 1974. When Hugh Johnson published his first *World Wine Atlas*, I took a magnum of the '69 to a party for him at the home of some mutual friends; it made such a hit with Hugh that he told the Wine Institute it was the finest California wine he'd ever tasted. They said, 'Which Cabernet Sauvignon?' and he said, 'It was Zinfandel.'

"Amador County had never been seen on a wine label before 1968," Corti went on. "The tradition there was to grow filler grapes for Gallo. They needed a fair amount of flavor and color; the grapes were picked after deer season in October, so they were pretty ripe. The home winemakers were Italian or Yugoslavian; they wanted ripe grapes, too. Why did they want ripe grapes? To make strong wines. Why did they want strong wines? Because they would keep. Delicate wine was never the strong suit of Amador County. The first wines made there were exceedingly powerful; they were *massive*, with very high alcohol. Before that Zinfandel had been made in the claret style from the North Coast—it was blended with Petite Sirah and Carignane, which tends to attenuate its overripe qualities. But in the sixties people newly interested in wine wanted to be overwhelmed with flavor. The early Amador Zinfandels were too intense; we thought they would live forever, like an Egyptian pharaoh. They didn't. But we still get these Neanderthals who *must* have late-harvest Zinfandels.

"We had a term in the wine trade back then," Corti said. " 'Santa Cruz Mountain Crude.' Ridge, Martin Ray, and David Bruce were trying to make wines with all the flavor possible. That's not always a good idea. David Bruce once had a tasting from twenty-two different casks; each was bottled individually, and each was more disgusting than the next. Back then anything different was deemed good; we made virtues of faults. We wanted to be pure, so we left our wines to nature. We didn't do anything to them—there was no rational control of malolactic fermentation or sulfur dioxide, and we made the customer swallow wines that were defective. We all have a lot of sins to pay for. Ridge made some incredibly poor wines. They'd *grow* things in them! They had casses and hazes of every imaginable sort! See that bottle standing up over there? It's a Ridge '67. It's refermenting. Come."

Corti led me out of the office and into his reserve cage. The cork on the wine he'd pointed out—a '76 Ridge, actually, whose label said, "1% residual sugar"—was protruding from the bottle neck, apparently forced out by carbon dioxide, created by refermentation of the unstable wine. "See this?" Corti said, warming sufficiently to the subject to abandon momentarily his excoriation of California. He was pointing to a 1959 Wehlener Sonnenuhr Beerenauslese. "It's one of the most famous wines of Germany. You'd expect it to be stable. Well, I came in here one day and there was a dark spot all over the floor. I said, 'What the fuck is happening?' I looked over there and saw some spots in the dust on those bottles. Then I looked down here and found the cork where it had blown out of the bottle."

The telephone rang, and we returned to Corti's office so that he could answer it. "Yes," he said into the phone. "It's still available." He began cleaning his fingernails with a letter opener. "I go to France on business," he said. "I go to Italy on business and pleasure."

After listening silently for another minute, he said, "Excellent. Ah, splendid. Wonderful," and hung up. A moment later a man holding a couple of wine bottles tentatively appeared in the doorway. "I wanted to leave you some samples," he said to Corti, who nodded curtly and said to leave them by the door.

"Probably the worst winery in Amador County," Corti said after the man had departed. "Actually I like to call it Amateur County. After all, who's to say that Zinfandel is the best variety for that region? Frankly, the Barberas have been more interesting. The best aging wine in Amador County right now is the Monteviña Montenaro; it's a combination of overripe Zinfandel and Barbera that didn't go through malolactic. I named it; it means 'mountain man.' I also created the name Monteviña, and of their Zinfandel Nuevo, which was the second or third carbonic-masturbation wine made in California. The first was Cuvaison. Monteviña made the first white Zinfandel from Amador County, in 1973. The grapes were picked early, so it really was white. The first Sutter Home 'white Zinfandel' was orange-red and made from Mission grapes—it was the only way Bob could get rid of them. The rest is history. Now we have these benighted assholes selling 'red Zinfandel.' My God, are we still preaching to the unconverted?

"It's unfortunate that we're a wine-producing country with only two wines," Corti said, with regard to the recent premium market. "Zinfandel is more characteristic of California than Cabernet is for red wine, just as Sauvignon Blanc is more characteristic of California than Chardonnay is for white. By 'characteristic,' I mean earthy, ripe, and aromatic. Zinfandel is very aromatic and pleasant; it has an aroma and spiciness all its own. But people are still trying to make wines from it that are more than the grape allows. And it's still less popular than it was twenty years ago. It's going to have to make new customers or win the old ones back. You know, the first Zinfandels in

California were called claret. But claret tends to be low in alcohol, with fairly high acidity. California Zinfandel now is more like a Rhône wine, less like a claret. I don't like many Zinfandels, quite frankly. Nalle. Rosenblum. Some Monteviñas. I have yet to taste a Ravenswood that excites me. They are sometimes *excruciatingly* tannic. For that matter, I don't much like the '84 Ridge Monte Bello either—especially for the price. Let's just say that some wines are laudable, while others are merely laudatory."

"What?"

"Some wines are praiseworthy," Corti said. "Others are merely praised."

After taking leave of Corti, I drove another hour east to Fiddletown, a tiny hamlet at twenty-five hundred feet in the foothills of the Sierra Nevada, where dogs are commonly found sleeping in the middle of Main Street. After I arrived, Bill Easton and I got into his car, a gold 1965 Buick, and drove the back roads into Shenandoah Valley, passing by the fifty-acre Eschen vineyard, from which the Ridge Fiddletown Zinfandel had come. As we rode, Bill—dressed in a straw cowboy hat and sheepskin vest—enumerated the components of the Amador appellation: its red volcanic decomposed-granite "Sierra series" soil—unique to the state—and its situation between the San Joaquin/Sacramento River delta (which contributes warm westerly winds early in the day) and the high Sierra (from which cool alpine breezes are sucked during the late afternoon and evening). Apparently, this position produces grapes that are uniquely high in both sugar and acid. Bill's evaluation of Zinfandel tastography paralleled Joel Peterson's: "In Sonoma it translates into raspberry," he said. "In Napa it's briary, less varietally distinct. Amador Zinfandel is more earthy—sort of big-bottom tobaccolike."

We parked the car at the Santino Winery, then walked across

the road to prune some vines. I toss this off rather casually, but the fact of the matter was that we were about to lay shears on the oldest Zinfandel vines in the state—and therefore, in all likelihood, the world. This was the ten-acre Grand Père vineyard, planted circa 1867 and recently purchased by Scott Harvey, the winemaker at Santino, who would soon be moving into a small house on the property.

The vines, like all old Zinfandel vines, were head-trained. They stood before us like rows of tiny, phantasmagorical trees—van Gogh could have had a field day with their twisted shapes in the sun. Some of the rows had already been pruned, and their lean, austere arms contrasted sharply with the dense tangles of spurs that trailed from the unpruned trunks, drawing a clear line of demarcation between the wild impulses of nature and the civilizing influence we were about to impose.

"Keep the vine open in the center," Bill said as we set to work. "You want the branches to form a bowl in the middle." Each vine had more or less six branches, which we cut to leave one cane per branch, two buds per cane. This would confer a low crop come summer, intended to conserve the energy of the vine and concentrate the flavors of the grapes. The ancient, brittle branches were covered by mosses and lichens, and the gnarled trunks shook as we clipped and cut them; they felt as if we might pull them right out of the earth, though their roots probably extended underground for some twenty feet.

"It's hard to hurt these old vines," Bill said, leaning into one with his shears, instructing me in the excision of knotlike little clusters of canes called budwells: Dig your blades into the base of the knot, give the shears a sharp twist, and the unwanted ball of wood pops out onto the ground. Very satisfying, Bill agreed—"like picking a scab."

After a while Harvey's wife, daughters, and father-in-law came walking along. In passing, they directed us to leave not two but three buds per cane. After they'd departed, Bill explained that Harvey's family was pushing for a bigger cash crop. Here it was in a nutshell, I thought: In France, controlled appellation wines must come from a crop that is limited by law, but no such rules exist in production-happy California. The Zinfandel vineyard where we stood was practically deserving of designation as a state historical landmark, but even it remained vulnerable to the economic pressures of grape growing (i.e., agriculture), which, in affecting families first and foremost, unceasingly exerted an insidious campaign for a less distinctive product.

After a while we knocked off and went up an adjacent hill to Shenandoah Vineyards, the largest and best known of Amador County's newer wineries. As soon as we entered the tasting room, we encountered the owner and winemaker, Leon Sobon—a slightly nervous, wound-up guy with a graying beard and thick eyeglasses, who was dressed in blue jeans and a plaid wool shirt. With his wife and six children, Sobon had moved to Shenandoah Valley in 1977 from Los Altos, where he'd been working as an engineer for Lockheed; he'd begun by making wine in the big, old-fashioned style, and then, to meet his winery's financial demands, hitched a ride on the white Zinfandel bandwagon (though that wasn't how he described it). Lately, however, his more refined version of red Zinfandel had been going through the roof—he said that it had been doubling in production for each of the last five years.

The '87 was being racked as we spoke. Sobon dipped a glass into it, swirled, sniffed, and offered it to us: a fruity, pleasant, medium-bodied, not very tannic claret—certainly nothing like the powerhouse Amador Zins of the past. "The old Amador County style has gone out the window," Sobon acknowledged (adding that his first vintage—the '77—still wasn't ready to drink). He explained that he now fermented his wine cooler and kept the skin time shorter to preserve the fruit and leave out the tannin. "We think we're getting it now to where it ought to be," he said. "People really seem to like this wine; it's very drinkable."

I mentioned the standard prejudice against Amador County Zinfandel—namely, that the warm weather tends to produce a pruny wine. Sobon termed this "a fallacy. We pick the grapes at twenty-two-point-five. They're not overripe. They're mature, and they make very well-balanced wine. The climate here is Region Three, on a par with Calistoga and Healdsburg. We don't get the peak highs that they get in the afternoon, but we don't get their morning fog, either, so our temperatures tend to be warmer early in the day."

"I seem to remember having to vacate my cottage in Jackson every day during summer between two and ten P.M.," I said.

"It doesn't get as hot here as it gets in Jackson," said Sobon.

Bill and I went back down to Santino. When we found Scott Harvey, he was talking on the telephone in German. Though he had grown up mainly in neighboring El Dorado County, Harvey was born in Germany and studied winemaking in the Rhineland Pfalz, a circumstance directly connected to the fact that he makes outstanding sweet white wines. Sitting in his laboratory, Harvey seemed Sobon's opposite: sandy-haired, mustachioed, younger, plumper—and more relaxed.

"Leon has a problem I don't have," Harvey acknowledged when we told him about our visit with Sobon. "Santino is paid for. But Leon had to finance his whole winery; I've got to give it to him for that. You know the old saying 'We will sell no wine before its time—and the banker says it's time.' "

When we mentioned the pruning instructions we'd been given by his family, Harvey said that usually, later in the winter, a frost would kill the third bud anyway; if it didn't, he might sneak back into the vineyard at night and do some secret pruning. "I think the same person should prune the same vineyard every year," he added. "And he should talk to the vine. That way the vine gets to know the person, and vice versa."

The sun was setting, so we locked up the winery, picked up Bill's wife, Jane, in Fiddletown, and went to dinner at Teresa's, one of Amador County's rare decent dining establishments, located outside the town of Jackson on a narrow lane lined with Italian restaurants. I still have the cork from a wine drunk at Teresa's in 1977 in celebration of something or other; my companion and I had lacked the funds for a full dinner, so Teresa herself arranged a couple of half portions, which still offered enough food for a football team. ("It doesn't matter how hungry you are when you enter Teresa's," wine writer and retailer Stanley Hock once wrote. "After huge portions of antipasto, minestrone soup, and salad, you greet your entrée with an odd mixture of awe and fear.")

Harvey had brought along a bottle of Zinfandel from the Grand Père vineyard, which offered a solid accompaniment to the foothill-Italian cuisine. "The flavors of Amador County wines marry well with our food," Harvey said. "I think there's a spot for them on the dinner table alongside things like venison or leg of lamb. Basically, it's a Rhône style. It's more European than most wine in California; like Burgundy or Chianti, Amador has one red wine: Zinfandel. There are two other appellations known for Zinfandel—Dry Creek and Paso Robles—but if you want Zinfandel that tastes like this, the only place you're going to get it is right here. We're the first *appellation contrôlée* in the United States; we require that 'Amador' wines be made from ninety-five percent Amador grapes, and we have a tasting panel to make sure that the wines meet a certain level of quality."

It seemed an appropriate time to raise Darrell Corti's question: "Who's to say that Zinfandel is the best grape for Amador County?"

"That's why we're experimenting with Rhône varieties," said Bill. "It's an attempt to find the best product for the region."

"That's going to be a thirty-year project," said Harvey. "It'll be ten years before we get a decent crop; another ten for the potential of the vines to show; then another ten for the wines to age enough to realize their potential. Any region has negative qualities that have to be worked out; I think the task of a winemaker is to figure out the problems of an area, then harvest the grapes and make the wine so as to maximize the positive qualities and minimize the negative ones. The French have been there for hundreds of years, but Mother Nature plays hell with their vintages, so they seldom get perfect conditions."

The check came, and Bill and Scott both lunged for it; fearing injury, I maintained a discreet distance. As we drove back to Fiddletown in the dark, Harvey said, "Eventually my finest wine won't be named after a grape; it will be called Amador. I want to be the guy who made Amador County work. It's really exciting to be in a region where you're in on the ground floor."

Bill noted that regional winemaking chauvinism was sprouting up all over: in Santa Barbara, in Oregon, in Virginia, on Long Island, even in Texas, for God's sake. Shifting into his other favorite mode, he posited that this trend toward regional diversity was "connected to the idea from radical biology that a diverse system is a healthy one." He also noted that "politically, Amador County isn't in the mainstream of California winemaking." Not only is it not near the coast, but it grows neither of the industry's prestige grapes, Cabernet and Chardonnay. This made me realize that Amador County was well suited to Bill's maverick self-image and that, as with most new waves—for example, the one that had spawned Ridge thirty years earlier—the concerns of Amador County winemakers were radical indeed in their traditionalism. While most contemporary California vintners exhibit a clear tendency toward hubris, each striving to make "the best wine in the world"—in context of, perhaps, but not particularly subordinate to the locations of their wineries—the overriding aim of Amador winemakers seemed to be a regional character with which they could both proudly and humbly identify. Historically this was no more innovative than the age-old European ideal, but in contratraditional California—the distilled essence, as it were, of New World civilization—it carried the weight of a revolutionary credo. Bill had been right to identify it with grass-roots bioregionalism, as it aptly expressed one motto of that movement—"Think Globally, Act Locally"—in the realm where culture and geography cross over: wine.

Soon after returning from Amador County, I went to the Sutter Home Winery to talk to Bob Trinchero. I drove up Highway 29 on a stormy winter day as low white clouds drifted through Napa Valley, intermittently obscuring the ridges of the Vaca and Mayacamas mountains. Amid the yellow mustard growing in the vineyards, enormous Victorian houses stood in their inimitably abrupt, haughty, solitary Napa Valley way. One such immaculate structure, though not quite so solitary (it fronted on Highway 29 in St. Helena, directly across the street from the Louis Martini winery), was the Sutter Home headquarters—a green-and-white gingerbread Victorian with a white fence protecting the date palms and orange trees that grew in its front yard.

I pulled into the parking lot alongside a BMW whose owners were just coming out of the building clutching a couple of bottles of Sutter Home White Zinfandel, and went into the tasting room, whose walls exhibited souvenir T-shirts saying, "Life is hell without Zinfandel" and "If you don't squeeze me I will be crushed." When I presented myself to one of the clerks, she phoned next door. Then she said, "Bob's expecting you at the big house."

The receptionist at the big house was recommending a hot-air balloon company to somebody over the telephone. She directed me upstairs to Trinchero's office, decorated with statues and classicalesque paintings on its beige walls. Trinchero himself wore a beige sweater, and he came around his desk to greet me. He also wore a gold neck chain and gold wire-rimmed aviator eyeglasses. He was in possession of a respectable paunch and a receding head of hair, which he combed straight back from his forehead. Somehow, his soft face and dark, shining eyes still gave him a little-boy quality. When I told him that this was the first place I'd visited that didn't have a car with a clever license plate out in front, he admitted that his car—which wasn't out in front—actually said "MR ZIN"; his wife's said "MRS ZIN." "Maybe I should get 'KING ZIN,' " he laughed as we sat down.

I asked him how long the winery had been in his family. "Ever since 1947," Trinchero said. "This house was actually built in 1884, when it was the Thomann Winery and Distillery. They were making two hundred thousand gallons of wine in 1880. In 1906 it was bought and renamed by a Mr. Lewenberger, whose wife was a Sutter. Sutter Street in San Francisco was named for her brother—not the Sutter who discovered the gold. My uncle bought the winery in 1947. My dad was the last one to come over from Asti, where the family had also been in the wine business. Hail destroyed my grandfather's vineyard there twice; after he replanted it the first time, it was reduced to rubble again three years later, just when it was starting to produce a crop. I was born and raised in New York City, where my dad was in food service, and we moved here in '48, when I was twelve years old. Napa Valley was still pretty provincial then—farming, agriculture, prunes, walnuts, cattle, tomatoes.

"In 1960 Dad and I bought my uncle out. My sister was married, and my brother was ten years younger than me, so it was just me and my dad. I took over as winemaker. We had no vineyards, but we bought only Napa Valley grapes. We used to sell jug wines locally—everything from vermouth to aperitifs to sparkling wines. We made fifty-two different wines. Our unofficial motto was: 'If You Can Roll It Through the Door, We'll Fill It Up.' About the nicest thing you could say about Zinfandel then was that it was a bulk varietal; since Prohibition, it hadn't yet recovered from the Central Valley mentality.

"Back then there were two types of wine drinkers: sophisticated cork sniffers who only drank imported wines and European immigrants who drank red wine with their meals. In the sixties middle Americans discovered wine, and Napa Valley grapes started getting more expensive. We were making jug wines for Darrell Corti and his brother and uncle then. One day in the spring of 1968 we were having dinner at their house, and Darrell went into his wine cellar and poured us an Amador County Zinfandel—a big wine that Charlie Myers had made from the Deaver vineyard. Two weeks later I met the Deavers and bought twenty tons of Zinfandel from them. Our '68 Amador County Zinfandel was the best wine I'd made up to that point; it bolstered my confidence as a winemaker and marketer. The year it was released—'71—we bought all the Deavers' grapes. We still do. We make red Zin from it.

"Three blockbuster wines from that year really brought a lot of attention to Zinfandel: the '68 Ridge, the '68 Mayacamas, and the '68 Sutter Home. The thing that killed Zinfandel later in the seventies was its price. As long as the consumer had a choice between a twelve-dollar Cabernet and three Zinfandels for four dollars each, Zinfandel had a future. But if he has to choose between a twelve-dollar Zinfandel and a twelve-dollar Cabernet—no way. There's talk now of a red Zinfandel comeback, but so far it's only talk; Zinfandel won't reach its former status until we rethink quality and price.

"One thing you can say about *white* Zinfandel is that's truly a consumer-built wine. Not a penny was ever spent on advertising. The industry thought it was a flash in the pan, and wine writers thought it was a bastardization if it wasn't red or white. Our *only* positive response was from the consumer. If you want to know the secret of Sutter Home's success, it was that we had the common sense to give consumers what they wanted instead of what we thought they should buy. We made the decision to become a consumer-driven winery, which basically means keeping an open mind and asking the customer, 'Tell us if you like this wine; if you don't, we'll make it so you do.' Some people think that makes me a heretic, but I'd rather be a live heretic than a dead traditionalist. If the consumer likes a little residual sugar in his wine, why not give it to him? The cork sniffer will pour it out, but the wine drinker will say, 'Hey, that's great!'

"I've had many lively discussions with these cork sniffers," Trinchero revealed. "When they say white Zinfandel is really pink, I say, 'Why do you call Chardonnay white wine when it's really yellow? Why do you call old Cabernet red when it's really brown?' But I might as well be talking to a painting; they're not listening. They and the wine writers have such a narrow focus that they just can't accept it. Nobody has built a wall of intimidation for the wine consumer like the wine writers. It's their elitism that really bugs me—they make people think they need a Ph.D. to appreciate wine. The difference between good wine and fine wine is a fleeting moment on the palate; it takes a lot of study and tasting to understand it. You want to smell oak? Here, grab a wood chip. You don't need four hundred words of vocabulary to describe *alcoholic grape juice*. I mean, how many people hang a Rembrandt or a Picasso in their house? But there are plenty of *prints* of Rembrandts and Picassos out there. I can enjoy ballet, but not under any circumstances can I tell you if it's a good, great, or mediocre performance—and I sure wouldn't go up to the conductor afterward and say, 'Boy, you sure blew it tonight!' People who drive Rolls-Royces don't feel compelled to tell Chevy drivers that they're stupid, but wine writers go out of their way to tell people they're jerks for drinking white Zinfandel. The reason white Zinfandel sells is that it's unpretentious. Americans eat pot roast, fried chicken, and hamburgers; they don't want to talk about wine at dinner. They just want to enjoy themselves and have fun. Look at the way beer is marketed: The people *always* look like they're having fun. When was the last time you saw a wine commercial that looked like the people were having fun? Until we decide to market wine the way other things in America are marketed, it won't make any inroads as a common beverage."

I asked him about the charge that grapes for red Zinfandel had become scarce because of demand for white Zinfandel. Trinchero called this "one of the unfortunate side effects of saving the varietal."

"If it weren't for the 'bastard,' white Zinfandel, there wouldn't be any Zinfandel left in this state," he said. "Five years ago I was buying Zinfandel for a hundred and fifty dollars a ton. When I saw what was starting to happen with white Zinfandel, I told growers it was the wave of the future, but they wouldn't listen. If they'd planted Zinfandel back then, they'd be in Fat City now that it's selling for seven hundred dollars a ton. But plantings are always five years behind demand. You know, the American farmer is amazing: As soon as the demand for a crop exceeds the supply, he kills the goose that laid the golden egg by raising his prices to an unreasonable level. There isn't much room for the price of white Zinfandel to rise beyond three dollars and ninety-nine cents a bottle, so our solution has been to go into the vineyard business. We recently bought six hundred and fifty acres of mixed red varieties in the Sacramento Valley and leased another seven hundred and fifty acres near Lodi, which we grafted over to Zinfandel—the largest grafting to one varietal in the history of the state. North of Sacramento, we're planting another twelve hundred acres to a clone selection from Davis that was developed exclusively for white Zinfandel. It has less color, less sugar, and larger production—ten to twelve tons per acre. Other big wineries are doing the same thing. Within five years we'll be growing forty percent of the grapes we crush; then the overall demand will drop, and we'll be able to tell the growers that we can't continue to pay their prices."

"Do you think the market for white Zinfandel is going to increase forever?"

"I don't know where the peak will be. This is more than a success; it's a phenomenon. There's been nothing like this before except coolers. And they got their business from the beer industry."

"What do other Napa Valley wineries think of you?"

"I don't think they know quite what to do with me," Trinchero laughed. "At first they didn't take me seriously. Now Mondavi's white Zinfandel is the best-selling seven-hundred-fifty-ml they've got, and over a fourth of Beringer's production is white Zinfandel. The growers do look at me kind of funny; now I make no Napa Valley wines, so they use me as an example of what could happen if wineries use the agricultural preserve without using the grapes. But I'm still on the appellation committee. The only families that have been here longer are the Martinis and Mondavis."

After we'd chatted awhile longer, I thanked Trincheo for his time. But as I got up to go, he suddenly launched into an unexpected diatribe.

"You know," he said, "there's no reason that Napa Valley should be better known than Sonoma. The grapes there are potentially just as good. It's just names. Make a list of the people who contributed to consumer acceptance and recognition in the industry: Martini; Mondavi; Chateau Montelena; Brother Timothy at Christian Brothers. How many wineries can you name in Sonoma Valley? They've got a chip on their shoulder about us now because we were more ambitious than they were. We did our homework. They're too fractionalized, whereas we've pulled together and become a cohesive force. At our meetings we never even discuss Sonoma Valley. Now they're pissed at us and they're trying to catch us. If we stop taking ourselves seriously, they could."

As I drove back down Highway 29, my latent image of Sutter Home revealed itself to me in the rain. It was the Sylvester Stallone among wineries: Both had started out as moderately serious, inconsequential Italo-American bit players; then— through sheer force of ambition and the savvy to appeal to the consumer—had become the eighties' box-office champs. The tastefulness of both might be roundly reviled, but no matter how uncouth they might seem, their popularity—and therefore their power—were beyond argument. To judge by Trinchero's unsolicited outbursts against such minor threats to his success as wine writers and Sonoma Valley, his power apparently mattered little in his desire for respect; yet his definition of success remained doggedly and entirely economic. Under such circumstances, it seemed inevitable that no matter how rich Napa Valley, Sutter Home, and Bob Trinchero might grow, the old jug producer would go to his grave in the grip of an inferiority complex. In his heart of hearts Napa Valley would forever be a struggling postwar agricultural region, and no matter what trends might come and go, Zinfandel would always be a bulk varietal from the Central Valley.

One rainy winter morning I arrived at Ravenswood to find the office freshly painted. The furniture had been rearranged, and about four tons of newspaper had disappeared to the dump. Where the cat-hair-infested couch had been, there was now a desk. At the desk was Ravenswood's new office manager, a pleasant, organized woman named Lynn.

Thijs Van Stigt was sitting in the office with his leg in a cast. He explained that recently he had woken up during the night and, discovering that his furnace was on fire, jumped out of bed and broken his foot. A few minutes later John Kemble, hoarse and sick with a cold, returned from the warehouse where he'd gone to get samples of 1986 wines. At eleven-fifteen, Joel walked in, wearing jeans, a ski sweater, and L. L. Bean duck-hunting shoes. He had just arrived from Lake Tahoe, where he was not shooting ducks but sliding down mountains in the company of his family. "It was Winter Wonderland up there," he reported. "Fresh powder, clear and sunny." Nonetheless, he had just driven three hours for a meeting that was about to take place.

For the next forty-five minutes everybody waited. John and Thijs commenced playing Dark Castle on the office Macintosh. The discussion turned to other computer games that simulate flight around San Francisco Bay; there was disagreement on the name of the one that allows you to crash into the Transamerica Pyramid.

After about half an hour Lynn called a local hotel. "He's on his way to Los Angeles?" she said. Joel rolled his eyes. "If this guy doesn't show up," he said, "my wife is going to kill me."

At five past noon I looked up and saw Ravenswood's CEO, Reed Foster, standing in the office, a canvas Patagonia shirt and a tie under his tweed sport jacket. Then I noticed two other men standing beside him. Both were bulky, and both were wearing trench coats; they might have been FBI agents or pro football players in street clothes. One—large, lumbering, bearded, booted—appeared to be a defensive tackle but turned out to be Jim Arsenault, manager of Macarthur Liquors in Washington, D.C., and progenitor of the California wine futures market. The other—broad nose, heavy brow, gap between his two front teeth, and a score of tiny embroidered wineglasses on his necktie—was not Jim Plunkett of the Oakland Raiders but Robert M. Parker, Jr., editor of *The Wine Advocate.*

"It's good to finally meet you," Parker said to Joel in a slightly high-pitched voice that gave him a sort of schoolboy quality.

Arsenault explained that he and Parker had been visiting Napa and Sonoma wineries for the past two days, tasting wines from barrel.

"We've been very pleased by the '86s," said Parker.

"It's another of these strange vintages," said Joel. "We thought we were going to be picking early; then the grapes didn't get ripe. Then there was a heat wave, and they all came in at once. In the end the delayed picking was probably good; the grapes got more mature, and it turned out to be a nice vintage."

Parker said he had to leave by twelve-thirty to catch a three o'clock plane from San Francisco. So, accompanied by the usual rock sound track (now playing: U2), Joel, Parker, Arsenault, and Foster went through the sliding glass doors into the winery,

211

which in winter was colder than the office by twenty degrees.

Innovations were unceasing. A wooden rack, screwed into the ceiling, had replaced Ravenswood's toilet tank as a wineglass holder. Joel distributed glasses; Parker asked for a spittoon. Apologizing, Joel fetched a white plastic bucket. "That's okay," said Parker. "I've seen the best and the worst."

Joel poured the '86 Sonoma County Zinfandel, explaining that it was a blend of three different vineyards: Dry Creek, Lyeth, and Cloverdale. Parker ran the wine through his teeth. "My God," he said.

Arsenault took one sniff and walked away, shaking his head and laughing.

"This is a gorgeous wine," said Parker.

"Every year it keeps its character," said Joel. "It's our most archetypal Zinfandel. Dickerson and Old Hill are the extremes at either end."

"Another kickass vintage from Ravenswood," said Arsenault, regaining his composure and rejoining the group.

"That is a great wine," said Parker.

Next Joel poured the Dickerson. Sucking and chewing at the wine, Parker's mouth seemed a device conveying information to his brain.

"Yummy!" it reported. "There's an explosiveness to your wines, but the balance is always there."

"Does this get new oak?" asked Arsenault.

"About thirty percent," said Joel. "We'll give it the final dose next month. The amount depends on the year and the structure of the individual wine. The cedar aspects of the Dickerson tend to interact with the oak and make it more pronounced."

"I think these are as good as your '85s," said Parker.

"They have a broader spectrum," said Joel. "They have more fruit than the '85s."

"The tannins might be a little tougher."

"That's because we haven't finished them yet. Toward the end we'll throw in some egg whites to soften them up."

Next came the Old Hill, the usual astounding agglomeration of deep dark fruit and mentholated spice.

"I think these are world-class wines," Parker said. "I hope you don't mind, but I'm serving a tasting soon at the Revue du Vin de France, and I'm putting two of your Zinfandels in with the Cabernets. Over there they usually see only the big producers, not the artisan wines."

"One of our '76s was taken to a tasting in France once," said Joel. "Somebody said it was like a beautiful woman with too much makeup. But it was the first wine to disappear from the table."

"Zinfandel has been maligned," said Parker. "It's fallen in and out of favor. But I think it's a great variety. There's no better proof than right here."

"I've got a question for you," said Joel. "Would you ever give a Zinfandel a perfect hundred-point score?"

"Yeah," said Parker. "I just haven't had the guts. First there's the question of whether it's ageworthy; my scores cut off at ninety for wines that won't age past two years. Chenin Blanc, for example, will never get a perfect score."

"There are some wines that people would never give a perfect score, no matter what," said Joel. "But if it's a classic of the varietal—"

"You know," said Parker, "I've been collecting wines since the sixties, and I've got a pretty nice cellar." Somehow one had suspected this. "You'd be surprised at how often I go down there and reach for a bottle of Zinfandel. I've got old Bordeaux and Burgundies, but a lot of times they turn out to be flat or in a dumb stage. But with Zinfandel, you always get something out of it."

"What I really enjoy is when people come here and tell me they drink only white wines," said Joel. "Then they taste our Zinfandels and go crazy. It's something they've never experienced before."

"You don't plan on changing the way you make it?" asked Parker. "I can't see why you would."

"We'll never be high tech," said Joel. "I'm not antitechnology when it's used for the proper purposes. But people use it to prevent problems that may not even exist. Technology is like modern medicine; it's applied prophylactically. I say, 'If it ain't broke, don't fix it.' "

"In California you get this fabulous fruit," said Parker. "But the food-processing mentality strips it all out. Consumers are getting more sophisticated, though. They're asking for more."

"Being a small winery, we can take risks that big wineries can't," said Joel. "Since I know what's happening at every point in a wine's development, I can make whatever changes need to be made. We're at a unique point in history where we can still make wine the way they did at the turn of the century, but with our technology we can detect problems early and take care of them if they arise. Today you can correct for H-2-S [hydrogen sulfide]; you can take care of off odors and off flavors with fining and filtration. Thus far we haven't had to do a great deal of that. We've been fortunate."

Parker put his wineglass down on the barrel that served as a tasting bar. "I really have to be going," he said. "I'm a fast taster; if you don't know what you're looking for, there's no sense pondering it. It's almost inexcusable to spend so little time, but I'll be back."

A month later a special section on Ravenswood appeared in *The Wine Advocate #55*. Parker wrote that the "articulate, confident . . . handsome Peterson, dressed in high rubber boots and an army flak-jacket," was producing "California's most exciting, exotic and flavorful Zinfandels." Referring to their "bold, dramatic, complex style," he said that the Ravenswood Sonoma Zin "oozes with character," that the Dickerson was "equally awesome, yet totally different," and that the Old Hill was "a blockbuster wine with a staggering wealth of fruit and a finish that seems to last several minutes." Parker predicted that "all of Peterson's Zinfandels in both 1986 and 1987 will merit 90–95 point ratings, which is quite amazing," concluded that "Ravenswood is making some of the greatest wines in California," and advised buyers to "get your reservation in now . . . Availability is tight but these wines are worth a special effort to find."

It's always hard to know if professional praise is heartfelt when uttered face-to-face, so—aside from its potential effect on the price of Ravenswood's wines, not to mention the size of Joel's head—it was encouraging to see that Parker's enthusiasm at the winery was genuine. When compared with his written account of it, however, his visit to Ravenswood made obvious the sheer subjectivity of wine tasting, to say nothing of Parker's tendency to get carried away. I'm referring, of course, to the fact that my notes contain no reference whatsoever to an army flak jacket.

In February Joel Peterson and I had dinner at Joe Swan's house.

Since the early seventies, when he was roundly acknowledged as making the most dramatic Zinfandel in existence, Swan's fortunes had changed. Other winemakers, alerted to the excellence of Dry Creek fruit by Swan wines, began to outbid him for his grapes. Then, in the early eighties, Swan had altered his wine style in the direction of less alcohol and more "elegance" on the grounds that such wines go better with food. His Zinfandel had become softer and more approachable but seldom excited the fanfare of old. As Charles Sullivan told me, "Swan Zinfandels are still outstanding, but now many others are as good." Sullivan theorized that when a winemaker reaches his seventies, perhaps he isn't quite so concerned with making wines that age. As a result, 1987 was the first year in memory that Sullivan had declined to cellar a vintage from Swan. Nevertheless, the wines remained exceedingly rare—they were sold only at exclusive restaurants, through Swan's own mailing list, and in a handful of fine wine shops in San Francisco and L.A.

I drove up to Swan's place at the end of one of the days of hazy, filtered sunshine that began the 1988 drought. Unseasonably balmy, cloudless weather had encouraged the trees to bud out along Highway 101, though the rains of January had left the hills a deep, brilliant green. Near Santa Rosa mustard grass was growing in the vineyards, some of which had been pruned and some of which hadn't; the latter vines trailed black tangles of spurs in the yellow-flowered grass, and pink almond blossoms lit up the roadsides in the setting sun. As dusk fell over the horse pastures, I was reacquainted with the odd, mysterious Russian River atmosphere—an almost eerily quiet realm of apple orchards, tourist resorts, palm readers, and the Bohemian Grove, where the leaders of the Western world gather each summer to "cremate care."

On a corner lot just off River Road, a sign said NICARAGUA IS NOT OUR ENEMY. As it happened, the mailbox on the same property said SWAN. The place contained ancient, unpruned grapevines, an old trapezoidal tank house, a swimming pool, a red barn, a hot tub, a house, and a group of ceramic swans. As I got out of my car, Joel pulled up in his Peugeot, his son asleep on the seat beside him. We left Morgan in this uncharacteristically quiet state and walked around behind the house. On the glass-enclosed back porch I noticed a string of red Christmas lights in the shape of chili peppers and five volumes on Thomas Jefferson by Dumas Malone. In the kitchen a cassoulet was being tended by several people: Swan's wife, June; her daughter, Lynn; Swan's son-in-law and winemaking assistant, Rod Berglund; and, in a blue down vest, a short-sleeved madras shirt, a pair of running shoes, and khaki pants with a handkerchief protruding from the back pocket, the white-haired patriarch himself.

For some reason I had expected a gruff fireplug guy. In fact, Joe Swan was tall, slender, quiet, and rather shy, with long, skinny arms and a full head of hair. He asked if we wanted to see the winery before it got dark, so Swan, Berglund, Joel, and I went back outside and, each clutching a wineglass, walked a few hundred yards up the road to a prefab steel building where Swan made his wine.

As Swan undid the padlock, Joel asked him if he was going to take grapes from Sonoma Valley again this year.

"I might buy them again if the vineyard can be pruned back

to where the production is more appropriate," said Swan. "I told her she puts too much crop on there. I noticed she left three or four buds per spur. That's not my idea of finished pruning."

"Well, if you don't want them, I'll take them," said Joel. "My Old Hill production fell from a thousand to six hundred cases this year because of Otto's pruning."

As we entered the winery, Joel exclaimed: "Joe, you've gone too high! I never thought I'd see it happen." I wasn't sure if he meant "too" or "two"—one row of Swan's barrels had a second row stacked on top of it.

"It's true," said Swan. "If you stack the barrels, you can't roll 'em." His other barrels were rolled forty-five degrees to keep the bung in contact with the wine, preventing evaporation. Swan removed the wooden wedge from underneath one of them, rolled the barrel upright, took out the bung, and dipped a glass thief into the hole. "What you don't drink goes back in," he said, releasing Pinot Noir into our glasses.

"Good cherries!" Joel commented upon tasting the wine. "Nice feel on the tongue; nice edge of astringency."

"You've got to have some of that tannin for aging," said Swan. "Pinot Noir is such a challenge—you really have to put a lot of thought into it. But I like what I've been getting. I'm going to graft my vineyard over to different clones of it in the next five years." He rerolled the barrel, and we moved on to his Cabernet Sauvignon, which I thought had a beautiful, characteristic Cabernet nose. When I told Swan so, he said, "Not *green* Cabernet, though. I pick it when it begins to lose its Cabernet character."

"It's funny," Joel said, smelling the wine. "Zinfandel fruit is accessible early; Merlot is a little more reticent; then you taste Cabernet at the same age, and it's just like this." He made a tight fist. "Are you still making only two barrels of it?"

"Two and a half."

Next we tasted the '86 Zinfandel: soft; earthy; round; fruity. Joel said, "You haven't lost your touch, Joe."

"You've really fucked up if you mess *these* grapes up," said Swan.

"Some people do it all the time."

"This is about six tons off a hill near here, and five from Willowside Road," said Swan. "I think this area is better than Dry Creek for Zinfandel—the wine has more elegance and finesse because the grapes ripen adequately without giving you high alcohol. The soil is light sandy loam above clay and the climate is cool. '85 and '86 were Burgundy heat-summation years—that's cool. For the last three years conditions during harvest have been perfect: The fog comes up the river late in the afternoon and lasts till ten or twelve o'clock the next day. Usually the only problem with picking is waiting till the acid's down. Picking Zinfandel is such a bitch; it's just a damn guessing game. This is about thirteen percent alcohol."

"Having made both fifteen and twelve and a half, I think thirteen is good," said Joel. "Fifteen is clearly too high; I find twelve and a half a bit thin."

"I have no problem with twelve and half," said Swan. "I think lower-alcohol wines are better with dinner. They last longer, too, because you haven't burned out the fruit by letting the grapes get overripe. One of my favorite Zinfandels is my '75; it has lower alcohol, and it's aging very gracefully. The only wine I ever made above fourteen percent was my '74 Pinot Noir—my building wasn't up yet, and I couldn't pick the grapes."

We went back outside and Swan locked up the winery. "I've been looking to Europe for my guidelines," he said as we walked back toward the house. "No matter where you go there, you can always find wine that's pleasant to drink with a meal. That's the way it should be. Lately I've been gravitating more and more toward Provence; I like the style of cooking, and the people are so nice! Not so stiff as in Bordeaux. The last few years I've been orienting myself toward Rhône methods, using a lot of stems and whole clusters. Zinfandel is similar to the Rhône grapes—it doesn't have a lot of tannin, so the stems help. The advantage of the whole clusters is that you get fresh, opulent fruit right away. With long fermentation, you precipitate out the hard tannins and end up with a better balanced wine. In the

Rhône they use a hundred percent of the stems. Those wines shouldn't be drunk until they're ten years old."

It seemed as good a time as any to ask Swan about the charge that he'd lightened up his style.

"Lower alcohol isn't lightening your style," he responded. "It would be if I pressed the wine at twelve degrees Brix, but not if it's in the fermentor for five weeks. I'd say I've *refined* my winemaking. My intention is still to make wines that'll last as long as possible, but ones that are better balanced in their youth. I like my wines better now than before. My older wines will taste better because they're older, but since 1980 I think I've gotten a more even bunch of wines. Particularly since '84, I've been making Zinfandel in a style I really like."

When we got back to the house, we went into the living room for hors d'oeuvres. On the wall hung a painting of the twenty-five-year-old Joe Swan, a self-portrait in the Thomas Hart Benton style of a hawk-eyed, slightly demonic-looking young man with the same full head of hair, only brown. Swan passed around his '75 Chardonnay, which at twelve years of age was rich and meaty with a brilliant nose and a deep golden color. Sipping the wine, Joel said, "I have to say that I owe you a debt, Joe. I got the nuts and bolts from you."

"Mainly I think you got the idea that Zinfandel could make good wine," said Swan. "*Beautiful* wine. People don't consider it noble, but I think some Zinfandels fit into that category. The problem is, you can count the people making *real* Zinfandel on one hand. I had some French guys down here after a Pinot Noir tasting in Oregon last year, and they were truly impressed by Zinfandel; they couldn't understand why more California wineries don't concentrate on it."

"One nice thing about Zinfandel is that the French don't have anything to compare it with," said Berglund.

"Truly good Zinfandel can hold its own in a lot of company," said Swan. "Somebody once thought my '73 was Pétrus. I've never been so put off in my life as by *The Wine Spectator*.

I sent them three different wines for an article called 'Zinfandels—Do They Age?' They never even mentioned the color. The *first* thing you mention on old wines should be the color. They said the '75 was a bad bottle; I've never *had* a bad bottle of my '75. It doesn't exist!"

"*The Wine Spectator* doesn't like flavorful wines," said someone whose name escapes me. "They like wallflowers—wines that are reticent and quiet. If a wine shouts, forget it."

"On the other hand, Robert Parker likes only full-blown wines," said somebody else. "That's a problem, too."

"He likes bacteriologically flawed wines."

"Parker has set himself a task that's like sweeping out the Augean stables. Nobody can taste that much unless he has a lot more time than Parker has."

"I'd like to know what Parker's controls on himself are," said Joel. "I know I can love a wine one day, then come back to it the next and wonder what was wrong with me. One-man wine tasting is definitely a problem."

"Dan Berger in the *L.A. Times* says that winemakers are starting to style their wines after Parker's taste," said Berglund.

"The problem with the wine industry," said Joel, "is that winemakers are trying to adjust to what they think the public wants. Growers are budding over every three years to the 'hot' varietal; then, by the time they get a crop, a different varietal is hot. Five years ago everybody was ripping out Zinfandel and planting Sauvignon Blanc. Now Sauvignon Blanc is dead in the water and Zinfandel's coming back."

"I never had any intention but making wine that I liked," said Swan. "I never focused on what the market might be. I've just been lucky enough to be able to sell it. I wouldn't be in business if had to make wine the way other people do. Putting residual sugar in Chardonnay! It's disgraceful. It's prostitution."

The cassoulet was dished up. We went into the dining room, where pictures of Swan's children, begotten over the course of four marriages, lined the walls. I happened to have brought along a bottle of Young Gentlemen's Nouveau, which Swan promptly uncorked. Upon tasting it, he announced: "If more nouveau Zinfandel was made like that in California, it wouldn't have gotten such a bad name." Buttons sprang off my chest onto the table, which I have to admit was rather embarrassing. Swan opened his '85 Zinfandel, and Joel brought out a bottle of his '85 Dickerson (aka '59 Mouton), which on this occasion struck me as extraordinary: One sip did things all over my mouth and then began sending occult vapors into my brain. "In light of this," Swan said, "I think I'll pull up a bottle of my '73."

He disappeared from the table and returned a few minutes later with not one but three bottles. "When I go down to pick out one of my own wines, I just can't find that many," he lamented.

"Same with me," said Joel. "I cancel out my '77 to '80 vintages altogether. I didn't think I was struggling stylistically at the time, but I was trying to duplicate my '76. But I didn't get good fruit, and when I did get it, I didn't know what to do with it."

For someone who claimed to have been frustrated in the cellar, Swan had done pretty well. His '73, '71, and '68 Zinfandels now stood before us.

"The '73 reminds me of yours," he told Joel. "It's voluptuous, unusual, exotic, almost Oriental. The '71 was picked early; it had lots of fruit and acid, and it still has it, which shows it didn't go through malolactic. With the '68 it all went into the fermentor—skins, stems, everything. I think I might have added yeast; I'm not sure. My number three son, Chris, was supposed to be punching it down, but probably it didn't get punched down. It was so purple and tannic that I had to fine it three times. Later I disgorged it from bottles and put it in French oak. Maynard Amerine said he hoped he'd live long enough to drink it."

I was tempted to go to the telephone and give Amerine a call, because on this day in 1988, the 1968 Swan Zinfandel— the first wine Swan made from his home vineyard, before his winery was even bonded—was ready. From the glass it sent a sweet announcement of the fact into the nostrils; then, drawn into the mouth, it coaxed a shower from the taste buds and glided *à point* across the palate. It never overstepped or understepped its bounds; everything about it—color, fruit, acid, tannin, oak—was in balance. It was a beautiful tightrope walker of a wine, muscular but well coordinated, perfectly proportioned in a tight shining outfit, pirouetting in the dark.

"I rest my case on Zinfandel," said Swan.

"The last time I tasted this wine was ten or twelve years ago," said Joel. "It hasn't lost any of its vibrancy. If anything, it's even more graceful and complex. Most '68s are showing a real pallor now; even the BVs are getting a little slippery. But this wine is still vigorous and intense."

"My '85 will come along like this," Swan offered.

"Oh, no, it won't," said Joel. "This is like few wines in the history of the world. It isn't even California. It's its own thing. It's a genie; you captured those grapes in the bottle, Joe."

I spent the rest of the evening in Aladdin's cave, wandering back and forth from one lambent treasure to another. Joel had previously told me that there were actually two Joe Swans: one a taciturn, almost gruff winemaker, the other an amiable, sociable host who appeared at the dinner table after 6:00 P.M. Sitting there with the latter, drinking transcendent old Zinfandels from vines growing outside the door of his farmhouse, surrounded by a tableful of his friends and family and pictures of his scattered children, I began to swell with a euphoria I've seldom known before or since. Joel had told me that we could spend the night there with no problem, so I made no effort whatsoever at temperance; therefore, when Joel announced at eleven o'clock that he'd better be heading home, I was stunned. I'd reached a point where I had utterly no confidence in my ability to operate an automobile, but not wanting to impose on the Swans, I weaved stupidly out to my car, started it up, and pointed it east. Somehow, through the grace of Bacchus, I managed to reach 101, and from there things got much easier. Compared with the curves along River Road, the freeway seemed straight as a bowling lane, and I sped home through the starry night, suffused with rapture and foolishness and love of life and Zinfandel.

In late February I visited a vintner who, over the past five years, had won more awards for Zinfandel than any other winemaker: Dr. Bernard ("Jerry") Seps, a former professor of European history who now made Zinfandel, and nothing but, at Storybook Mountain Vineyards.

I already knew a couple of things about Storybook Mountain. For example, I knew that Jerry Seps, like Joel Peterson, had learned his craft from Joe Swan. I also knew I could look long and hard before I'd find another Zinfandel that was less like Joel Peterson's. Where Ravenswood was brawny, opulent, and aggressive, Storybook Mountain was—for the first several years of its youth, anyway—lean, austere, and reticent; to put it in Paul Draper's terms, the two styles offered a textbook example of rich versus elegant. However, where Draper largely attributed those qualities to the weather and ascribed them to particular vintages, Seps and Peterson seemed to achieve them year in and year out, regardless of climatic deviation. Considering that both wineries were renowned for the same varietal and both winemakers had been schooled by the same teacher, this clear, consistent divergence in style was rather remarkable. It also seemed potentially instructive, since the one trait that the two wines shared was that both were very well built.

The winery was located above Calistoga off Highway 128, just below the Sonoma County line—as far north as a person can go and still be in Napa Valley. As I closed the swinging gate and drove up the gravel access road, I thought I'd never seen a more beautiful site for a vineyard. Rising directly behind me was Mount St. Helena, mottled green and cloudy gray in the winter weather. A neat stone wall paralleled the road to the winery, where twelve stainless-steel fermentors stood on a concrete pad next to a hillside. I parked my car beside a stand of redwoods and walked into a cave in this hill. Rows of spotlit barrels receded down a tunnel into the bowels of the mountain; I called out, "Hello," and a man appeared in the dim, distant recesses. As he approached, I saw that he was dressed in blue jeans, black rubber boots, and a denim jacket.

This was Jerry Seps—a soft-spoken guy of about fifty, with kind blue eyes, a gray beard, and hair that wafted out from his temples before disappearing altogether from the top of his head. Accompanied by a stick-and-tennis-ball maniac—a dog he identified as two parts retriever and one part shepherd—Seps led me into his cave, at the far end of which was an upright German oval oak tank, carved with the winery's fairy-tale-like insignia: a fox, a vinifera leaf, and a cluster of grapes. "We named this place Storybook for three reasons," Seps explained, turning off a hose. "To begin with, it was started a hundred years ago by the brothers Grimm—a pair of Germans named Jacob and Adam. Jacob's citizenship papers were signed by Jacob Schram, who introduced Zinfandel to Napa Valley. The second reason is that I think fine wine is like a storybook—it enhances your life, adds another dimension to it."

I noticed that the ceiling of the cave was covered with a papery gray substance that rubbed off at my touch; Seps described it as an "alcohol-related mold." He said that the caves had been dug by Chinese laborers in the nineteenth century and that he'd bought the place in 1976, having been interested in wine for some twenty years. He'd put himself through college with a job as a sommelier at the Ahwahnee Hotel in Yosemite Valley; every other week he got three days off, and he'd come down to Napa Valley and "fell in love with it." He'd gone on to get a doctorate in history, taught for a time at Stanford, and eventually gained tenure at California State University at Dominguez Hills in Southern California. But Napa Valley had continued to haunt him.

"There wasn't any *need* for me to do this," Seps said. "But I wanted to do something right, and I thought it would be creative to resurrect a top estate in the Napa Valley. Plus, I thought, if I'm ever going to do this, I should do it while I'm still strong enough to work.

"When I bought this place, it had been abandoned for over a decade. In 1964 a fire had leveled the house, the winery, and the vineyard, so it was really wild. Carl Doumani from Stags Leap had looked at it and been told that only six acres were plantable—and those were noncontiguous. But five varieties of grapes were still growing here, including Zinfandel that had been planted during the 1880s. The early planters tended to use the hills for Zinfandel; the air and foot drainage are better here, and heavy valley soil thickens the vegetation too much. The grape is not humidity-tolerant—it has a tight bunch and thin skin, and it'll rot.

"André Tchelistcheff used to say that the best Zinfandel came from the 'red clay loam in the hills above Calistoga.' Only about five percent of Napa Valley has soil like that. The only Bordeaux vineyard that has it is Pétrus; the best wines of Australia come from it; in Germany the wines from Schloss Böckelheimer Kupfergrube have it—the vineyard is on top of an old copper mine. We're between the Sonoma Valley mountain system and the Napa Valley mountain system here. Breezes come right over that ridge, so this vineyard is ten to fifteen degrees cooler than the town of Calistoga. The eastern exposure is ideal in the California context—you get a long, gradual growing day with a lot of sun, but not the warmest sun of the afternoon. So the grapes develop good acid and a low pH. This land is also great for Cabernet Sauvignon and good for Sauvignon Blanc, but there is no *better* land for Zinfandel—the grapes develop more depth, character, and spice. So we came here, evaluated the land, planted Zinfandel—and then fell in love with the grape. As far as I'm concerned, berries and spice are an ideal combination."

Seps led me into his tasting room—a high-ceilinged central part of the cave, where spotlights illuminated red, blue, and gold ribbons and the different colored labels on Storybook Mountain bottles: blue for estate bottlings; maroon for grapes that Seps got from Sonoma; white for the estate reserve, Seps's premium product and the most expensive Zinfandel that money could buy.

"We originally came here to raise grapes, not to make wine," Seps said as we tasted through his vintages. "At first we stored Cabernet in these caves, but Al Brounstein from Diamond Creek advised me to consider making wine. The price paid for mountain-grown grapes isn't enough to make a profit, but if you're turning out a quality product, it becomes economically viable. We had pride in our grapes, and we wanted to carry things all the way through. So we put in water, electricity, and cement floors and reinforced the corners of the cave; I took courses at Davis and read a hell of a lot. Eventually I sent Joe Swan a card and said I'd like to work for him at no charge. He was a pragmatic choice—his were among my favorite Zinfandels. The key thing with Joe was respect for the product, plus his desire to bring out the most in the grape. It gave me a path to follow, even though I might deviate from it to fit my own taste. Joe feels strongly about things, but he's not opposed to changing if it means he can make a better wine. I think his wines are much more approachable now than they used to be."

We walked back to the mouth of the cave and looked out over the vineyard. The sloping hills were terraced and lined with Seps's immaculate vines. "We're organic farmers here," Seps said. "We use no insecticides or herbicides. Instead we do companion plantings—berry bushes host wasps that feed on the parasites in the vineyard. All the weeds are hand-hoed, and in the Burgundian fashion we ask the vines by the forest to carry only half the load of those on the flatter, heavier soils. In May and June we regulate every vine's crop load according to the width of the wood and the amount of vegetation. In September we drop all the unripe fruit. Every location in the vineyard ripens differently, so we handpick the grapes by half rows over a six-week period, getting about three tons to the acre. I try to pick between twenty-two-point-two and twenty-two-point-seven degrees Brix, with about a three-point-one pH and point-nine acid. Acid is important to me. I want an intense wine, but you can achieve intensity in different ways—by being heavy, thick, and viscous or by achieving a lingering, clean intensity on the palate. The latter is what we're looking for. Joel Peterson takes his grapes riper than I do; I like a leaner wine.

"You know, Zinfandel was originally introduced to California as a fine claret—a rival to Europe. The Ravenswood style has become somewhat dominant for Zinfandel, but— Don't misunderstand me, they're well-made wines, but I think some aspects of that style obscure the finer qualities of the grape. Very ripe grapes make Zinfandel unidimensional; you miss the subtlety, the spice, the complexity, and the aging capability. [As far as Ridge is concerned,] I think Petite Sirah and Carignane coarsen the wine. And American oak can be very aggressive—it has a lot of tannin and wood extraction that isn't flattering to the wine. Ours spends a year in small oak—forty percent French and sixty percent American, which we ameliorate by using air-dried wood. In our ovals we use German oak from Spessart. You seldom see Riesling exhibiting any oak because of the hard, tight grain. We leave the fermenting wine on its skins for thirty days and keep the temperature in the low seventies. I think heat can produce off odors, so our fermentation is both cooler and longer than most other Zinfandel producers. With long fermentation you transform the tannins so that you taste them farther back in the mouth—they don't feel as rough. We do induce a malolactic fermentation, but the high acid and low pH tend to inhibit its completion. We usually have to filter to prevent it from happening in the bottle. My wife, Sigrid, and I taste from each barrel in a competitive way three times a year. Every barrel has a number, a correspondingly numbered bung, and a mark on the bung, so that it always fits the same way."

As I looked out over the vineyard, listening to Seps describe his fastidious viticultural and enological practices, Storybook Mountain exuded two things: a lot of money and a lot of work. I certainly didn't agree with everything Seps said—if the truth be told, his tight, Teutonic Zinfandels weren't my cup of tea— but his commitment was impressive. More than anyone else I'd met, Seps seemed to devote his entire existence to his product, from the dirt up.

He had told me that there were three reasons for his winery's name. He now revealed the third.

"When, in your mind's eye, you imagine what a winery should be, it's like a fairy tale," Seps said. "Even after all the hard work, we still feel that's what this is. Usually I'm in bed by ten and up and doing something by six; except for meals, I'm working the whole time, six and a half days a week. We make about five thousand cases, and our wine is sold in thirty-five states and a hundred and eighty restaurants. Even so, the bank's still carrying us; we're still losing money. But we're doing something we want to do, something we believe in. And that's important."

On a rainy day in late winter Joel Peterson sat in the Ravenswood office surrounded by bottles. The labels were all handwritten or typed with the names of different wineries: '86 Monteviña, '87 D'Agostini, '87 GBZ from Alexander Valley, '86 Jones Ranch from Paso Robles. All constituted "tryouts" for the Vintner's Blend—the low-priced, high-volume Zinfandel that Joel puts together each year, partly from lesser wines made at Ravenswood but largely (about 60 percent) from wines produced elsewhere.

"Swanson's off," Joel said as John Kemble came in from the winery. "I offered them six dollars a gallon; then they cut their offer back to half the original amount and said they wanted six-fifty. I said I'd be happy to take it if they want to barrel-age it for me. I'm paying six dollars a gallon now for wine that's been in French oak for a year."

Joel tossed a piece of paper onto a desk in exasperation. "For me the equivalent of Dante's Inferno would be sitting in a room tasting samples forever," he said. "Every now and then you come across a good one, but you have to go through fifteen bad ones to find it. Sometimes the defects are small enough that you can bury them in the blend; you use the positive attributes of some to blend out the negative characteristics of others. For example, a wine that's high in acid but has nice oak would brighten up other wines that are low-to-medium in acid but very flavorful and ripe. So samples that might not work as individual wines might still work in the blend. You just have to be careful not to blend in a major defect."

Joel locates his blending wines through various means. Sometimes his friends at other wineries have a surplus that they're willing to sell cheap. Sometimes he works through brokers on the bulk market—a highly competitive and political prospect because some producers won't sell to other producers for reasons having as much to do with personal history and ego as with economics. In 1986, because of the demand for white Zinfandel, the going price for Zinfandel on the bulk market had soared from four to seven dollars a gallon. Joel located eleven thousand gallons of Zinfandel that he found "soft and pleasant with a light citrusy odor—not real distinctive but a good base wine"—at an Alexander Valley winery that specializes in decent, affordable wine. This winery happened to be short on Chardonnay, so Joel bought some on the bulk market (from wineries that might not have been willing to sell it to the Alexander Valley winery) and traded it for the Zinfandel. He blended that with his own oak-aged Ravenswood lots, plus 5,700 gallons of Zinfandel whose fermentation had gotten stuck at a nearby winery in Sonoma. The latter wine was high in alcohol, volatile acidity, and residual sugar, but it had a ripe intensity that Joel liked; so his next task was to balance it with something *low* in alcohol and VA, something young and fruity. He chose an over-cropped Carneros Zinfandel that had been picked prematurely but was free of condemning defects, rounded it out with a rich, berrylike product from Paso Robles, and injected a bit of backbone with a tannic Napa Valley Zin that had spent some time in oak.

Plucked from the inferno of 450 samples, these wines would essentially constitute the '86 Ravenswood Vintner's Blend. But up to the last minute before bottling, Joel continued to taste other samples as they arrived, on the chance that he still might find something interesting to throw in.

"One thing I think you've got to do in this business is offer a wine that isn't expensive," Joel explained. "Wine should be an everyday phenomenon—you need something to keep your palate in shape during the week, in between the luxury wines that you treasure and pull out for special occasions. We actually have individuals who order twenty-five cases of this stuff for themselves."

Indeed: Ravenswood released its 1986 Vintner's Blend on March 1, 1988; it received an 85 rating from Robert Parker and an 86 from *The Wine Spectator,* which in singling it out as a "Best Buy," called it "Full-bodied and herbal. . . . Nicely concentrated and moderately tannic. . . . A good value." By March 31, one month after release, all seven thousand cases of the wine had been sold. As a direct consequence, on April 8—the day before his forty-first birthday and twelve years after founding Ravenswood—Joel quit his job at Sonoma Valley Hospital, becoming a full-time winemaker for the first time.

Nineteen years earlier, in the summer of 1969, another new full-time winemaker—Dave Bennion—was "feeling pressed." As president of Ridge, Bennion was the winery's *only* full-time employee, responsible for everything from grape growing to winemaking to labeling to bottling to sales (which were still achieved primarily through word—and stimulation—of mouth). As the '69 harvest approached, Bennion also faced the task of bottling ten barrels—some six hundred gallons—of 1967 Château Montrose that Ridge had imported from Bordeaux. Remembering the articulate young man he'd met at a tasting the year before, Bennion fished out the slip of paper, dialed the phone number of the Anchor Steam brewery, and inquired as to the whereabouts of Paul Draper. Fritz Maytag told him that Draper was difficult to reach in Chile but that he'd soon be returning home.

Draper met with the Ridge owners as soon as he arrived in California. He started work at Monte Bello in September, when he and Bennion tasted from each of the ten barrels of Montrose, determining that each differed slightly from the next. "I recognized immediately that Paul had a better nose and tasting ability than I would ever have," Bennion says. As the self-effacing Fritz Maytag explains it: "Paul and I were rare in California. We were young, astute, and business-oriented, and we'd been carefully tasting, for practical commercial reasons, Cabernet Sauvignons from around the world. In 1966 there weren't very many people tasting ten Cabernets at nine o'clock in the morning and spitting them into the sink. If you gave us a Latour and a Louis Martini"—Maytag snaps his fingers—"we *knew.*"

For precisely the same reason, Draper and Maytag knew what they were tasting when Bennion invited them to his house and poured them the 1959 Monte Bello Cabernet that he'd made on his porch ten years earlier. "Paul came over and told me, 'You've got to try some of this!' " Maytag remembers. "It was so big and intense—I thought it was the best California Cabernet I'd ever had." Maytag had been laboring under the assumption that "serious" aged red wines were as rare in California as he and Paul Draper were.

For his part, Draper considered some Ridge wines "truly great, while others were sheer disasters. Dave's '62 and '64 were damn near perfect, but in '66 the entire Monte Bello vintage had gone to vinegar." He did think that Monte Bello Cabernet had "a chance to be one of the world's great wines because climatically the vineyard is right on the edge. It has a liveliness, a complexity, and an excitement that safer vineyards miss."

Draper's first task at Ridge was to supervise the bottling of the '67 Montrose. As a result, for the first time in history Ridge blended all the barrels of one wine into a uniform lot before bottling. In the fall Draper worked the harvest—a warm one, as it happened, which produced very ripe grapes. In accordance with Ridge traditions, most of the Monte Bello Cabernet was fermented in open tanks with its cap of grape skins submerged; Draper, however, having recently gained familiarity with the traditional practices of Bordeaux, fermented one lot by "non-action," with a closed tank and no pumpover (i.e., no mixing of the skins with the juice). As it turned out, Draper's batch went dry with no problem, while the main lot stuck at 1 percent residual sugar and was barely rescued from an illegal level of volatile acidity by malolactic fermentation. The following year the Ridge owners, impressed by Draper's experience and intelligence, invested him with full responsibility for the winemaking, beginning the modern era at Ridge Vineyards and the transformation of an offbeat scientists' hobby into one of the most respected winemaking operations in the world.

To perceive the nature of Paul Draper's effect on Ridge, it's necessary to understand the atmosphere before he arrived—not only at the winery but in the country in general and the San Francisco Bay Area in particular. As Hew Crane summed it up in his written account of the early history of the winery: "Ridge started in the post-Korean and fallout-shelter times, and matured during the Vietnam era, a period of intense social unrest." The summer that Draper bottled the '67 Montrose was the summer of Woodstock; the San Francisco hippie era had crested, but its effects were being felt in the back-to-the-earth movement, which asserted itself particularly strongly in the Santa Cruz Mountains. Where the Bennions lived—the vicinity of Stanford and Menlo Park, a few years earlier the site of the government's first experiments with LSD—the *Whole Earth Catalog* was just getting off the ground, boosted by all its attending values.

Imbued with exactly those ethics, I myself hitchhiked through the area on my first visit to California in the spring of 1971. Apparently I was a little bit too late since, according to Sue Crane, "three-quarters of Ridge's staff was acquired hitchhiking on the freeway. Dave Bennion listened to young people's stories and became interested in them; they needed a place to crash." As her husband wrote:

> Ridge became a way station and refuge for a large number of people. During that period, any young person who happened by Ridge tended to fall in love with the place . . . there were three houses at Ridge that were continually filled with all manner of living arrangements. We enjoyed these people very much as a group, but they also caused us a great deal of grief. . . . We had to con-

tinually balance our empathy for their causes with the urgencies of a complex and rapidly growing winery operation. . . . To some of these people, regular work was anathema. Most of them hadn't the foggiest idea of how complex and costly it was to create a viable economic entity within an old established industry and in such a remote location. Some felt they were automatically entitled to high salaries and to all of the other amenities. Ecology freaks objected to our use of herbicides in the vineyard, even though, as in our approach to wine production, we use absolutely minimum amounts of every chemical, and we require each one to be easily biodegradable.

Herbicides were especially disturbing, of course, to employees who'd secretly planted marijuana on the premises. On spectacular, supernal Monte Bello Ridge, psychoactive drugs proved quite popular; one Ridge acolyte—a full-bearded red-headed individual named Jerry—reportedly ate LSD sixty-four days in a row, and bottling was frequently performed by someone who held a 750-ml glass vessel with one hand and a joint of primo sinsemilla with the other. Though Bennion himself was not a druggie, the winery's operations had to conform to this altered state of reality.

David Noyes arrived at Ridge toward the end of this time. A bright, painfully shy kid who, in rebelling against a strict physicist father, had barely managed to graduate from high school in Palo Alto, Noyes had made fruit wine and mead at home. A friend of his family recommended him to Ridge, and Bennion started picking him up in the morning and driving him up to the winery, where he helped out in the vineyard and with bottling. The outward expression of Noyes's alienation was an inability, or unwillingness, to speak; during his first couple of years at Ridge, he hardly said a word. Now an open and articulate (if still slightly awkward) man, he fondly remembers harvests when "we'd be crushing grapes into the evening, eating walnuts from the trees and drinking port that the owners had imported. People would take off in the afternoon and hike down to Stevens Canyon for a beer; later somebody would have to drive down there and pick them up. Every day there was a communal lunch with a bottle of wine, and if the discussion was interesting, it tended to go on and on. Dave Bennion might not be there, but he didn't care; he enjoyed life as it went." Under such circumstances, Ridge's progress toward profitability resembled that of a mountain range rising from the earth. After a full ten years of operation the place was still producing only three thousand cases of wine per year.

Onto this scene in 1969 strode Paul Draper—he of Choate, of the Colli Berici and custom-made suits, of Bordeaux, Paris and the Sorbonne, of Chile and of New York. "We worried about Paul at first," Hew Crane wrote—but not for any of the above reasons. In the eyes of the owners, the chief cause for concern was that Draper "was a philosophy major from Stanford. Would he be the philosopher among what we prided ourselves as—'doers'?" Ten to twenty years younger than the winery's founders, Draper occupied a professional and personal position partway between them and the crew of part-time employees; in enological sophistication, however, he was ahead of everybody. As Charlie Rosen succinctly put it, "Paul was a wine snob."

By that time Ridge wines had become noted for (1) their intensity, (2) their purity, and (3) their lack of polish. With regard to the last, Hugh Johnson wrote that "André Tchelistcheff often uses the image of a smoothly polished ball to describe a mature, elegant wine. That is how a great wine should and does feel on the palate. A young unbalanced wine also is a ball, but it has stray flavors sticking out, like arrows, in all directions. In this image a weighty Ridge Zinfandel certainly is a purple sea urchin in youth, perhaps forever." As Noyes explains it, "Dave wanted maximum flavor and extraction, and he made the wines with long maceration and minimal handling. His philosophy was 'If the grapes can do it, let them do it. We want everything they have to offer.' He didn't want to do *anything* to the wine unless it showed that it needed it. He'd rack it only once or twice and leave it in the barrel for two or three years until all the activity died out. When Paul came, we began following the Bordelais schedule of racking six or seven times before bottling. He was more focused; Dave was more experimental."

Draper describes his attitude this way: "With methods that the rest of California hadn't used for fifty years, Ridge was making some of the best California wines of the day. Many people thought our grapes were the equal of first-growth Bordeaux. But the wines lacked finesse, and the outside world wasn't perceiving that we were as serious a winery as we were. I think Dave's aim was to make good wine, but not one of the great wines of the world. That wasn't rigorous enough for me. I liked the democratic atmosphere at Ridge, but it was all chiefs and no Indians—and some of the practices were just too loose. We were using a German crusher with spinning steel spikes in its grape hopper; you could lose your hand in it, and some of these guys were *stoned*. I was embarrassed by Ridge's reputation of being unprofessional and eccentric; I wanted to bring in more professionalism, a chance for the pursuit of excellence."

Noyes agrees that "in 1970, it was hard to get an overriding sense of what the purpose of the place was. Dave Bennion was a wonderful person to work for—he put no strictures on you at all, and he was one of the few people I've ever known who truly let you be yourself because *he* was so truly himself. But it was hard to fathom where he was coming from. When Paul came, there seemed to be a purpose for what we were doing. I like structure; Paul provided it."

Indeed, Draper turned out to be just the sort of doer that Ridge required. To begin with, he was fluent in French, Italian, and Spanish—a not insignificant lingual portfolio for a California winemaker. As an example of the sort of structure he provided, he says: "I actually asked people if they were going to be around to help bottle." Where Bennion seemed to run his life and his winery according to whatever idea was ascendant in his cortex at the moment—he'd begin a business meeting with an hourlong description of a meal he'd eaten the night before—

Blanche Rosen recalls with apparent amazement that "you could always come to Paul and get a direct order." Draper put up a chalkboard and instituted a work calendar, and using funds provided by the corporation's new stockholders, completely overhauled the winemaking equipment. From Fritz Maytag's suppliers at Anchor Steam, he ordered an array of new hoses and clamps to supersede the plastic home-winemaking fittings that the owners had previously employed, and he replaced a bruising impeller pump with one so gentle that it could move a tomato without damaging the skin. He supplanted the small redwood fermentors with stainless steel (easier to clean), designing the tanks himself, as well as the custom-made stainless grids that kept the grape skins submerged. He also helped supervise the remodeling of the upper winery, which obtained a new roof, a new cement floor, and several new doors where none had been before. To accommodate the multileveled layout of the building, Draper invented a combination spray-ball and suction pump that washed all the barrels in place without requiring them to be unstacked and removed from the cellar.

The barrels themselves—previously all used—began to receive annual infusions of new oak. Thanks to Philippe Dourthe, his friend in the Médoc, Draper had seen a turn-of-the-century French study that—somewhat amazingly, considering that the study was performed in Bordeaux—rated French oak last in quality behind Baltic, American, and Yugoslavian. Draper conducted blind tastings of wines aged in wood from France, Illinois, Missouri, Kentucky, and Arkansas and decided that he liked the best American samples as much as he did the French. The immediate advantage was that *Quercus alba*—American oak—was less expensive than French. Also, when it came to the winery's bread and butter, Draper could proclaim that "Zinfandel is the American grape. It doesn't need French oak; it needs American oak!" (Of course, the Monte Bello Cabernet was also aged in American oak, enabling Draper to assert that Ridge wasn't interested in making "imitation Bordeaux.")

Before coming to Ridge, Draper says he had "everyone else's

opinion of Zinfandel: that it was a minor grape, that it was fun, but not one of the great varieties. Monte Bello Cabernet was the reason I wanted to be here. But in '69 we also made five barrels of Jimsomare/Picchetti Zinfandel. I was leery of it at first, but as I tasted the wines through the following year, it was the one that intrigued me the most. It was so intense, flavorful, and interesting. I'd never smelled anything like it; it was beyond my ken. It took a year for me to become fully convinced, but by the time we bottled it, I saw that Zinfandel was a serious grape with serious potential."

During Draper's first couple of years at Ridge he and Dave Bennion functioned as cowinemakers. Draper was responsible for the red wines; Bennion worked mainly with whites. This arrangement was doomed from the start. If the reader has not yet so gleaned, both Bennion and Draper possessed strong personalities that were approximately as congruent as canine and feline. Where Bennion was scattered, Draper was disciplined; where Bennion was spontaneous and sometimes heedless, Draper was deliberate and sometimes calculating. Where Bennion lacked certain social skills—before a crowd of strangers, he'd blithely set about picking his nose or cleaning his teeth with used dental floss—the polished Draper had (in Hew Crane's words) "a bearing that one associates with a private-school background. . . . Even in jeans, or wearing rubber boots in the cellar, he always looked as if he just stepped off the stage of a TV commercial." Moreover, while Bennion was struggling to support a wife and four children, Draper continued to lead what Fran Bennion calls "a high-flying bachelor life." Even after joining Ridge, Draper continued to reside in San Francisco, more than an hour's drive away; often he would depart for a date at the end of the day, leaving the others to clean up.

"Dave's day at Ridge didn't begin or end," remembers Sue Crane. "The winery was his life. But Paul had a limit. Dave didn't like that." Bennion destested snooty wine events, but his great love was pouring wine at informal tastings where he accepted all comers on equal terms. By contrast, he found Draper—a frequent guest at the Bohemian Club who had no problem donning a tuxedo—to be disinterested in spending time with ordinary visitors. "Paul thought a winemaker should be a bigger cheese than I did, with meals at expensive restaurants and so on," says Bennion. "I got as much satisfaction from having people come around and love our wines after they'd tasted the best ones from France. Or by making good wine from Zinfandel, a grape that hadn't been considered very special."

"Appearances didn't matter to Dave as long as the substance was there," says David Noyes. "With Paul, appearances are more important. He wants to have his wines accepted in the Bordeaux tradition and to have Ridge accepted as a first growth of California; he needs a model for what he does. Dave was more confident of his own desires."

The upshot was that within a few years of Draper's arrival, an informal division developed at Ridge. The upper winery, where the winemaking took place, was Draper's domain; the downhill facility, which housed the business offices, became the province of Bennion, who soon gave up responsibility for winemaking and instead concentrated his attention on the vineyards. Thereafter every Ridge label carried two separate notes: One, describing the wine in the bottle, was written by Paul Draper; the other, declaring the winery's position geographically and philosophically ("Ridge wine is made with an emphasis on quality and naturalness that is rarely attempted"), was signed by Dave Bennion. The duality of the voice was significant, as by the mid-seventies there ceased to be anything other than professional communication between the two men.

This situation seems remarkable, considering that during this period Ridge was building a reputation as one of the great wineries of the New World. Perhaps, just as grapevines require a period of stress in order to produce the most intense fruit, so the strain between Bennion and Draper concentrated the character of Ridge wine in the seventies. At any rate—whether through Draper's winemaking skill, his talent for public relations, or both—Ridge wines began winning unprecedented acclaim from the time he arrived on the scene. Bennion continued to oversee Ridge's vineyards and to procure new ones as the winery's production increased; perhaps to escape discomfort at Monte Bello, he'd pack a lunchbox and disappear, living on bread and cheese and red onion, sometimes sleeping under grape trucks in vineyards far from home. Following Draper's arrival, new sources of Zinfandel were secured in the mountains above Napa Valley, in the orchards and benches along the Russian River, in the foothills of the Sierra Nevada, and along the Mendocino coast. As the grapes came in and were vinified, Ridge unleashed an unprecedented explosion of Zinfandels upon the world. Year in and year out, the Ridge Geyserville, the Ridge Occidental, the Ridge Fiddletown, the Ridge Lytton Springs, the Ridge Paso Robles—all made and marketed separately, with the vineyards identified on the labels—ranked among the great wines of the vintage. A wine that Draper helped make in his first year—the 1970 Ridge Jimsomare, for which he predicted drinkability in the year 2000—was lauded as history's ultimate achievement with the mystery grape ("the single greatest bottle of Zinfandel I have ever tasted"—Robert M. Parker, Jr.). California's "ubiquitous orphan"—the workhorse, the plebeian, the second-class citizen—had risen from its obscure origins and was knocking at the door of nobility.

Soon after Paul Draper arrived at Ridge, his friend Fritz Maytag planted Zinfandel, Cabernet Sauvignon, and Petite Sirah in his York Creek vineyard on Spring Mountain, west of Napa Valley. The budwood for the Cabernet came from the Monte Bello and La Questa vineyards; the budwood for the Zinfandel came from the Trentadue and Picchetti ranches. New plantings of Zinfandel weren't very common in 1971, but Maytag says he "thought it was possible that Zinfandel might become our Bordeaux." As with Draper, Bordeaux was his benchmark for fine wine. "Burgundies are erratic and not all that rational," Maytag explained to me the day I visited him at his brewery in San Francisco. "Italian wines vary. But Bordeaux has order and romance and science and gravity. Big, rich Bordeaux that age are the wines that melt men's minds."

It's been said that Burgundy—earthy, fleshy, fecund, *feminin*—tends to seduce the sensualist, where Bordeaux—tannic, concentrated, muscular, *masculin*—appeals more to the aesthete. While these two proclivities need not be mutually exclusive, on the scale described, Zinfandel probably belongs more to the sensual than to the aesthetic realm—as Draper himself says, it's romantic as opposed to baroque, an orchestra to Cabernet's chamber quartet. While Draper frequently cites sensuousness as an element in great wine, his avowed standard of historical excellence is Château Latour, the most robust and long-lived of clarets. Inevitably, from the moment he arrived at Monte Bello, Ridge wines—Zinfandel included—began to be measured by that yardstick.

"When I produced the '71 Monte Bello," Draper once told me, "my partners said, 'My God, what have you done? This is the lightest wine we've ever made.' *But,*" he quickly added, "it was as big as any of the '70 Bordeaux." For a while during the seventies Draper maintained a nominal interest in big, blustery Zinfandels; it was, after all, the heyday of the late-harvest ethic, and as he himself says, when he was in his early thirties, he was capable of sitting down to dinner several nights a week with a fifteen-percent-alcohol wine. But as time went on—as Draper himself aged and matured—his native instincts for balance, structure, and harmony rose inexorably to the top. He retained Ridge's basic orientation—idealizing naturalness and purity above all, he was biased in favor of long maceration and against filtration, and he even returned to fermentation on natural yeasts (Bennion had been using commercial strains)—but over the next decade Ridge wines became noticeably less big and brawny, more elegant and refined. Increasing production may have been partly responsible for this change—as greater volumes of grapes entered the winery, a given wine might spend less time on the skins before being pressed to make way for the next—and the attending shrinkage of long-term storage space might also have contributed to earlier bottling (i.e., less barrel age). At any rate, by the time I met him, Draper had—in the terms of one of the Bay Area's plethora of pithy wine-shop newsletters—"evolved from an innovator of modern dance into a master of classical ballet. Vinously, this means he has gone from making brash, attention-grabbing wines based on heavy extraction to making subtler, finesse-influenced wines which have more polish." In other words, after Dave Bennion relinquished the Ridge wine-making to Paul Draper, Ridge wines became less and less like Dave Bennion and more and more like Paul Draper.

As mentioned earlier, my first response to the latter style of wine was not positive. Over the next few years, however, numerous developments effected a change in my attitude. For one thing, I learned that during the era that produced the first Ridge wines I'd tasted, the winery had been waging a pitched battle with the dreaded Brettanomyces—a sulfur-resistant yeast that converts alcohol into water and acetic acid. In the past decade Brettanomyces has become widespread in California, owing to the proliferation of wineries; traveling from one facility to another in barrels, it can be arrested (and then only partially) only by chlorine or sterile filtration. If it infiltrates a wine, it can give rise to activity within the bottle and generate peculiar qualities; within limits it adds a level of interest—e.g., the "barnyard" or "sweaty-saddle" aspects of some Burgundies and Châteauneuf-du-Papes—but with regard to Ridge in the early eighties, the consensus seems to hold that Brettanomyces got beyond the limits of acceptability.

Draper's first instinct had been to tolerate it; he once told me that he'd "rather have Brettanomyces as part of the characteristic, as long as it's not at all dominant, than sterile-filter our wines." In time, however, the aforementioned "damp wood, mushroomy" problem forced Draper to face the facts. Ridge underwent a drastic increase in its level of sanitation, the barrels were indeed washed with chlorine, and the entire 1982 vintage was sterile-filtered. The '82 harvest was enormous, and in an effort to concentrate the wines, Draper drew off a considerable amount of free-run juice after crushing the grapes (assigning it rare "Ridge White Zinfandel" status a year later). Unfortunately this had the ultimate result of making the red wine too tannic. The combined upshot of all these factors was that 1982 was one of the worst vintages in the history of the winery.

In early 1984 Dave Bennion was asked by his partners to resign the presidency of Ridge. The reasons were various, but the most important seemed to be that Bennion's organizational discipline was inadequate to the task of running a winery of the size that Ridge had become. The onetime hippie haven was now producing more than forty thousand cases of wine per year—far from colossal by industry standards, but still more than twelve times as large as it was when Paul Draper joined on. As it happened, 1984 was also the year that Ridge got a handle on its Brettanomyces problem, as well as the first in a string of superb California vintages. These circumstances are borne out by such wines as the '84 Monte Bello—considered Ridge's best estate Cabernet bottling since 1977—and the '84 Geyserville Zinfandel, the wine that singlehandedly rearranged my personal view of Ridge.

To recount how this transpired, I suppose I'll have to divulge certain details of a cherished bachelor ritual—namely, the solo steak dinner, a common devotional practice that includes as a sacrament the better portion of a bottle of wine. As the reader might guess, there isn't anything very complicated about it. In the form into which I was initiated, one selects from the grocery store a long, thin russet potato, cuts it crosswise into eighth-inch disks, and deep-fries the disks (with garlic) in oil. As the potato is relinquishing its nutritional value, a token green vegetable is also steamed. The steak should be boneless: a rib eye or New York cut, though filet mignon will suffice. Grilling is best, but if time or weather don't permit, a cast-iron pan is heated until smoking as the beef receives an ablution of spices; the steak is then seared quickly on both sides, though the interior should remain quite rare. This can be tricky, since under such superheated conditions the meat goes from purple to pallid pink in a matter of seconds. The utmost vigilance is thus required— no small order, since another major element in the rite is the consumption of at least one glass of Zinfandel by the time the meal is ready, at which point the rest of the bottle should follow in whatever proportion personal decorum dictates. This ceremony should take place only at the end of a day that makes its necessity apparent: a wearing shift, a heavy workout, the completion of an arduous task—whatever. It thus cannot be planned much in advance, so the bottle of Zinfandel should be kept at the ready, like a condom in the wallet or a revolver in the glove compartment.

On the occasion under discussion, the bottle I had in reserve was the '84 Ridge Geyserville, a wine that I, having been unmoved by recent Ridge offerings, anticipated without much in the way of expectation. Therefore imagine my surprise when I poured a small amount into a glass, swirled, sniffed, and was *riveted by a rich, briary nose brimming with black cherries, roasted chocolate, and toasty oak.* Immediately upon sipping the wine, I recognized what was meant by the "rich claret" style I'd heard so much about. The wine was full but not overpowering, sensuous but not too fleshy, oaky but not overly tannic. Its complexities were held together in perfect balance—*so* perfect, in fact, that balance itself was the wine's major hallmark. It was Zinfandel, to be sure, but its main distinction lay in the fact that it was also something greater.

Given my previous reactions to Ridge wine, I naturally wondered what was responsible for my experience of this one. Was it the simple fact that Ridge had cleaned up its act? Or was it, perhaps, my own growing sophistication? In the course of my research I'd obviously spent a lot of time with Paul Draper; and little by little, I suppose, his enological philosophy was working an effect on me. Moreover, I'd been tasting quite a bit of wine— and under such circumstances, one's palate inevitably becomes more refined, whether one intends it to or not. Eventually I got to where I could pick out a Ridge wine at a blind tasting, not simply by its American oak but by its balance and restraint, its tastefulness and harmony—its aristocracy, if you will. I still maintained my stylistic preference for "rich" over "elegant," but all in all, I became somewhat better equipped to see merit in wines that weren't utterly titanic.

The difficult part—as far as the Young Gentlemen's Culinary Society was concerned—was that as I came to appreciate the subtler aspects of wine, I was less willing to sacrifice its nuances to hot, spicy food. After a while it seemed to me that the only red wine (and make no mistake, *red* wine was the only kind that the Young Gentlemen considered legitimate) capable of "standing up" to such cuisine was not even Zinfandel in general, but Ravenswood Zinfandel specifically. Thus it seemed to me that if we ever planned to drink any other kind of wine with dinner, we would perforce have to reduce the amount of pepper that we put in the food.

To the other Young Gentlemen, this fancy new attitude of mine represented nothing less than a policy of willful emasculation. The one hunter—i.e., sportsman, rifle shooter, duck subduer, venison procurer—in the group went so far as to pronounce himself *constitutionally incapable* of making the food less spicy. The growing schism was dramatized one night when I offered to bring some aged Cabernets to dinner; as the hour of the meal approached, the member who was acting as host for the evening—somebody who made a specific point of *not* cultivating any special interest in wine, aside from his appreciation of its properties as an alcoholic mouthwash—informed me that he was preparing Cajun meat loaf. When I surprised him by showing up with Zinfandel instead, he explained that he'd merely been trying to choose a dish "that would stand up to the wine." In the face of my creeping cork sniffery he clung tenaciously to the ideal that Wine Is Meant to Be Drunk (and So, presumably, Are We). As far as I was concerned, this continual demand that the food and the wine square off in some kind of culinary cockfight was becoming rather wearing.

It appeared that an age-old ideological rift was threatening to tear our once-joyous group asunder. To put the matter in proper mythic perspective, you might say that Apollo and Dionysus were confronting each other over the Young Gentlemen's table.

This choice of imagery is not accidental. The philosopher whom Paul Draper singles out as his old college favorite, Friedrich Nietzsche, began his first book, *The Birth of Tragedy*, this way: "We will have done much for the science of aesthetics when once we have perceived . . . that the continuous development of art is bound up with duality of the Apollinian and the Dionysian, in much the same way as generation depends on the duality of the sexes, involving perpetual conflicts with only periodic reconciliations. . . . These two very different impulses run side by side, for the most part openly at variance, each continually rousing the other to new and mightier births, in order to perpetuate in them the warring antagonism that is only seemingly bridged by the common term Art. . . . "

In Olympian mythology, Apollo is the god of poetry, music, oracles, healing, manly youth and beauty. Dionysus (aka Bacchus) is the god of wine and the vine. To restrict one's view of these two deities to such narrow roles, however, is to miss the wider influences ascribed to them, not only by Nietzsche but by such other twentieth-century thinkers as Carl Jung, Walter Otto, Joseph Campbell, and James Hillman. In his book *The Homeric Gods*, Otto attributes to Apollo the "spirit of clear-eyed cognition . . . destined to produce not only the arts but eventually even science. It was capable of looking upon the world and existence as form." For Jung, Apollo gives rise to the "perception of inner images of beauty, of measure, of controlled and proportioned feelings," as opposed to "what breaks out in [the Dionysian] state . . . pure affect, something instinctive and blindly compelling." To put this dialectic in Freudian terms, Dionysus represents the unconscious, unchecked id; Apollo, the conscious, repressed superego. To put it in terms of the Young Gentlemen's Culinary Society, my new attitude toward wine— one that, to the others, appeared to advocate "detachment, dispassion . . . clarity, formal beauty, farsighted aims, and elitism" (James Hillman, *Re-visioning Psychology*)—was Apollonian, whereas the opposing view—one that seemed to promote "a passionate-painful overflowing into darker, fuller, more floating states" (Nietzsche, *The Will to Power*)—was Dionysian.

As it happens, Paul Draper is well versed in this sort of thing. He annually attends at least one Jungian seminar/retreat, where, among other things, he studies poetry and archetypal psychology and comes into contact with the likes of James Hillman. When I asked Draper what had inspired him to undertake such studies, he put the blame on Thoreau, who said he went to Walden because he "did not wish to discover, when it came time to die, that I had not lived." Draper expanded on this explanation by telling me a story about one Rabbi Zescher, a "very holy man" who, on his deathbed, was being attended to by one of his disciples. The disciple was dozing off when Rabbi Zescher suddenly sat up. "Are you all right, Rabbi?" asked the startled attendant. "Yes," said Rabbi Zescher, settling back. "I had a dream that I had died and was taken before God. I was sure he was going to ask me, 'Rabbi Zescher, why weren't you more like Moses?' Instead he asked me, 'Why weren't you more like Rabbi Zescher?'

"I always had the problem of *puer eternus*, the eternal child—the feeling that I wasn't yet living real life," Draper told me. "I'm a Pisces—I flow very easily through this world. I was the Italian Paul Draper, the French Paul Draper, the winemaker Paul Draper. But I never confronted the question, Who am *I*, Paul Draper? When I began to wonder about that, Jung started to make an impression on me. Jung encourages you to ask: 'To what degree do we know who we are and respond out of who we *truly* are?' "

According to Jung, anyone's psychological process is governed by one of four functions. Some guide themselves and their relations primarily through thinking; others—their opposite—define the world through feeling. Still others comport themselves according to impressions made on their senses, while their opposite type operates according to intuition. Draper says that, in Jungian tests, thinking is his lowest function; the one that occupies the dominant role in his consciousness is, rather, intuition. This is consistent with Draper's predominant picture of himself: as a "natural" winemaker; as a Pisces (i.e., an intuitive, artistic, impractical dreamer); as a person who idealizes the Mediterranean and the Dionysian; as an undergraduate who enjoyed Nietzsche "because he let the chaos in." Yet when one scrutinizes Draper's life, it can hardly escape notice that rather than reflecting a sustained impulse to "let the chaos in," it exhibits a marked compulsion to keep the chaos *out*. Everywhere Draper has gone (Italy, Paris, Latin America, Ridge) he has functioned largely as an imposer of order. While I'm prepared to accept the idea that he operates mainly by intuition—especially if, as Jung maintains, such a person "perceives the outer primarily through the medium of the inner, sometimes even at the expense of reality" (to wit, Ridge's Brettanomyces problem in the early eighties)—on the basis of the evidence here gathered, it appears that if there was ever a Dionysian on Monte Bello Ridge, his name was David Bennion. Indeed, compared with the compulsive, earthy, indulgent Bennion (he whose guiding principle was "If the grapes can do it, let them do it"), the civil, cerebral, classically educated Draper seems downright Apollonian.

Paul Draper aspires to the Dionysian, it seems to me, in the same way that certain white musicians aspire to blackness: to unite themselves spiritually (all right—*bodily*) with the roots of their art. The admiration may be genuine, the urge heartfelt; but ultimately, Draper is no more Mediterranean than Mick Jagger is African-American. This is not to call Draper (or Jagger) a hypocrite; it's merely to observe that like many of us—though in a somewhat more sophisticated way—he idealizes impulses foreign to his nature and hankers for things impossible for him to attain.

I have aired these notions with Draper, and he has predictably (that is to say, Apollonially) resisted them. To refute my identification of him with Apollo, he points out how disorganized he is in his personal life, how he realized way back in prep school that he wasn't cut out to be an orderly engineer (Bennion's first career, after all), how for him wine is "a connection to the earth and the blood and the body, not to the spirit." He insists that his ideal is "the *conscious* Dionysian"—the union, as it were, of the body and the intellect—and says that his main problem with Bennion "was that he typified so much of what I saw, and didn't like, in myself."

As far as similarities between Draper and Bennion are concerned, I can attest to the willingness of both men to pursue any conversational path, whether or not it pertains to an immediate order of business. Also, it must be said that where Bennion was renowned for his illegible notes, Draper's handwriting also fails to answer one's expectations of a lucid personality. Moreover, I understand that one might still wonder: If science stems from the inner clarity and detachment of Apollo, how exactly did it come to pass that a group of Silicon Valley electrical engineers created such powerful, primitive, uncontrolled—i.e., such Dionysian—products as the Ridge wines of the sixties?

On this point, Draper's fellow Jungian Fritz Maytag has a hypothesis. "Ridge was the mistress of rational scientists," Maytag told me that day at his brewery. "The scientist always falls in love with a chorus girl—someone in whom the 'higher' mental functions are not, shall we say, well developed. Not that she can't dance or sing like a bird; that romantic, *spiritual* energy is just what he's looking for. Scientists at play want unquantifiable, deep marvelous stuff."

According to Jung, while any individual is primarily governed by only one of the four functions—thinking/feeling, sensation/intuition—his or her mental process will normally be "seconded" by a function from the other pair—for example, intuition supported by feeling, or thinking supported by sensation. The other functions remain repressed in the unconscious, where they retain the potential of breaking out in uncontrollable moods or seizures—a phenomenon referred to as enantiodromia. According to Joseph Campbell, enantiodromia represents "a 'running the other way,' which is a term borrowed from Heraclitus, who thought that everything in time turns into its opposite. . . . Jung's concept is that the aim of one's life, psychologically speaking, should be not to suppress or repress, but to come to know one's other side, and so both to enjoy and to control the whole range of one's capacities; i.e., in the full sense, to 'know oneself.' And he terms that faculty of the psyche by which one is rendered capable of this work of gaining release for the claims of but one or the other of any pair-of-opposites, the Transcendent Function."

To my mind, Maytag's model provides a perfect example of enantiodromia. The Ridge founders were people primarily disposed toward thinking who, in their "other lives," sought out something to which they could relate primarily in terms of feeling or sensation. In particular, the story of Dave Bennion, who started out as a teetotaling scientist and ended up a hedonistic, no-holds-barred winemaker, seems a particularly stirring example of an enantiodromiatic life. For Paul Draper, the urge to explore his other side has not been such an unconscious process; steeped as he is in Jungian psychology, Draper, who wants nothing so much as to "know himself," is fully aware that the Mediterranean represents "the other side of the Anglo-Saxon character," and as a result, he seeks it out as part of his personal therapy—the Jungian process of individuation. Apollo being the god of healing, one might even argue that Ridge itself realized its full potential only through Draper's application of the so-called Transcendent Function; after all, he effected the place's transformation from a struggling, inefficient Dionysian enterprise into a respected, successful "consciously Dionysian" one.

The path was not without stylistic pitfalls, however. As Hillman explains:

> therapeutic psychology [or, for our purposes, Draper's approach to winemaking at Ridge] has an inherent contradiction: its method is Apollonic, its substance Dionysian. It attempts to analyze the collectivity, the downwardness, the moisture of libidinal fantasies, the child, the theatricality, the vegetative and animal levels— the "madness," in short—of the Dionysian by means of

the distance, cognition, and objective clarity of the other structure. . . . A therapeutic psychology [or an approach to winemaking] which would transform the unconscious (Dionysian) into consciousness (Apollonic), no matter how imaginatively sophisticated its method, continues in the main line of our tradition. Even where it may encourage Dionysian experience, the experience is for the sake of consciousness. . . . Despite programmatic intentions about "integrating the shadow" and "joining the opposites," analysis [or any such approach to winemaking] must unavoidably continue to cast shadow yet further upon matter, body, and female.

Of course, in a sense, all winemaking—which, like all therapy and even art, is a means by which uncontrolled impulses are channeled to meet the constraints of civilization—*must* remain rooted in order, rationality, and repression; otherwise, society would be awash in "totally natural" wines (and people) that are constantly refermenting and blowing their corks. The consummate gentleman Paul Draper understood this better than did the semibestial Dave Bennion, which is why Draper ultimately succeeded where Bennion did not.

Jung explains how, soon after coming to Ridge, Draper might have come to feel about his cohort:

. . . in the Dionysian state the Greek [i.e., Bennion] was anything but a 'work of art.' On the contrary, he was gripped by his own barbarian nature, robbed of his individuality, dissolved into his collective components, made one with the collective unconscious. . . . To the Apollonian side [i.e., Draper] which had already achieved a certain amount of domestication, this intoxicated state that made man forget both himself and his humanity and turned him into a mere creature of instinct must have been altogether despicable, and for this reason a violent conflict between the two broke out.

Nevertheless, as Nietzsche pointed out, art depends on precisely this conflict for its sustenance and survival—and that may go deeper than anything else to explain the quality and character of Ridge wine during the seventies. One might assume that Draper stayed on at Ridge, despite his alienation from Bennion, for reasons of professional expediency; where else, after all, would he find such sympathetic enological employers in 1969? But as we come to understand what Bennion and Draper represented to each other—consciously and unconsciously—we see that greater forces than material security were at work on Monte Bello Ridge. As Otto poses it in *Dionysus, Myth and Cult*:

> Should we not ask whether Apollo could not have wanted this association for reasons other than greed or expediency? Could he not have been driven by an inner necessity to supplement the scope of his own domain by the proximity of the other—and just this other one—to show the world that only the two together signify the whole truth?. . . . Is it not more sensible to believe that Apollo and Dionysus were attracted to each other and sought each other out—that Apollo had wanted this close association with his mysterious brother because their realms, though sharply opposed, were still in reality joined together by an eternal bond? . . . In this union the Dionysiac earthly duality would be elevated into a new and higher duality. The eternal contrast between a restless, whirling life and a still, far-seeing spirit. . . . Apollo with Dionysus, the intoxicated leader of the terrestrial sphere—that would give the world total dimension.

"And with this marriage," Otto concludes, "Greek religion"— or, for our twentieth-century purposes, California winemaking—"would have reached its noblest heights."
The conscious Dionysian: Ridge Zinfandel.

In April I made one last trip down the Nimitz Freeway to talk to Dr. David Bruce, the dermatologist who, according to Darrell Corti, in 1971 had made twenty-two different Zinfandels, "each more disgusting than the next." As one of the California Revolution's early independents, Bruce was a charter member of Corti's "Santa Cruz Mountain Crude" school, an experimentalist who strove to produce the purest, strongest wines he could. Similar to that of many of his fellows, Bruce's winemaking had since become more refined; unlike some of them, he had now quit making Zinfandel altogether. Nevertheless, it was one of the wines for which he had initially gained renown—particularly in its late-harvest incarnation—so I wanted to hear what he had to say about its place in the Revolution.

The winery was on Bear Creek Road, on top of the Santa Cruz Mountains with a distant view of Monterey Bay. At the entrance was a coat of arms—or, rather, grape bunches—with the inscription "Est. 1964." Pinot Noir and Chardonnay grew on the surrounding slopes; black rubber storage tanks were upended by the driveway, as was a black Labrador retriever. A car with Arizona license plates was parked next to the winery, which bore a sign saying, COME IN—HONK AT HOUSE. The door was open, however. I entered and saw a young woman—the Arizonan, presumably—talking to a lean, rangy-looking man in a blue corduroy shirt and jeans. The man had healthy, angular features; graying hair flopped over his forehead. The woman was asking him which Cabernet was his favorite.

"Right now the '83," he said. "You can taste the sun in the '82; the '84 has loads of cherry fruit, but the '83 is wonderfully balanced." As they talked, I surveyed the ribbons and citations and shelves of wine. A sign on one of them asked: WHO HAS MADE CABERNET FOR 26 YEARS? DAVID BRUCE, THAT'S WHO!

When the woman departed, I introduced myself to the man: David Bruce. He locked up the tasting room and, accompanied by the dog, we went up the hill behind the winery into the Douglas firs. We came to an enormous house with stained board-and-batten siding and a multilevel redwood deck. A rather cloudy swimming pool was built into it. Climbing a series of staircases, Bruce told me he'd been born in San Francisco and raised in Palo Alto and had begun making wine in 1959, the same year as the Ridge founders.

"Back then there was only Ridge, Martin Ray, Hallcrest, Bargetto over here, and Dan Wheeler down in Soquel," Bruce said, escorting me into his curiously (compared with the opulent exterior) unfurnished dining room. "I was a Martin Ray disciple—I used no sulfur dioxide in my wine for ten years. Dan Wheeler felt that the more horrible things wine went through biologically, the better; he'd put wines in jugs for five years to stabilize them before bottling. He made a lovely Riesling champagne. I made a lot of wines that were considered curiosities: some Pinot Noir whites; a full-blooded red Grenache; a dry Gewürztraminer. In California it had always been made sweet. In '71 I individually labeled seventy different wines. People thought of me as a high-alcohol guy solely because of the late-harvest Zinfandels I made in '69, '70, and '71. I put them in the barrel right after they were fermented; some came out sweet like port, and others came out dry. The dry ones developed awkward tannin, threw an enormous amount of sediment, and developed a pruny quality, which any high pH will do. They were made wrong, really. If I had it to do over again now, I'd correct the acidity, and the sweet ones would probably drink even better.

"Ridge and I must have bottled hundreds of different Zinfandels," Bruce said, sitting down in a reclining chair and putting up his feet. "My problem with Zinfandel"—he pronounced it with the accent on the last syllable: "Zin-fn-*del*"—"was that whereas I sold my '64 for three dollars and fifty cents a bottle, I could sell my '81 for only four dollars, and it took three years to get rid of the stuff. So many wineries were coming on so fast, and the value of the dollar made European wines cheap; French was what was selling, and Zinfandel wasn't French. It's a shame because I always thought Zinfandel was something that could attain true prominence—even greatness of a sort. The bunch at Davis said it would live only five, six, or seven years, but we all knew that wasn't true. I remember having the '41 Nervo Zinfandel at a friend's house and thinking it was Bordeaux.

"I was discouraged about only one aspect of Zinfandel: It's hard to get rid of the chocolaty quality in it. In any bunch of mountain grapes you'll get one green and five shriveled, which creates high alcohol; there's an overconcentration that creates a sort of mummification effect. It really bugs me. Zinfandel has one great advantage, though: It will have wonderful fruit early and still go on and do great things in the bottle. So maybe you can have your cake and eat it, too.

"I should go down and get an old bottle of Zinfandel," said Bruce. "I haven't done that for a long time." He disappeared into his temperature-controlled cellar, and returned a moment later holding an unlabeled bottle. Keeping it almost horizontal, he braced the bottom against the kitchen counter and twisted a corkscrew in from the side. Then he decanted the wine into a clear glass pitcher, where it showed a venerable burnt-brick color against the white Formica.

"Let's see what we've got," said Bruce, pouring a small amount into two glasses. "This is the 1968. The grapes came from Ken Burnap's vineyard over on that ridge." He gestured across the pines to the northeast. "To my mind, these were some of the best Zinfandel grapes ever to come out of California—and from an area that rarely gets this ripe. This wine was enormously complex, right from the beginning."

With a graceful, elegant motion of the wrist, Bruce swirled the glass back and forth in a way than recalled Paul Draper. After sniffing and sipping, he announced: "It isn't aging as gracefully as it should. The tannins are unwieldy, and the mouth feel isn't what I'd like it to be. It has to do with the acidity. I can smell a little yeast, a little H-2-S, a little activity in the bottle. Of course, we didn't understand those problems at all back then."

I found the wine appealing: smooth, velvety, slightly spicy; a trace of tannin, but not much. The only drawback was the absence of any acidic bite.

"A neophyte in the wine business might think this is a hell of an interesting wine," said Bruce. "It has a lot of flavor, as high-pH wines always do. But it isn't a wine that drinks well. It reminds me of what the Italians say about some of their old wines: It has a tarry quality. Notice the sweet follow-through? You'd never find that in a European wine. It comes from the high pH. This wine has one major fault: The acidity was wrong."

Bruce poured more of the wine into our glasses. "California went through a fulcrum point around '79 or '80," he said. "That was when we got a handle on acidity. It was like the fifties in France—they'd made more dirty wines than you could shake a stick at, but they cleaned up their act around '59 and '60. The French themselves never understood acidity because the areas of the finest wines didn't have a problem with it. But now that they're overcropping their vines, they're getting pH creep, and they've got to learn winemaking. Bordeaux is fruitier now than it used to be—you don't hear the term *infanticide* used so much now when they drink them young—but the tannins are more bitter, and the maturing wines don't have quite the velvety quality that they once did. They aren't waiting for bottle bouquet; they're going more toward the California thing. We, on the other hand, are starting to learn how to blend Cabernet and develop wines that will age. It's almost like we're going toward the same point in time."

The room was beginning to get dark; looking toward the windows, I noticed that the sun had set. Bruce switched on a light over the dining-room table and got some bread and cheese from the kitchen. Then he decided that another Zinfandel should be opened for purposes of comparison. Again he disappeared into the cellar, and again he emerged holding a bottle horizontally. "This is the '66," he said. "It was made from basically unripe grapes. It wasn't as warm a year, so the acid was higher. Also, this was aged in American oak."

True to his expectations, the '66 was livelier in the mouth than the '68. It actually seemed younger, though it didn't have as much flavor.

"I like this nose quite a bit better," Bruce said, swirling his glass. "It's very rare for a wine to hold its fruit all that time. This thing's twenty-two years old, but it's still got a long ways to go. And it was made by a neophyte who didn't know very much about winemaking. It still needs another ten years; the acidity's really too high. In the other one, it's too low. Let's try blending them and see what we get."

Bruce reached across the table and poured wine from each pitcher into our glasses, approximating a fifty-fifty mix.

"Wow, how about that!" he exclaimed upon tasting it. "It tones down the intensity and brings out a kind of buttery style." Oddly, I noticed more tannin in the blend than I did in either of the individual wines. Still, there was no question that the combination of the two was the best wine on the table; if I'd had my druthers, I probably would have preferred three parts of the smooth-rich-spicy '68 to one part of the lean-sharp-intense '66.

"If we could put our talents to Zinfandel today, I bet we could make wines that would live thirty or forty years," Bruce said. "I especially think that with the kind of background and knowledge I presently have, I could make a Zinfandel that would be really lovely. If I had it to do all over again— I don't know, it would be fun, but you can only spread yourself so thin. I feel the greatest wine ever put in a bottle is Pinot Noir, so that's where I want to invest my time and energy.

"You know," Bruce said, " 'great' wine is defined as wine having lovely characteristics. But part of that greatness is holding those characteristics for a long time, so you have to wait awhile before you can say whether a wine is great. Until recently we didn't know how to make Zinfandel in the great style. Now we do—so we're just in the incipiency of finding out what it's capable of. And I have a sneaking hunch that Zinfandel is capable of doing something truly lovely."

A door slammed in a different part of the house. A moment later Bruce's wife, Jeannette, came in, returning from a dog show in San Jose. She immediately shooed the black Labrador retriever out of the house, commenting rather harshly on the dog's cleanliness (or lack thereof).

"Nonsense," said Bruce. "He's immaculate." Then he admitted that we were "in our cups." He asked Jeannette to sit down and join us; when she reluctantly did (her own dogs were still in the car), Bruce poured her a glass of the '68 and challenged her to identify it. After taking a couple of sips, she said: "1986 David Bruce Pinot Noir."

Bruce smiled. "I had two calls recently about my '74 Lodi Zinfandel," he said. "Both of them thought it was a very Burgundian-style Pinot Noir." As I retasted the '68, it did seem to exhibit a certain sweet, earthy, "Burgundian" quality; it was getting better and better as it sat in the pitcher. "That H-2-S quality is blowing off now," Bruce acknowledged. "It's opening up. In a couple of hours it might be pretty interesting.

"Oh, well, wines are fun," Bruce said, placing his glass on the table. "Your organoleptic perception is always changing— your sense of smell, taste, vision, and touch. So it's impossible ever to attain the ultimate. Maybe that's good, huh?"

At six o'clock on a Sunday evening in late July, seven men gathered at Bill Easton's wine shop, Solano Cellars, in Albany, California. Present were Rod Berglund of the Joseph Swan winery; Darrell Corti of Corti Brothers Grocers in Sacramento; Paul Draper; Charlie Myers of the Harbor Winery (who made the catalytic 1965 Zinfandel from Ken Deaver's vineyard in Amador County); Doug Nalle; Joel Peterson; and Charles Sullivan.

Behind the tasting bar, their identities concealed behind brown paper bags, were some two dozen wines. I had spent the previous week driving around the San Francisco Bay Area and the North Coast wine country collecting them; varying in age by more than fifty years, they included many of the most famous Zinfandels ever made, as well as some of the most lauded wines of recent years. They had come from Napa Valley, Sonoma Valley, the Mayacamas and Santa Cruz Mountains, Amador County, Knights Valley, Alexander Valley, Dry Creek Valley, and the Russian River area.

My stratagem was this: All the people present had patiently submitted to my questioning; at my behest, all had spent considerable time expounding upon the question of what constituted the "best" Zinfandel—about what the grape could or couldn't, or should or shouldn't, do. Still, no consensus had been reached; the Zinfandel taste mystery remained unsolved. Perhaps, I thought, if I gathered these people together in one room and confronted them with the very wines in which they'd invested so much oral and intellectual energy, some sort of ultimate clue might present itself. With many of the most historic Zinfandels from the past half-century lined up alongside one another, the highest and best use of the grape would surely come forward, and the secret of Zinfandel might be unlocked.

All the wines had been donated to my cause either by the wineries that made them or by individuals who owned them. Most of the men had previously met, but many hadn't seen each other for years. They milled about and reminisced while Bill Easton and I decanted the wines and arranged semicircles of glasses on the bar. Bill's wife, Jane—eight months pregnant—was also preparing a dinner, but first the wines would be tasted in three flights. The first flight consisted of nine older wines; the second contained seven younger ones; the third included four late-harvests. The younger wines would be ranked in order of preference. The more varied, complex, older wines would not, but would be extensively discussed.

Rod Berglund thought the first wine—unbeknownst to the tasters, a 1941 Louis Martini Private Reserve from the Monte Rosso vineyard in the Mayacamas Mountains (hence a standard-bearer from the days when almost nobody produced varietally labeled Zinfandel)—was "faded but still lively. It's obviously very old, but a real pretty wine for what it was." Joel Peterson found it "very smooth, with some acid and freshness . . . perhaps a little thin, but still a really interesting and fun wine to drink." Charles Sullivan unabashedly called it "a wine to be admired. It's going; it will be gone soon. But still a very, very good wine."

Paul Draper acknowledged the wine's quality—"it must

have been more balanced than half of these other wines when it was bottled, in order to have held this well," he said—but still thought he could probably "do with about one of these per year." Charlie Myers admitted that he "might be speaking from a peasant-style winemaking background, but it seemed fairly senile" to him. Doug Nalle—no peasant—agreed that he preferred "wine with more freshness."

Darrell Corti chided the naysayers. He informed them that "this wine is pretty much drinking *history*. The color is something you should pay attention to—it's the color of a traditional Barolo when it gets to be twenty years old. The pigment isn't stable, so it begins to look very brown; obviously it wasn't *black* when it was made, but nevertheless, it's wine of a piece."

Berglund thought the second wine was a "typical old Zinfandel—not very complex, but not objectionable." Joel found it "of moderate interest—intense, round, and dusty—pretty solid." Sullivan, however, went all out and declared it his favorite wine in the tasting. "I love the flavor," he said simply. "It's a little bitter and astringent, but ten years from now I think I'll like it very much."

Draper panned the wine, it seemed to me, as bluntly as he is capable of denouncing anything outright. "It does not excite me," he said. "If I'm going to wait this long for a wine to come around, I want that gritty tannin to be resolved. I'd just as soon drink something else with my dinner." Myers agreed that it was "a rough mouthful, but, as the writer Roy Brady used to say, 'Never met a tannin I didn't like!' It's a fairly austere wine in the mouth, but I like the nose very much—it's a clarety kind of nose. In the old days, before any of you were born, it was a commonplace that old, properly made Zinfandel acquired a clarety character."

"Wetmore wrote in 1889 that if you want to make Zinfandel into claret-style wine, you have to make sure it isn't too alcoholic," Corti countered. "I don't like the alcoholic taste of this wine, but I think it's a good example of typical old Zinfandel. It has the sort of character that made Zinfandel interesting in the forties and fifties—the same sort of character that we *don't* like in wines in the sixties, seventies, and eighties."

"I would have thought this was from the late sixties," said Draper.

"I think it's at least a decade older than that," said Corti.

In fact, it was the 1968 Sutter Home—the first commercial wine made from the famous Deaver vineyard in Amador County, the Zinfandel that kicked off the Amador winemaking revival in the late sixties, owing largely to Corti's efforts.

The third wine was a big hit. Bill Easton called it "extremely beautiful, elegant, and interesting—a Pandora's box of complexity." Sullivan named it his second favorite; Berglund thought it was "altogether more complex and better balanced than the previous wine." Draper agreed that it had "repaid the aging it's gotten, which the previous wine did not for me. The tannins are chalky but not gritty. My God, the complexity of this wine is just lovely. If this is the new style, it's what we're looking for."

"I guess I'm the outlier," said Nalle. "I appreciated the aromatics; it changed every five minutes. But I objected to the bitterness. I don't think it will necessarily fall away." Darrell Corti, however, gave the wine "two stars" and ranked it first in the flight. "This is what the ancients had in mind when they described Zinfandel as a 'California claret-style wine,' " he said, then added, "I think it's probably one of Ridge's wines."

Actually, it was the 1976 Ravenswood—Joel Peterson's first Zinfandel. "That's a very nice wine," Corti reiterated, apparently aware that he'd just done something he'd never done before—i.e., tasted a Ravenswood wine that excited him. (I, for my part, thought it smelled like turnips.)

The fourth wine had arrived the day before by Greyhound bus. As a result, it was thoroughly shaken up and still not cleared entirely of sediment. Joel said it was "a shame it's cloudy because it probably influences the entire character of the wine. It seems relatively simple and slightly acetic on the palate; but it also has that dusty quality that coats the tongue and a wonderful ripe berry nose. I think it's probably much more interesting than it's showing us right now." Draper, for his part, simply found it overripe. Berglund thought the wine was "murky not only in appearance but in aroma. It reminded me of generic, old-style California red wine." Nalle, however, called it "one of my favorite wines, sediment notwithstanding. It's complex, with some chocolate, prunes, and mint. I think it was probably great a few years ago; now it's good." Myers liked the finish—"one of the lengthier finishes here." But Corti said he was "not particularly fond of it. It smells like everything I don't like about Amador County Zinfandel."

Indeed, it was the 1968 Corti Brothers Reserve Selection—the same Amador Zinfandel as the previous one made by Sutter Home but aged by Corti himself in French oak. When he saw the label, he shrugged.

Draper thought the fifth wine "had some real interest. It's chalky but balanced; of the developed noses, it had quite a lovely one." Sullivan thought "the cedar flavors were a bit too much, but it has a certain earthiness to it. Also, a definite varietal quality." Berglund and Easton, however, thought the wine's fruit had faded—especially relative to the strong element of wood—and Joel found it "old, charred, and slightly harsh." Corti, as usual, was the most brusque; he said it had "the tired, slightly weedy smell of wines of medium quality that are now old and falling apart."

It was the 1935 Simi Zinfandel from Sonoma County, the wine that Paul Draper had once tasted at a dinner where an Englishman confused it with an old Bordeaux.

Before the discussion had begun, Darrell Corti was the first person to finish tasting and evaluating the wines. While waiting for the others to catch up, he silently pushed my sixth glass toward me, then followed it with a note. "Are they all Zinfandel?" it asked. Now, as the wine came up for discussion, Corti said he thought it had "a Cabernet Sauvignon stench—the smell of fresh, short green stems." Still, he considered it one of the two best wines in the tasting, "aromatic and delicious."

Berglund thought the wine "had more elegance than the

others." Nalle called "highly attractive and atypical. It's unique and it's good, though I couldn't figure it out. It's odd in the pack, but I'd drink the whole bottle if you put it in front of me." Sullivan also said he "had a lot of trouble with it. At first I put 'clear varietal definition.' But now I can't taste any Zinfandel." Draper said, "If it's Zinfandel—which I think it is—it's clearly a claret style. It's not a big wine, so it doesn't hold up against the bigger wines here. But it's very well balanced—one of the best-*defined* wines on the table. It has a lovely, earthy, mushroomy nose of a kind that I like."

Finally Joel came out with what some of the others seemed to be thinking. "I think this wine is a ringer," he said. "I think somebody threw a Bordeaux into this tasting. This has all the characters of a complex old claret—it's very perfumy, with some cedary qualities and some tannin, but very smooth at the same time. Really a racy wine, very nicely done."

I don't suppose I should have expected to fool these guys. Since so many stories about fine old Zinfandel compare it with Bordeaux, I thought I'd try to throw the group off by including the genuine article: a 1964 Château Beycheville, donated by Joel's mother, Frances Garbalano. I was secretly hoping that somebody would trash it—ideally as an example of how Zinfandel doesn't age. Instead, they'd fingered it as "odd in the pack" and heartily sung its praises. *C'est la vie.*

The seventh wine was no claret. It was big, full, dark, spicy, exotic, and altogether provocative. Berglund found it "the most massive wine of the group, very complex and powerful. Not out of balance, just real dense and rich. It has youth, but also a lot of mature components. It's very unusual." Corti thought it was "sappy and fresh and nicely developed" and ranked it alongside the '68 Sutter Home. So did Draper, though in his book that position didn't have much prominence; he thought the wine had "big and uninteresting flavors—piney and resiny with hard, undeveloping tannins in the body. Not a sensuous wine; not my style of Zinfandel."

"It's not my style either, but I put it at the top of the group," said Nalle. "I think it's interesting and unique. It's big but not alcoholic; it has extract without being too bruising. I think it's a hell of a wine."

Myers said, "This wine shows that we really like Zinfandel as long as it isn't very much like Zinfandel. This is just not typical of the bloody grape. It's dark; it smells different; it tastes different; and we love it. Ergo, logic is logic: We don't like Zinfandel."

From the descriptions, the wine sounded suspiciously like a Ravenswood. Indeed, Joel Peterson now admitted that he "should disqualify myself from commenting on this wine because I'm much too close to it. It's one of the wines I tasted long ago that made me say, 'Zinfandel—you can do something with that grape.' This wine hasn't changed appreciably since 1972. I find it very, very powerful and interesting—like Charlie says, almost an aberrancy among Zinfandels. A mutant, but a wonderful thing." He thought it was the '68 Swan, and he was right.

I found the eighth wine very soft and elegant, with a nose not unlike that of the '64 Bordeaux. Myers, however, thought it "smelled like some wines that had the misfortune of having malolactic fermentation take place in the bottle. It blows away as the wine sits in the glass, but it's 'different.' " Nalle disliked the wine's "vegetal component"; Corti thought it had a "cooked," overripe-chokecherry quality. "It's hard," he said, "mature, but hard." Sullivan said, "I think it's a case of *de gustibus non disputandum.* [Roughly, 'There's no accounting for taste.'] I didn't care for the flavor as much as some of the others, but I'm very much impressed by the way it's put together." Joel agreed and added that it had a "super finish" and "a nice, soft, ripe, full, earthy, rich, elegant nose. But it also has a thing that I associate with American oak—almost a lactic quality which softens the wine in a strange way." Draper agreed that it was "one of the few wines where the oak really came into the nose as well as the taste. I think the oak makes it fairly austere, and with that austerity, I don't think it's going to develop as well as I like from here on out."

The wine was the 1973 Ridge Geyserville, widely considered

the finest Ridge Zinfandel of the seventies. "Really?" said Draper when the label was unveiled. "I would have expected more." (Indeed, he may have had a right to; this wine had, sometime earlier, spent thirty-six hours warming up in the trunk of my car.)

The final wine didn't show very well. It reminded Joel of "dried green tea—harsh, simple, slightly acetic." Bill Easton thought it was "very resinous, with a sour edge to the flavors"; Corti termed it "old-tasting, with unappealing silage and incense aromas"; Berglund found it "faintly dill-like and exceptionally tart for the fruit—a little odd." Nalle said it struck him as similar to the '68 Swan, "but for the opposite reasons. It's complex, it does so many things . . . but finally, I couldn't handle the acidity."

When Draper's turn came, he anounced that the wine "could have come from only one place. I don't think I made it, but it's from Monte Bello Ridge. That smell—'dill' is perfect—has been in almost every single vintage of Zinfandel from the old vines up there. The sourness is probably very high acid. It's really too cold an area to grow Zinfandel—in cool years, you can't get it ripe."

The wine was the 1968 Ridge Jimsomare, made by Dave Bennion.

If a consensus were to be drawn from the above, it would seem to support the conventional Zinfandel wisdom. The most popular wines were the youngest one, the one that didn't taste much like Zinfandel, and the one that wasn't Zinfandel at all. The oldest wines were treated with ambivalent respect in one case and polite dismissal in the other. However, those who consider Zinfandel a "junk grape" would still be forced to recognize that some of the wines were very fine, none was without interest, and all had paid dividends beyond ten years of age.

So how about at five years of age?

Some of the wines in the second flight were:

The 1984 Ravenswood Old Hill. Joel Peterson's first vintage from the Sonoma Valley vineyard, made during the fall that I worked at the winery.

The 1984 Ridge Geyserville. The wine that changed my mind about Ridge, from the first vintage of the post-B&B (Bennion and Brettanomyces) era.

The 1985 Nalle. The wine that made such an impression on me on Christmas Eve and later on the members of the San Francisco Vintner's Club (plus a great many other critics).

The 1984 Joseph Swan. First of the recent, "accessible" Swan Zins, made from a vineyard near the Russian River with low alcohol and some whole-berry fermentation.

The 1984 Santino Grand Père Vineyard. The one Amador wine in the flight, made by Scott Harvey from the vineyard that Bill Easton and I had helped prune in January (the oldest Zinfandel vineyard in the state).

The 1984 Storybook Mountain Reserve. Made by Jerry Seps from his estate vineyard at the hilly northern end of Napa Valley.

For reasons of economy and fatigue, many highly regarded Zinfandels—those from Lytton Springs, A. Rafanelli, Shenandoah, Summit Lake, Sky, Rosenblum, Sausal, Kendall-Jackson, Karly, and Hop Kiln, to name a few—were not included. The wines in the tasting were chosen for what they represented—stylistically, geographically, or previously (in this book). The one exception was the 1984 Grgich Hills from Sonoma County, a Zinfandel grown and fermented by Sausal and then finished by Mike Grgich, the winemaker who crafted the Chateau Montelena Chardonnay that won the famous 1976 tasting in Paris. I put it in at the last minute, for two reasons: It had been getting rave reviews, and it represented a rarity in postrevolutionary California enology—a fine red wine consciously prevented from undergoing malolactic fermentation, thereby resulting in a slightly simpler, fruitier style.

About two hours before the tasting, the wines were transferred from bottles into glass pitchers in order to oxidize them. Since it's unusual to find sediment in wines so young, Bill Easton and I weren't concerned about clearing the wines by decanting them. I suppose we should have borne in mind that Ravenswood wines are unusual: When the Old Hill was poured into a carafe, a sizable share of sediment appeared, clouding the wine and contributing to the controversy when the final votes were counted.

The wine that finished last in the flight was the '84 Swan, which some of the tasters seemed to consider defective. Joel perceived a "gassy edge in it—a tanky quality that indicates it's been doing something in the bottle." Draper noted the whole-cluster, carbonic quality, which he said "brings with it the chance of some tankiness"; he also didn't perceive much varietal character.

"That's my objection," said Sullivan. "It's not Zinfandel. It's not raspberry; it's not boysenberry. It's more like a Châteauneuf-du-Pape." Myers thought it smelled like Kool-Aid. Corti, however, ranked the wine third and called it "a valid Zinfandel type. As they've been telling us at the Los Angeles County Fair for the last eighteen years, light-bodied wines have to be given the same respect as heavy-bodied wines. I put down: 'Good light style; too simple and fruity for serious wine.' However, we'll sell more of this kind of wine than any other."

The next-to-last-place wine was my darling, the '84 Ridge Geyserville. Joel found the nose "slightly aberrant—complex, but kelpy. It also had a bitterness in the finish that seemed out of keeping with the wine." Myers thought he smelled sulfur in it, and even Draper admitted that it had "a stink. There's a lot of complexity there, though." He ranked it second; Sullivan and Nalle ranked it third. Sullivan "loved the Zinfandel raspberry," while Nalle said it had "extremely nice aromatic qualities, with simple but pretty fruit." Corti said it reminded him of a young Rioja.

The fifth-place wine was the Santino Grand Père, though from the comments, one wonders how it managed to finish that high. Corti called it "chalky and flat-tasting, with not enough extract for the style. It didn't have the characteristics of red wine." Joel agreed. "If you blindfolded me and told me it was white, I would have believed you," he said. "It smells like red Chardonnay."

"*Barrel-fermented* Chardonnay, with latex kicked in at the end," specified Nalle. "A couple of Trojan rubbers, maybe, or some other prophylactic."

"You'd better patent that or Gallo will be selling it," Myers advised.

The '85 Nalle finished fourth. In this company, it tasted light, candied, and zesty. Interestingly, Berglund called it "a wine writer's wine"; Corti chose "a good Chinese-style wine—sort of sweet-sour. It smells like blue cheese or Botrytis—a bunch of Zinfandel grapes that got rained on." Draper agreed that it was "over the line in VA" and ranked it last. Joel said, "It would have been really good except for that twist [of volatile acidity]."

"Oh, I don't know," said Sullivan. "I think it's okay."

"Well, let's face it," said Draper. "All of these wines are *okay*."

"No," Nalle admitted. "It's dying. It had a stuck fermentation; when I bottled it, it was advanced. Now it's heading off into the sunset."

In third place was the '84 Storybook Mountain Reserve. The nose was just that: reserved. The flavor, however, was exuberant. Joel called it "nicely balanced—a good middle-of-the-road Zinfandel" with a "soft, sweet cherry nose and a nice pepper-and-spice quality." Berglund found it "dense, bright, and lively, with good acid." Draper, however, thought the acid and tannin were too aggressive. Corti, who ranked it second, still termed it "astringent for no good reason."

"Given that astringency," said Draper, "I'd like to see more richness."

"You're supposed to buy a bottle of richness and dump it in," said Corti.

Only two wines remained now, of course. Between them, the cloudy Ravenswood and the fruity Grgich Hills monopolized

271

the first-place votes. Individual reactions to them, however, ranged across the landscape. Half the tasters ranked the Ravenswood first, but Corti placed it last and Draper put it next to last. Predictably, Corti found it too tannic and aggressive. Draper agreed that "there's a roughness to it. I thought it might be too much oak, but with the sediment, it's hard to know what you're tasting." He and Corti both ranked the Grgich Hills first. Corti praised its full, fruity flavor; Draper, its ripe nose. Easton called it "showy." Sullivan found it complex and "gave it a good score, but thought it tasted slightly concocted."

"*Concocted* is a good word for it," said Joel. "Somebody did a great job of balancing all that fruit with a little French oak. It's very soft and appealing right now, but it's the difference between a Beaujolais and a Bonnes Mares. I don't think it's going to go a long way."

"There's no reason it can't be a Bonnes Mares of Zinfandel," Corti insisted. "That wine is going to last a long time."

Myers censured Corti and Draper, proclaiming that the Ravenswood was "clearly number one—it has a *tremendous* nose. Sure, it's distressed because of the cloudiness; but hell, a professional allows for these things." Sullivan called it "a truly great wine, one of the best young Zinfandels I've tasted in years."

When Joel's turn came, he dug in his heels. "I tasted this wine a month ago," he said, "and it's not cloudy at all. It's really interesting and complex, with all sorts of angles: mint, anise, cedar. . . . The VA is a little high, but you can't assess the tannin because of all the sediment. Certainly the wine I had a month ago didn't have all that woolliness. Unfortunately this bottle has been mistreated and mishandled."

He might have just said that he would have expected more. The Ravenswood finished second in the standings by one point.

During the meal that followed (grilled pork loin; wild rice pilaf; fresh corn-and-roasted-pepper salad; summer fruit in Zinfandel sauce), the first wines to disappear from the bar were the '64

Beycheville, the '76 Ravenswood, the '68 Swan, and the '41 Martini. Berglund went out to his car to fetch bottles of Swan's '75 and '87, and Corti pulled out two more bottles of an Amador Zinfandel that he'd made in 1970. One had been aged in wood, one in glass; both were delicious. We also opened another old Martini (both bottles donated by Louis P. himself); this one, made in 1955, actually seemed farther over the hill than the '41.

Corti and Myers then had to drive back to Sacramento, leaving the others—not very sorrowfully, it seemed to me—to evaluate the late-harvest Zinfandels. I won't go into a lot of detail about these since by that time the company had lost the finer parts of speech and was having trouble telling the difference between the various wines, all of which were roundly reviled as too harsh, too alcoholic, and too hard to drink—"not sensuous" in Draper's phrase, "good for tying a headache on" in Joel's. Actually, Sullivan did think the wines were sensuous, "in the sense that if you walked out on a drill field and saw a platoon marching toward you and heard the bark of the drill sergeant, you'd say, 'That is a *sensuous* sound!' " Both he and Nalle expressed a preference for Bushmill's and soda. Berglund said he "wouldn't want to drink these wines and *definitely* wouldn't want to have made them" but was "glad somebody did, if only to see what would happen." Nalle thought that, if grapes were going to be picked so ripe, the fermentation should be forcibly halted so as to make the wine more sweet and less alcoholic.

"That's what the '69 Bruce was like," said Sullivan. "About six to eight percent sugar. Boy, with chocolate with gooey red stuff on it, it's great!"

I took that as a signal to reveal the presence of the '69 David Bruce in the tasting.

"Are you kidding me?" Sullivan cried. "Get out of here! The bottle I had a year ago was *sweet*! We had it with a goddamn square of black gooey stuff with red things on it!"

A moment before, he'd said the *red* stuff was gooey.

Next I unveiled the '68 Mayacamas, the wine that had effectively begun the late-harvest craze of the early seventies. Sullivan, who still owned one bottle, announced that he would now never drink it. "That one's really gone away," agreed Joel. I, however—proving myself a Young Gentleman to the last—thought it was still quite tasty, mouth-filling and rich.

The third wine was one that Robert M. Parker, Jr., called "the single greatest bottle of Zinfandel I have ever tasted"—the '70 Ridge Jimsomare. I found it better balanced than the other wines, with an earthy, European-style complexity, but Draper simply called it "too rich. It started out awkward, came into its own, and then quickly became too tough. Parker probably had it in its heyday. I'll take the compliment, but I'd go with the '70 Occidental."

On cue, the '70 Ridge Occidental—for Draper, Ridge's best late-harvest Zinfandel of the seventies—came out of its bag. "It's too strong," Draper said, shaking his head. "But I still prefer it to the Jimsomare. This one is at least fifteen percent Petite Sirah."

Everybody swirled, sniffed, and sipped the wine again. "I think it has some nice herb tones to it," Easton offered.

"Actually, it tastes better to me now," said Joel.

Berglund, who a moment earlier had declared that he didn't care to drink it, now nodded and said, "Nice wine."

"Yeah," said Sullivan. "It's starting to taste better." He looked up from his glass and grinned. "Funny things happen when you know what they are," he said.

Funny indeed. As I watched these men's tastes change minute by minute, saw them defend or denounce their own products (as well as others they'd once lauded or hated), and heard them argue about whether a given wine was an example of sublimity, senility, or sensuality, I knew that the mystery of Zinfandel wasn't going to be explained—not by them, not by me, not tonight, not ever. After all my questions and all their answers—after all my *driving*, for God's sake—I now saw that, despite the multifarious leads indicating that this Zinfandel caper had the earmarks of a murder case, a kidnapping case, a case of mistaken identity, a case of elegant versus rich, or perhaps a case of nolo contendere, it had turned out to be a different kind of case altogether—one that by definition couldn't be solved.

As Charles Sullivan had said earlier in the evening, it was a case of *de gustibus non disputandum*. In the end, people's responses to the wines revealed less about the wines than about the people—their backgrounds, their prejudices, their haphazard biologies. Indeed, if someone (Haraszthy? Dionysus?) had set out with the intention of obfuscating America's enological identity, he couldn't have chosen a better grape with which to do it. In the mirrorlike relationship between wine and human beings, Zinfandel owned more reflective properties than any other grape; in its infinite mutability, it was capable of expressing almost any philosophical position or psychological function. As a result, its own "true" nature might never be known. If it could truly be called anything, it remained truly Californian and hence truly American—something that, having originated elsewhere, was continually reinventing its image, its history, and its taste. For all its distinctiveness and idiosyncrasy I was finally forced to recognize that Zinfandel, in its endless guises, would always be the mystery grape.

As David Bruce had said: "Maybe that's good, huh?"

EPILOGUE

Ravenswood's top three 1987 Zinfandels—Old Hill, Dickerson, and Sonoma County—received two 93 ratings and a 90 respectively from Robert M. Parker, Jr. Predictably, the same wines didn't fare as well with *The Wine Spectator*, which bestowed upon them scores of 87, 86, and 88 and termed them "intensely tannic." (Parker had chosen "phenomenal.") The '87 Ridge Geyserville Zinfandel received a 90 from the *Spectator* ("lush . . . gorgeous . . . richly concentrated"), while Parker gave it an 88 ("elegant and supple").

The '87 Young Gentlemen's Zinfandel won a bronze medal in the home winemakers' Zinfandel division at the 1989 Sonoma County Harvest Fair. The judges' tasting notes variously described it as delicate, flowery, light, and sour. The following year—1988—the fermentation was heated up and the wine was left on its skins for twenty-five days; the result is big, dark, fruity, spicy, intense, and delicious. Inexplicably, it also received a mere bronze medal at the fair; one particularly faint-hearted judge called it "harsh."

Despite its location directly above the San Andreas Fault, Ridge suffered no serious damage in the Loma Prieta earthquake of October 1989. Unfortunately David Bruce, whose winery is situated five miles from the quake's epicenter, lost ten thousand gallons of Cabernet and Chardonnay as barrels and stacks of cases fell to the ground and smashed. In nearby Los Gatos, Charles Sullivan watched his entire historic bottle collection disintegrate in the dining room, but not a single bottle was broken in his sub-gazebo wine cellar, which had been designed with the possibility of earthquakes in mind.

In March 1988 Dave Bennion died in a car collision on the Golden Gate Bridge. On his way to look at a vineyard in Mendocino County, Bennion apparently crossed the center divider into oncoming traffic and ran head-on into a truck. An autopsy revealed no alcohol in his system nor any evidence of heart failure. As he had recently returned from a viticulture conference in New Zealand and Australia, his wife, Fran, theorized that Bennion may have forgotten himself and was driving on the wrong side of the road.

At about this same time Joe Swan developed a pain in his groin. Initially he thought it was a pulled muscle, but X rays revealed a hairline fracture in his hip. An indistinct gray area on the film inspired a biopsy, which apparently proved negative. The hip bone was pinned, but the pain persisted. Finally Swan traveled to the Mayo Clinic in Minnesota, where his hip was found to have deteriorated and his condition was diagnosed as malignant. The hip joint was replaced, but the cancer had already spread to his lungs. Chemotherapy was unsuccessful, and Joe Swan died the following January at his home near the Russian River.

In June 1988 Munro ("Chip") Lyeth, Jr., the photographer and pilot from whom Joel bought Zinfandel for his Sonoma County Zinfandel blend, crashed his single-engine plane in a vineyard while performing air stunts for a picnic and burned to death near Geyserville in Alexander Valley.

In late summer of 1988 I again accompanied Joel Peterson on his pre-crush rounds of Zinfandel vineyards. Again the poplars were turning yellow in August. One of our stops, as it had been the previous year, was at Lyeth Vineyards; Joel and I drove the hills with Tom Mauritson, the temporary vineyard manager, and then repaired to the family's house, where Cathy Lyeth, a slight brown-haired woman with a pile of papers on her kitchen table, was overseeing the sale of the '88 grapes. She and Joel agreed that Ravenswood would again take ten tons of Zinfandel; Mauritson asked Joel if he might be interested in a long-term contract. Joel said that he would.

Joel departed on a two-week trip to Canada. When he returned, he learned that Lyeth no longer intended to sell him the grapes. The weather had been warm, the harvest was approaching, and when the newly widowed Cathy Lyeth was unable to locate Joel, she decided to sell her Zinfandel elsewhere.

She sold it to Ridge.